THE VILLAGE OF S____
1837

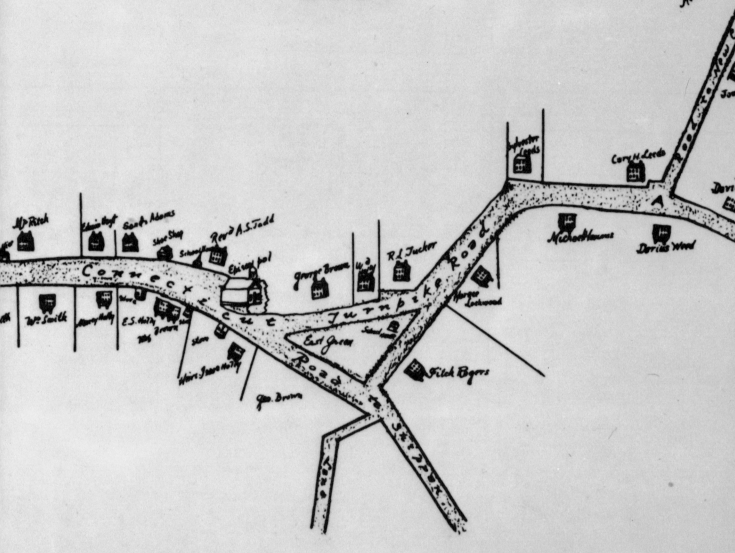

STAMFORD

STAMFORD

An Illustrated History

Estelle F. Feinstein & Joyce S. Pendery

"Partners in Progress" by Marie Updegraff

Picture Research by Lissa Sanders

Introduction by Don Russell

Produced in cooperation with the
Stamford Historical Society, Inc.

Windsor Publications, Inc.
Woodland Hills, California

In Memory of Virginia T. Davis and Carl Lobozza

Windsor Publications, Inc.
History Book Division
Publisher: John M. Phillips
Editorial Director, Corporate Biographies: Karen Story
Senior Picture Editor: Teri Davis Greenberg
Senior Corporate History Editor: Karen Story
Design Director: Alex D'Anca
Marketing Director: Ellen Kettenbeil
Sales Coordinator: Joan Baker

Staff for *Stamford: An Illustrated History*
Senior Editor: Jill Charboneau, Jim Mather
Text Editor: Lissa Sanders
Production Editor: Lynn Kronzek
Picture Editor: Nancy Evans
Assistant Editor, Corporate Biographies: Phyllis Gray
Corporate Biographies Editor: Judith Hunter
Editorial Assistants: Kathy Brown, Patricia Buzard,
    Lonnie Pham, Pat Pittman
Designer/Layout Artist: Ellen Ifrah
Sales Manager: Michele Sylvestro
Sales Representative: Letty Carro, Hannah Dresser

Illustration Credits
Unless otherwise indicated, black-and-white illustrations are from the collection of the
Stamford Historical Society.
Color Photography by Simon Wolfe for Windsor Publications.

Library of Congress Cataloging in Publication Data

Feinstein, Estelle F.
   Stamford: An Illustrated History.

   "Produced in cooperation with the Stamford
Historical Society."
   Bibliography: p. 196
Includes index.
1. Stamford (Conn.)—History. 2. Stamford (Conn.)—
Description. 3. Stamford (Conn.)—Industries.
I. Pendery, Joyce S., 1930-   . II. Updegraff,
Marie. III. Stamford Historical Society. IV. Title.
F104.S89781-114-3
ISBN 0-89781-114-3

CONTENTS

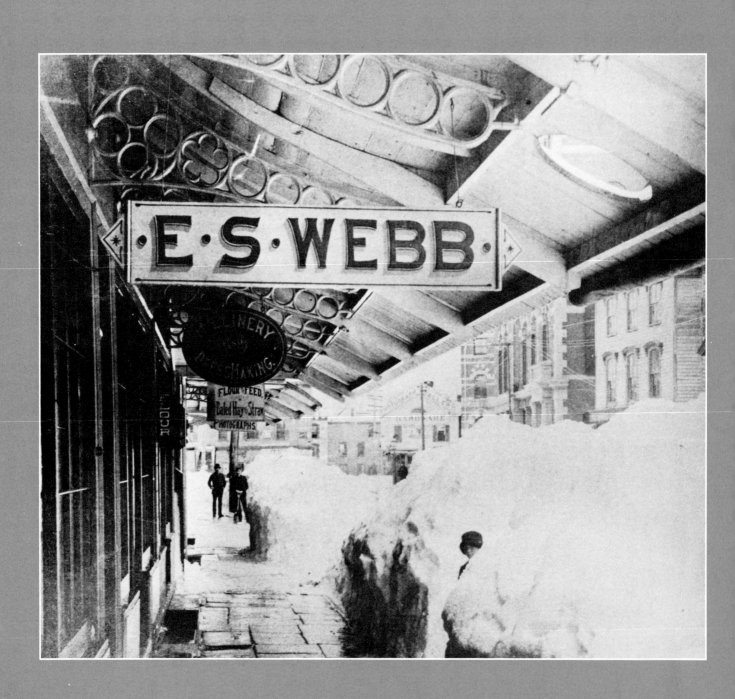

Introduction

While most of my friends were out riding their bicycles, I was usually seated at the kitchen table, munching on an apple, and pouring over a book titled *Picturesque Stamford*. It was bound in leather, gilt-edged, and looked very large to a boy in his teens. *Picturesque Stamford* was published as a souvenir of the 250th anniversary of Stamford in 1892. It was, until the publication of *Stamford: An Illustrated History*, the last comprehensive history of its magnitude about Stamford. I enjoyed reading in *Picturesque Stamford*, about the establishment of my hometown, and its growth into a vibrant city, able to maintain an identity of its own although located close to New York City. The constant reference use of that history book inspired me to walk the wooded paths and streets of Stamford in search of the places where historical events occurred—even to the spot that is reputed to be where the original deed was signed when this land was purchased from the Indians.

Since the publication of that book Stamford has undergone many changes. From a manufacturing town, and research city, to its present state of housing the headquarters of Fortune 500 corporations. All of this growth has brought with it problems and joys. These are put into perspective by this new volume's authors; they trace the history of Stamford from its beginnings, created by Wethersfield dissidents, to the present day.

The pages of this book are so vivid and detailed in their descriptive historical fact that you will find yourself taken back in time. And you will gain a new perspective about Stamford. One that will build more respect for the many political processes and decisions that were made through the years. Like most historical narratives you will find that the story encompassed here will create within you a feeling of loyalty for those events that preceded, and in many ways paved the way, for the good fortune that we enjoy here in 1984.

The fascinating pages here will take you from the Puritan Settlement on the Rippowam, through the formative years of the borough and town, to city and thriving metropolis. Through all of the pitfalls and triumphs of war, the Great Depression, and the painful evolutionary process that was caused by the abandonment of the city by its one major industry, you will find that Stamford rose to the occasion.

The narrative, coupled with the fine and rare illustrations, make this a book to be studied by every member of the community—native, or just arrived. Now it's evident that space should be made on all of Stamford's bookshelves for this new and most comprehensive study that takes us to the present day.

Don Russell
Columnist
The Advocate
Stamford, Connecticut
1984

PURITAN SETTLEMENT ON THE RIPPOWAM

In its origins Stamford was a Puritan village, the westernmost product of the social and political culture of New England. In its economic and social development, it was inevitably drawn into the orbit of New York. Heir to two traditions, Stamford has known both prosperity and decline; but prosperity has been the more familiar partner.

The story of Stamford began on the first day of July in 1640. Two Indian chiefs, Ponus, Sagamore of Rippowam, and Wascussue, Sagamore of Shippan, affixed their marks that day to a treaty which transferred a vaguely defined tract of land along both banks of the Rippowam River in return for 12 coats, 12 hoes, 12 hatchets, 12 looking glasses, 12 knives, 2 kettles, and 4 fathoms of white wampum (shell beads). The Indians of the northern bank of Long Island Sound, who were loosely linked to the Siwanoys of the lower Hudson Valley in their use of the Algonquin language, had pursued a semi-sedentary way of life for thousands of years. Reduced by a recent smallpox epidemic and other diseases and wars to a handful, they reserved to themselves only "a piece of ground [of] meadows, upland grass, with the rivers and trees."

The purchaser on that July day was a Puritan captain, Nathaniel Turner, who was acting as agent for New Haven, a town only recently planted on the Quinnipiac River. During the spring and summer of 1641, twenty-nine men, accompanied by their wives and children, arrived at the Rippowam River site and began to build a new community. They came, however, not from New Haven, but from Wethersfield, a village still further east. On April 6, 1642, the newcomers formally adopted the name "Stamford" for their plantation. Perhaps they had the English cathedral town of Stamford in Lincolnshire in mind; or perhaps they were aware that "Rippowam" denoted "cliff of rocks" in the Siwanoy dialect and thought "stone ford" an apt translation.

But the roots of Stamford—as well as those of New Haven, Wethersfield, and hundreds of other New England towns—went deeper than the opportunity for mere land acquisition. They lay in the driving Puritan impulse which brought thousands of men and women from England across the ocean in the early 17th century. Committed to the Calvinist beliefs in original sin, predestination, and salvation, they hoped to build a model church and society based on the Bible and purified of the corruptions of the Church of England and the royal Stuart regime.

To 1665

Facing page: Stamford's earliest days, always a source of great interest, were recreated by enthusiastic Darien "Puritans" and "Indians" in this 1913 historical pageant.

When the Massachusetts Bay Company initially secured a charter from the King to establish a colony, the Puritan leaders planned to establish a homogeneous community. While on board ship, Governor John Winthrop spoke eloquently of his dream of building a "city on a hill." But neither Winthrop nor any other Massachusetts leader could contain the restlessness which arose in the new country. Within a year Boston was surrounded by neighbors seeking more space and better land. A new society, unplanned and unforeseen, arose in the American wilderness.

A pattern for constructing communal institutions within the Puritan framework evolved with amazing speed. In each town the first concern was spiritual. When seven virtuous men selected themselves as the "pillars" and signed a covenant, a "Church of Christ" was planted. A minister, or two ministers, always university-trained, were chosen and ordained with the approval of the congregation. The church grew with the admission of morally upright men and women who freely attested to their Christian beliefs and conversion experiences. As towns multiplied, the Congregational Church network evolved and was accepted as the established church of the colony, which every inhabitant was required to support and attend.

The second concern was practical: economic and political survival. The Bay General Court assigned a specific area to each new town which in turn controlled admission of new members. Without guidance from Boston, much less London, the adult male settlers gathered in town meetings and made decisions on land divisions, planting of crops, and all issues of significance to a new community. Each town was effectively an autonomous religious community and democratic polity, supported by its own

agricultural economy.

Once the hiving process had begun, it could not be halted. In 1634 residents from Watertown, a village near Boston, made a settlement at Wethersfield on the Connecticut River, an area outside the Bay Colony's official jurisdiction. Other migrants from Bay towns formed Windsor and Hartford during the next two years. By 1639 delegates from the three river towns—Hartford, Windsor, and Wethersfield—under the charismatic leadership of the Reverend Thomas Hooker, formulated the Fundamental Orders of Connecticut and set themselves up as a full-fledged Colony. The Orders provided for the election of a governor and established a General Court, composed of the governor, magistrates, and town deputies, all chosen by the freemen of the towns.

It was a bold act. Neither King nor Parliament had authorized the creation of the Colony of Connecticut. England, however, was preoccupied with turmoil at home, from the accession of Charles I in 1625, through civil war and the execution of the King in 1649, to the end of Oliver Cromwell's Puritan dictatorship in 1660. During those 35 tumultuous years New England was left largely to its own devices, and the people of Connecticut took full advantage of the freedom.

For a short period after the founding of the three river towns, further expansion down the Connecticut Valley or along Long Island Sound appeared blocked. The fierce and independent Pequot tribe, who controlled the eastern Connecticut shore, represented a formidable barrier to settlement. But when the English destroyed the Pequot camp near Mystic by fire in 1637 and hundreds of Indians perished, the tribe's power was broken. English settlement followed swiftly.

An ambitious new Puritan effort began in 1638 when the redoubtable Reverend

John Davenport and the wealthy merchant Theophilus Eaton led their followers from London to the mouth of the Quinnipiac and founded the town of New Haven. They intended to construct a rigorous Bible state and a thriving seaport. They also quickly entered into a race with the Connecticut River towns to establish satellite plantations. While the Connecticut Colony accepted Stratford and Fairfield in 1639 and Norwalk in the early 1650s, New Haven men founded Milford and Guilford by the end of the 1630s. Daniel Patrick and Robert Feake purchased the manor of Greenwich in 1640, perhaps as agents for New Haven, but after two years turned the village over to New Netherlands. In securing

Rippowam in 1640, Turner acted on behalf of New Haven. The purchase constituted another link in the New Haven chain, and New Haven may have had a shrewd notion of who would fasten the link.

News of an ugly rift within the Church of Christ at Wethersfield, organized in 1635, had spread across New England. Four of the seven pillars and a minority of the congregation were locked in a bitter struggle with three of the pillars and a majority of the congregation over an issue that remains obscure. When the Reverend Davenport, among others, tried and failed to resolve the dispute, he suggested that one faction leave. He also undoubtedly pointed out that an attractive tract to the west, purchased from the Indians just a short time before, was available in return for payment of £33 to New Haven and agreement to remain part of the New Haven domain. The suggestion resolved the crisis. The group that chose to stay yielded the original church covenant to the migrants but remained in their homes and town.

The seal of the State of Connecticut fittingly proclaims, "He who transplants, sustains." But to carry out a transplantation, much had to be done. Each of the future settlers had participated in the forming of Wethersfield in Connecticut, and perhaps a third had taken part in the establishment of Watertown in Massachusetts a decade earlier. A solemn meeting was held in Wethersfield on October 19, 1640. Twenty men, including four pillars, made the decision to form the Rippowam Company, to purchase the western grant from New Haven, and to settle on it. Nine others joined them. It was voted that the Reverend Richard Denton and his family would arrive at the site by mid-May, 1641, and the others by the end of November. Each of the 29 agreed in writing to provide a specific number of bushels of corn the following spring to defray the New Haven debt. Seeking "contentment and satisfaction," the company proceeded to award home lots. As each man stepped outside, the rest decided on his share, ranging from 3 to 28 acres, roughly in proportion to his contribution in corn. A body of five townsmen, composed of the minister, two pillars, and two major investors, were charged with ordering the affairs of the new plantation in the spirit of "equity, peace, love, convenience." Matthew Mitchell, a once-prosperous landowner who had lost friends and property in Indian attacks, and a younger man, Francis Bell, were given the responsibility

for making lot layouts the next spring. Whether the 29 men realized it or not, and although it had taken place in Wethersfield, the first town meeting of Stamford had effectively been held.

On October 30, two representatives of the Rippowam Company, Andrew Ward and Robert Coe, arrived in New Haven. Five days later they signed a contract to purchase Rippowam for £33. On behalf of the company, they promised to hold one-fifth of the land for one year for possible New Haven claimants—a promise they were not required to fulfill—and to remain under the jurisdiction of New Haven—a promise that many later deeply regretted.

It is unlikely that any of the 29 men had ever visited the Rippowam site, but perhaps some had explored portions of the embayed Connecticut coast. The river estuaries and salt marshes were rich in herring and oysters, fish and shellfish; the salt meadows and numerous necks contained abundant cord grass and salt hay for cattle; the red cedar or juniper of the upland and the oaks and maples supplied ample firewood; the forests sheltered deer and beaver; and the myriad brooks and streams provided fresh water. Against these advantages were deterrents: rock-strewn land; rumors of designs by the Dutch only 40 miles westward; and fears of Indian attacks, chronic on a frontier. Perhaps the settlers assumed that the Rippowam Indians would abandon their seasonal rounds and settle on their reserved patch, which may have been in the inland area now known as Springdale.

To this day we do not know if the company arrived in families or together, by sea or land, with or without their horses, oxen, cattle, sheep, and swine. By the first winter they had felled trees, sawn planks, and built the meeting house and some two-dozen homes. The first houses were probably rude and low, constructed around a central open hearth. They may have been placed at intervals along an east-west path that paralleled the Sound and along a north-south road that paralleled the river. Main Street and Atlantic Street follow similar routes today. At the intersection stood the meeting house. No doubt it was a simple, one-story wooden structure, about 30 feet square, with a pitched roof, bare in the interior except for benches on the sides and a platform for the minister. It was surrounded by a stockade and served as the community's fort as well.

In the primary matter, religion, the settlers at first faced no difficulty. They had only to continue to worship under

the covenant which they had carried with them. Each adult presumably shared the conviction that religion was the foundation of the social order, and each was expected to lead a virtuous life, to attend services twice on Sunday, and to keep a watchful eye on the behavior of neighbors.

But trouble soon arose. The minister, Dr. Denton, a graduate of Cambridge, 50 years of age and blind in one eye, was described by Cotton Mather as "an Iliad

in a nutshell not least among the seers of Israel." Others also praised his honesty, piety, and learning. Yet the congregation and the pastor were ill-matched. (Perhaps he offended by his unorthodox belief that the children of the non-churched should be baptized at birth.) In 1644 he left Stamford, along with a third of his parishioners, and established a church at Hempstead, Long Island, under the protection of the Dutch.

The Denton departure produced a crisis. A Puritan town without a minister was unthinkable. Legend holds that two planters, Francis Bell and George Slawson, immediately began a journey on foot to the east. They found the Reverend John Bishop, probably in Taunton, and persuaded the minister, who had been trained in England and in Massachusetts, to walk back with them. Tradition also insists that Bishop carried his Bible in one hand and his staff in the other on the whole trek.

With the arrival of Bishop, the town was spared further ecclesiastical upheaval. The minister frequently haggled with the town meeting over his salary, which was paid in winter wheat, pork, and Indian corn, and he often inveighed against backsliders and dissenters, such as Richard Crabb and his wife, a pair of quarrelsome Quakers in neighboring Greenwich. Nevertheless he remained the pastor for half a century, until his death in 1694.

In the crucial matter of survival, the community initially relied on a semi-cooperative economy based on grain cultivation and stock raising. To assure a harvest of winter wheat or corn, the inhabitants adopted the open-field system they had known in England. The town meeting opened four common fields: the South Field, just west of the harbor; Rocky Neck, a peninsula just east of the port; East Field, still further east along the shore; and North Field, an inland

This is an anonymous artist's conception of Stamford's first meeting house (and fort), which stood near the intersection of present-day Atlantic and Main streets. Photograph by Don Piper.

area above the South Field. Each householder was assigned one or more strips in each field in proportion to his investment, and an attempt was made to balance the acres of salt meadow, pasture, and upland that each received. A pitch, or lottery, decided the order in which each proprietor chose his strip in the field.

During the first quarter-century the population remained small. A total of 55 known settlers arrived during the first two years, but 17 families departed for Hempstead, Long Island, in 1644. In the 1660s there may have been 40 to 50 households, fewer than twice the number of original planters.

Cultivation expanded slowly, too. A survey made in 1650 showed that 1.5 square miles, or 960 acres, had been plowed. During the first two decades no new fields were opened. At the same

time a movement away from the system of common cultivation and toward individual cultivation and consolidation of strips soon appeared. As early as 1650 several private, compact farms, some as large as 70 acres, had been formed through sales, exchanges, and grants.

The family was the primary economic as well as social unit of each town. While the husbandman supplemented his work in the fields with stock-raising, fishing, and some hunting, his wife took responsibility for preparation and preservation of food, spinning, weaving, sewing, and child-rearing. It was the wife who also frequently cultivated the beans, peas, pumpkins, squash, and other vegetables, and perhaps some tansy and hollyhock, in the home lot. Daily care of the animals often devolved on the children. The young boys of the village took charge of the cattle and sheep and

The residence of the Reverend John Bishop, pastor of the First Congregational Church for 50 years (1644-1694), is pictured in this rendering from the early 1900s. The site is at the intersection of Atlantic and Park streets.

herded them on the ample common meadows and pastures. Loose animals were placed in town pounds; however swine, if ringed, were allowed to roam free.

For governance, as for religion, the newcomers had a ready-made mechanism. The town meeting, begun in Wethersfield, continued in Stamford. Although records of the sessions held between 1642 and 1664 are scarce, the meetings were undoubtedly primarily concerned with such things as allocation of strips, adjustment of grants, construction of roads and bridges, enforcement of fencing regulations, and control of wandering or dangerous animals. Setting and collecting the tax rates were urgent issues. The first list of officials included a board of seven selectmen, fence viewers, pounders, and highway surveyors, and the number and types of offices increased steadily.

The town meeting was also the agency of first resort for resolving land disputes. When a quarrel over boundaries arose, the meeting appointed a committee of three "indifferent" men to investigate, and the freemen usually accepted the recommendation of the committee. Occasionally contentious parties resorted to the courts.

The town meeting also undertook responsibility for negotiation of further treaties with the Indians. The Turner purchase of 1640 had left the town boundaries unclear. Several generations of community leaders tried to confirm and enlarge the town territory beyond the original purchase, which secured the areas now known as the Waterside and Shippan. First came an effort to increase the land to the east. In 1645 Andrew Ward and Richard Law signed a treaty with Piamikin, Sagamore of Roaton, for cession of the section between Pine Brook and Five Mile River. However the town of Norwalk claimed the same plot

and cited a treaty with another Indian chief as proof. Only in 1685 did Connecticut firmly fix the boundary between the two neighbors at Five Mile River.

Next came an attempt to clarify the provisions of the original treaty. In 1655 a new agreement with Ponus and his son, Onax, reaffirmed the Indian reserve and defined the town of Stamford as 8 miles in breadth and 16 miles in length, a total of 128 square miles. The boundaries ran from Five Mile River in the east to the Mianus River in the west, from Long Island Sound to the present New York line. Today this area encompasses portions of Bedford and Pound Ridge, New York, about a third of New Canaan, and all of Darien. (Modern Stamford, a little more than 38 square miles, is less than a third the size of the town of 1655.)

During the next decades the promulgation of three more treaties effectively terminated all Indian claims. In 1668 a son and a grandson of Ponus ceded the last Indian possession in Stamford, the tribal reserve, and were given 20 acres in a "convenient place." In 1687, after decades of bargaining, Chief Winbock and his four sons gave up Long Neck for "diverse considerations." Finally in 1701 the Sagamore Catona and 15 other Indian leaders affixed their marks to a document which solemnly reconfirmed all the Indian deeds and quit claims and reaffirmed the boundaries of Stamford. The number of Indians who were resident in the Stamford area in 1640 is unknown; a Connecticut census revealed that not a single Native American lived in the town by 1756.

Despite its achievements in organizing church policy, landholding, and Indian agreements, the government of Stamford, during its first 24 years of existence, was continually disturbed by the interventions of New Haven, the parent plantation. In

1643, two years after the founding of Stamford, the leaders of New Haven created the New Haven Colony, or Jurisdiction, composed of the plantations of New Haven, Milford, Guilford, Stamford, Branford, and Southold on Long Island. Colony government included a governor, a court of magistrates, and a General Court composed of governor, deputy governor, magistrates, and two deputies from each of the six towns. Like the Fundamental Orders of Connecticut, the charter was home-grown, unsought and unsanctioned by English authority. Unlike the more liberal Connecticut polity, the franchise was expressly limited to members of approved churches. The law code, based on the Mosaic model, enforced religion and morality rigorously. Trial by jury was

unknown; and particularly annoying to Stamford, colony magistrates sat with locally elected deputies or judges to hear purely local cases.

New Haven was 40 miles east of Stamford and separated from it by a series of towns that were part of the Connecticut Colony. To bridge the gap, both village and General Court tended to rely on two men, Richard Law and Francis Bell. On the one hand the Stamford freemen repeatedly elected them as deputies to the court or legislature. On the other hand New Haven appointed them as constables to administer the plantation or trial courts. Both men enforced the laws vigilantly, increased their holdings measurably, and gained in prestige steadily. Law lived in the center of the village, served as

Wheare as The Inhabitance of ye Towne of Stanforde have purchased Severall Tracks of Lande as may more plainly appere By Deeds under ye hands of Severall Indians Sagamors & other Indians ye one under ye hands of Taphase Son of ponase & penehay (s) Son of onax; barringe Deat ye 7th of January 1667 & ye others under ye hands of nowatonimons & other Indians

Know Yea That I Catona Sagamore & wee whose names are under written Doe for us our (e) heairs & Suckesers, acknoleged & Conferme all the above Deeds of Sale; & Doe by these presents quitt Cleame & Relinckwish all our Rights, Intreses & pretences unto any parte or parsell of Lande meadows or priviliges whatsoever: within ye bounds or Limitts as by sd Deeds may appere: unto ye Inhabitance of ye Towne of Stanforde; To them there heairs & Sucksesers forever to possess & Injoy in a full & free maner: & for wonte of Deu & Reguler bounderys in sd Deeds, wee ye sd Catona & other Indians doe by these presents: Sett & fix bounds to sd Deeds as followeth: to say: westwarde as far as ye west bounds of bedforde purchase by marked Trees: & by ye east bounds of bedforde purchase; bounded north by ye South Side of bedforde purchass: & by ye Ston hill on ye Northeast Side of bedforde & To Run from ye sd Ston hill upon a Straight Line eastwarde unto ye uper Ende of ye Longe ponde: & from thence an east Line untill It meets with a Line Drawn ; north from ye uper Ende of five mile River: which is ye East Line of our severall purchases: & wee ye sd Catona & other Indians Give Grante & quit Cleame unto all ye Lands meadows Trees feedinge Grounds Rivers pooles & other priviliges yt Doth belonge to ye sd Lands & meadows within and to ye Southwarde of ye North bounds above mentioned unto ye Sea: unto ye sd Inhabitance and there heairs forever & also Doe Ingage to free sd Lands from all former sales, Gifts morgages or Incombarances whatsoever: beinge ye True & Reall sucksessors of ye sd lands & meadows within the sd bounds as above is mentioned: and also Doe acknowlege by these presents to have Received of ye said Inhabitance a Concederable & valuabl Sum of mony for all ye sd Lands & meadows within ye bounds from ye Salt Sea unto ye sd North bounds above mentioned: It is to be understud that ye above sd Catona & other Indians Doth by these presents Conferme all ye sd old Deeds: of Taphase: ponase & penehay (s) old onax & also young onax also yt Deede made to Capt Turner in behalfe of ye Towne of Stanford & also yt Deede of nowatoneman That Is to Say a quitt Cleame to any parte or parsall of Lands & meadows within ye sd bounds as above mentioned: In witteness of Truth wee whouse names are underwritten have hearunto Sett our markes or names & Seales in Stanforde, this eaight Day of July, 1701 Inter Lined in ye Twenty fift Line with ye words; & also yt Deede of nowatonemans.

selectman for 33 years, and kept the town records. Bell and his wife, Rebecca, were the parents of the first white child, Jonathan, born in Stamford. The goodwife was proud enough of her wardrobe to describe it scrupulously in her will and to bequeath it to her daughters.

Despite the ministrations of Law and Bell, resentment against theocratic New Haven rule mounted year after year in Stamford. Town residents claimed that Stamford received little benefit from taxes collected by the colony and that the suffrage restrictions were unfair. A plethora of accusations brought against Stamford youth for blasphemy, drunkenness, fighting, carousing, seduction, fornication, bestiality, and other transgressions of the "blue laws" of New Haven rankled. The presence of officious New Haven magistrates on the local bench added to the irritation.

For Stamford, however, the most outrageous failure of the colony government was its self-righteous refusal to defend the exposed community from assault. The General Court referred to Stamford as "the fronteere towne," but shrank from demands by its deputies for protections against the Dutch and Indians in the west. Early in 1642 the town, impatient, passed a special levy and secured the services of Captain John Underhill, a veteran of the Mystic battle, a professional soldier, and a colorful adventurer. He gained permission from the court to form a Stamford "train band," or militia unit, in which all village men between the ages of 16 and 60 were required to serve. But, even after war erupted between the Indians and New Netherlands in the Hudson Valley during the summer of 1643, Underhill could not obtain a military commitment from New Haven nor from any other New England colony. New Haven preferred to avoid entanglement and

piously preached peace to Stamford even after an Englishman, traveling between Stamford and Fairfield, was murdered and a Stamford woman was attacked in 1644.

As devastating attacks on Westchester towns multiplied, the Dutch retaliated with a series of assaults against the Indians on Staten Island, in the Greenwich area, and on Long Island. They also hired Underhill away from Stamford. In February or March of 1644 Underhill led an expedition which burned down an Indian village and killed its inhabitants somewhere in the Mianus River vicinity. The massacre ended serious Indian resistance and dissipated the sense of panic. Even the murder of John Whitmore, a respected deputy, in the woods in 1648 did not raise apprehensions of a general Indian uprising. Suspicion focused instead on an individual, Taphance, son of Ponus, who was finally tried in 1662 and fined a mere £10.

Widespread panic struck again, however, during the period of the first Anglo-Dutch War of 1652-1654. Although the military engagements took place in northern European waters and produced a resounding English victory, there was genuine fear that the Dutch in New Amsterdam (New York City), with the aid of Underhill, were stirring up a vast new Indian confederacy and planning a joint sea and land attack on western New England. Several sagamores from Manhattan provided confirming testimony.

During the wartime period the New Haven General Court recommended that Stamford take defense precautions, but it refused to reimburse militiamen for "watching and warding" and contented itself with a tax abatement for the town. The other leaders of New England temporized, too, particularly after Peter Stuyvesant, governor of the Dutch territory, assured them that he had no

Facing page: The fourth and final treaty between colonists and the few remaining Indians in the Stamford area, executed in 1701, clarified Stamford's boundaries and summarized previous grants and payments. In this version of the treaty, the handwriting of the original has been transcribed into type but the spelling and punctuation have been retained. Courtesy, Ferguson Library

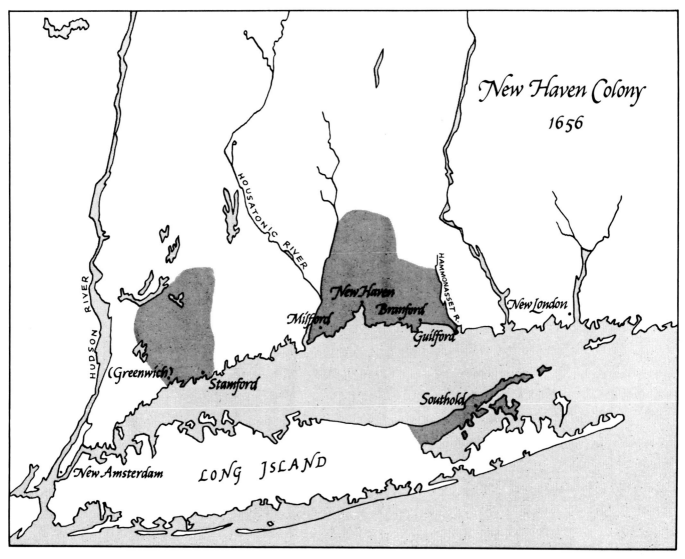

plot in mind.

As early as August, 1653, Law and Bell warned the court that Stamford rebels were threatening to pay no taxes "because nothing [was] done against the Dutch, and. . .they [the Stamford settlers] have been in bondage a great while." By November magistrates from New Haven, who had journeyed to Stamford, found the plantation "in a mutinous way . . . full of discontent." At a town meeting Robert Bassett, John Chapman, William Newman, and Jeremiah Jagger—three respectable farmers and a sea captain—denounced the New Haven Court. They repeatedly demanded the widening of the

franchise and compared the lot of Stamford freemen to that of slaves. In March, 1654, the four were brought before the General Court and charged with voicing treasonous sentiments and making preparations to form an army and lead a rebellion. Just how strong was the movement to form a separate coastal colony is unknown. Confronted with hostile testimony from witnesses, each of the four finally confessed his guilt and declared his remorse. In the end each suffered only a fine.

In one area New Haven did listen to Stamford. Responding to a bitter complaint by Stamford deputies on lewd behavior in Greenwich, and with the consent of the other New England colonies, it asserted authority over Greenwich in 1756. New Haven ordered the residents of the hapless town to pay rates to, obey the constables and courts of, and go to church in, Stamford. Greenwich did not regain an independent voice for six years.

The general restlessness pervading Stamford during the 1650s found an outlet in the next decade. The catalyst was the end of the Cromwellian regime and the restoration of the Stuart monarchy in England in 1660. For the first time the very existence of the colonies of Connecticut and New Haven and the validity of all individual property claims were in utmost danger, since Charles II might invoke the royal power to set aside unapproved charters. Members of the General Court of Connecticut responded quickly. They decided to send their brilliant and well-connected governor, John Winthrop, Jr., (son of the late Bay Colony founder and governor) to England to obtain a royal charter.

New Haven, under the leadership of the stubborn Reverend John Davenport and Governor William Leete, hesitated. The magistrates toyed with the notion of removal to the Delaware and meanwhile gave shelter to "regicides" (three men held responsible for the death of Charles I). Ultimately they sent a letter to Winthrop and requested him to seek a charter for New Haven, too. Winthrop may or may not have received the letter before his departure from Boston.

In London Winthrop's labors on behalf of Connecticut were remarkably successful. On May 10, 1662, the Charter for the Colony of Connecticut passed the Great Seal, the final step on the road to royal sanction. The charter retained the colony's traditional democratic frame of government. Much to the distress of New

Haven, it also incorporated the entire New Haven Colony, with the exception of Southold, within the boundaries of Connecticut.

As soon as the charter arrived in Hartford in October, the General Court of Connecticut invited all inhabitants of the towns of the New Haven Jurisdiction to take oaths of allegiance. It appointed local constables to collect rates and enforce the laws. In Stamford, where resentment against New Haven remained strong, there was little hesitation. Along with Greenwich and Guilford, it cheerfully joined Connecticut in 1662.

New Haven was stunned. For two years Davenport and Leete tried every political device to abort union. But another, and greater, peril arose. In August, 1664, the Royal Navy captured New Amsterdam without a shot. Supported by his brother, the King, the Duke of York not only established the Province of New York in the former area of New Netherlands but also asserted claim to all the land eastward to the Connecticut River. Fearful that the duke might try to pursue his claim to Connecticut land, including their own, the stalwarts in New Haven opted, on January 5, 1665, to place themselves under the jurisdiction of Connecticut. Broken-hearted, Davenport left New Haven for a pulpit in Boston and never returned.

The year 1665 marked a turning point in the history of Stamford as well. Its first phase, as a contentious Puritan outpost on the Rippowam, was over. Community institutions to care for the spirit, the economy, and the government were in place. The Indian threat had been subdued; the Dutch had been removed; and the officious interventions of New Haven had been eliminated. Stamford, by heritage a great-grandchild of Boston, settled into its role as a small, stable country town at the far western edge of Puritan New England.

Facing page: The New Haven Colony, to which Stamford owed allegiance until 1662, covered a wide area, as shown in this map by John O.C. McCrillis. Courtesy, The New Haven Colony Historical Society

II VILLAGE OF THE CONNECTICUT COLONY

Left in peace, the village of Stamford turned inward after 1665. As in other New England towns during the next century, the first generation, who had crossed an ocean to live and celebrate Puritan ideals, was succeeded by new generations, who had grown up in America and were eager to master their environment and build their fortunes while retaining their traditional ways.

Underlying the parochialism of the village was extraordinary homogeneity. Extrapolations from tax rolls indicate that the town numbered about 300 in 1680, just under 600 in 1701, and about 1,640 in 1735. Colony censuses put Stamford's population at 2,768 in 1754 and at 3,563 in 1774. On all these lists only a limited number of surnames—almost all English—recurred frequently. Hoyts, Scofields, Smiths, Webbs, Weeds, and Waterburys abounded. Marriages took place with neighbors or with sons and daughters from nearby towns. Settlement by outsiders was discouraged; between 1701 and 1727 the town meeting formally admitted a mere 20 persons as inhabitants. By the mid-18th century, patterns of cousinship were dense and intricate.

The only significant minority were the blacks, who arrived with the first English settlers. Slaves listed only as "Thomas" and "Miriam" were part of the household of Robert Bates in 1641. In his will Bates ordered them set free at the time of his death or when they reached 40 years of age. Other owners, however, continued to bequeath a "Negro man" or "Negro wench" to their heirs throughout the 18th century. Even after the Revolution, wealthy individuals, such as John and James Davenport and the Reverend Daniel Smith, continued to hold slaves.

Free blacks lived in Stamford, too, though their presence is more difficult to document. The regimental rolls of the French and Indian War include "Mark, a Negro." Samuel Bush, "a man of African descent," is listed among the soldiers of the Revolution. But, for reasons unknown, the total number of blacks fell drastically from 120 in 1754 to 86 in 1762 to only 60 in 1774.

The growth of population was due almost wholly to natural increase. Six, seven, or eight children or more were common. Despite deaths from diptheria, small pox, dysentery, typhoid, and other illnesses and fatalities from accidents, most of these children grew to maturity.

In the New England town virtually everyone held a place in the family, where the father was the legal head and the mother played a vital role. Apprentices, servants, and young kinfolk were treated as part of the household. Widows and widowers remarried quickly. The Reverend Moses Mather, a pastor of towering influence, married in turn Mrs. Hannah Fell, Mrs. Elizabeth Whiting, and Mrs. Rebecca Raymond and fathered

1666–1755

six sons and one daughter. To accommodate the large families, more spacious houses were constructed. The fireplace was moved out of the center; a full second story and rooms were added; and furnishings grew more elaborate.

For the first generation of fathers, there was no shortage of acres to bequeath to sons and sons-in-law. After 1665 the town meeting of Stamford at first continued its conservative policy in granting lands. As the strips in the first four fields were integrated into individual farms, the town gradually opened new fields along the coast from Shippan to Runkenheag and in the north in the New Field above the Rocky Neck peninsula. Mergers and expansion of private farms in these sections followed. Yet at the end of the 1670s, the town had allotted only one-third of its domain.

The pattern of landholding was transformed in the 1680s by two events. First, political considerations reduced the total town acreage by almost 40 percent early in the decade. In 1680, Stamford planters, with the consent of town and colony, set up the village of Bedford on the northernmost tier of Stamford. Three years later an exchange of land between the Colony of Connecticut and the Province of New York, which settled a longstanding boundary dispute, gave to New York all the area of Stamford that lay 10 miles north of the shore. The northern boundary, which proved permanent, was known as the "eight mile line," because it lay eight miles from the Post Road. As a result, from 1683 to the end of the 18th century, Stamford encompassed an 80-square-mile plot, ten miles in length and eight miles in width.

The second catalyst of change was the land policy adopted by Connecticut in 1685. In that year King James II, who had just ascended the throne, proposed the establishment of a single Dominion of New England, which would include the entire royal sphere from Maine to New Jersey. The scheme jeopardized both the Charter of 1662 and the title of every landowner. Townspeople were so incensed that Stamford sent neither rates nor deputies to Hartford one year. Connecticut is supposed to have saved its charter by hiding it in an oak tree when the putative governor-general of the Dominion, Sir Edmund Andros, appeared in Hartford. To safeguard the land tenures the General Assembly ordered the governor to issue patents to, and to designate proprietors for, each town. The Stamford Patent of 1685 clarified the town boundaries with Norwalk and Greenwich. The roll of proprietors was led by the Reverend John Bishop and included Richard Law and his sons-in-law, Jonathan and John Selleck, Francis Bell and his son, Jonathan, and four prominent landowners.

The colony initiative precipitated an extraordinarily rapid division of the remaining town lands, about two-thirds of the total, between 1687 and 1699. In the six divisions carried out during the dozen years, the number of proprietors who received shares varied from 50 to 75. In the final assignment of the interior "Long Lots" in 1697-1699, no attempt was made to set up common fields. Instead 69 proprietors received "extravagant" grants in fee simple. Since many of the farmers did not have the means to cultivate such large portions, located several miles from the village center, they frequently gave them to their offspring, as they came of age, or bequeathed them to their numerous progeny.

Actual layouts of the Long Lots were achieved by 1707. In effect, the process of making the common land private had been completed over a period of 66 years. A narrow, oblong area above the North Field and New Field, known as the Sequest Land, was held as a commons for

Right: This map shows the effect of the land-division process and the rise of parishes during the first century of settlement. From Stamford From Puritan to Patriot 1641-1774, by Estelle F. Feinstein, 1976

One of the few pre-Revolutionary buildings to survive the age, the Frederick Webb house (photographed at Main and Clinton streets in 1943) was built in 1723.

a few decades longer, but it, too, ceased to exist by the time of the Revolution.

The conclusion of the land-division process deprived the Stamford town meeting of the issue with which it had been most concerned and had a critical impact on attendance. By the mid-18th century many young farmers, who resided far from the village center, showed increasing reluctance to travel miles for meetings. Only desultory annual sessions were held; the mill rate remained low; and a small group of affluent landowners filled the posts of selectmen and deputies for long periods.

While almost every family engaged in farming and cattle- and sheep-raising, enterprises and crafts supplemented agriculture from the start. Beside muscle and wind, water power provided the main source of energy for simple machines. As early as September, 1641, the town meeting voted to build a gristmill and dam at the common charge. The structure was probably located at the falls of the Rippowam where the Main Street Bridge now stands. When the mill

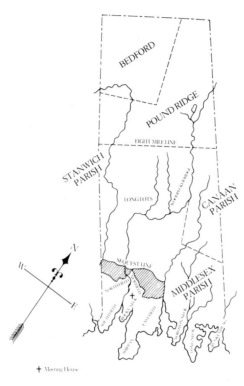

LAND DIVISIONS AND PARISHES
OF COLONIAL STAMFORD

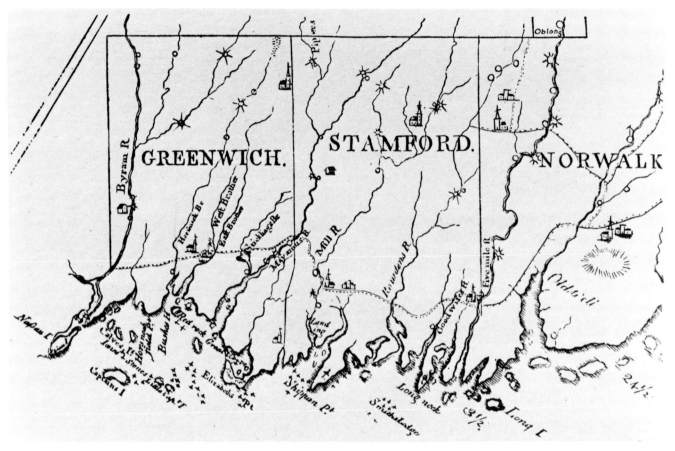

collapsed within a year, another assessment was quickly levied. In 1662 a seven-part covenant with an individual, Richard Webb, was signed for the operation of a mill at the falls by Webb and his heirs. At one point, late in the century, the charge fell on Widow Hannah Finch Webb, but she was forced to sell the mill and dam back to the town.

Requests to build other gristmills and dams on the Rippowam and on other streams multiplied. As Puritans became Yankees, ingenuity flourished. Sawmills, "sider" mills, and fulling mills for the production of woolens proliferated before the first century was out. Jonathan Bell was instrumental in constructing an early tannery and Jeremiah Jagger erected one of the first slaughterhouses.

Artisans were welcomed, and even solicited with offers of free lands and houses. Blacksmiths, gunsmiths, carpenters, hatters, tailors, shoemakers, coopers, and even two silversmiths, Jarvis Munson and Isaac Reed, set up shops in or near their homes. Some women, particularly widows, managed small stores and inns. As the town expanded in the 18th century, outlying mills and shops often became the centers of new neighborhoods, such as Woodpecker Ridge and Long Ridge in the north and Shippan and Middlesex in the south.

Overland trade was hampered in general by a lack of hard money and in particular by poor roads. Local highways followed no comprehensive design. Built piecemeal for the convenience of farmers, sometimes along old Indian trails, they usually meandered north to south and were narrow, stony, dirt cartways. The only lateral artery, which connected Stamford to Norwalk and Greenwich and

Above: The Patent of 1685 clarified the boundaries between Stamford, Greenwich, and Norwalk. Facing page, top: The Newman gristmill operated from 1726 to 1918. In the late 1960s restoration efforts, including refitting it with working machinery, received widespread support. Bright hopes for restoration were crushed, however, when the mill was destroyed by arson soon after work began. Facing page, bottom: This 1730 caudle cup is a rare example of 18th-century Stamford silverware. Photograph by Norma and Louis David. Courtesy, First Congregational Church of Stamford

the larger world, was known by a cluster of names: Main Street, the Boston Post Road, the Country Road, the King's Highway. Whatever its appellation, travelers rarely had a good word to say for it. When the intrepid, 38-year-old Sarah Kemble Knight journeyed by horseback from New York City back to her home in Boston in 1705, she found the Stamford portion of the Post Road fraught with "many and great difficulties, as bridges which were exceeding high and very tottering and of vast length, steep and rocky hills and precipices." Almost 40 years later, a Dr. Alexander Hamilton, a young Southern physician (no relation to the later celebrated statesman), made a similar trip and commented that "the country here is exceeding rocky, and the roads very rough."

Trade by sea was far less daunting. A report by a "Gentleman [of] his Majesty's Customs" described the Stamford harbor as "safe and good . . . 60 vessels of 100 tons may lie at anchor here with safety." Oystering and fishing predated the first white settlers and have not yet ceased. Local carpenters, such as Richard and John Mills and John Leeds, built barks and sloops. (Shipbuilding records were ill-kept, sometimes intentionally, to thwart British tax authorities). Beginning in 1641 small ships plied the coves of the sound with cargoes of wheat, fish, hops, and other products and even ventured to New Amsterdam when trade with the Dutch was forbidden. With the fall of New Netherlands in 1664, Stamford traders made increasing contacts with international merchants in New York City, rather than with wholesalers in Boston, a business pattern that has persisted.

Traffic between Stamford and the West Indies apparently flourished, but its extent is unclear. Vessels sailed out carrying wheat and other grain, lumber, horses, salt beef, and salt pork and sailed back loaded with sugar, molasses, salt, and rum. There was undoubtedly evasion of the tariff duties and the Navigation Acts by which the British sought to control colonial trade, and there may have been outright piracy. In 1702 the General Assembly, in its "Act for the Prevention of Undue Trade," included Stamford as one of the "Lawfull Ports." In 1769 the Commissioner of Customs in Boston recommended the appointment of a "Preventive Officer" in Stamford.

Two brothers, Jonathan and John Selleck, incontestably the richest citizens of the town at the end of the 17th century, were the leading figures in all phases of maritime commerce. They had married two wealthy sisters, Abigail and Sarah, the daughters of Richard Law. (The patriarch, angry that his only son had settled in Milford, had not favored the male heir but divided his estate equally among his three offspring.) The Selleck brothers, besides sponsoring inter-colonial, Caribbean, and European expeditions, invested heavily, furiously, and profitably in real estate. Among other undertakings one of the brothers bought a warehouse at the landing. In

1700 the governor of New York, the Earl of Bellomont, in defending himself against smuggling charges, insisted that Selleck

does us great mischief with his warehouse, for he receives abundance of goods from our vessels; and the merchants afterwards take their opportunity of running them into this town. Major Selleck received at least £10,000 worth of treasure and East India goods brought by one Clarke of this town from Kidd's sloop and lodged with Selleck.

Since the British did not pursue the charge, the connection of the Sellecks with the notorious Captain Kidd or other pirates remains mysterious.

In a society that was growing more stable, affluent, and deferential, the brothers also inherited the political mantle of their father-in-law. John Selleck was captured on the high seas by the French in 1689 and never returned. But Jonathan, a man of fierce temperament, served repeatedly as selectman, deputy, assistant, county commissioner, major in the militia, and judge of the Fairfield County Court.

Much as commercial expansion and land speculation interested enterprising townsmen, neither economics nor politics was the source of the major issues that agitated the community as a whole in the century following the incorporation of Stamford into Connecticut. The church and religion, in all its varied aspects, were the consuming interest and produced the strongest challenges to the even tenor of village ways.

The meeting house itself stirred disputes. By 1669 the population had outgrown the 30-foot-square building. After two years of debate, the town meeting voted to build a 38-foot-square wooden structure, with posts 12 feet high. Tradition holds that the first bell in Stamford was hung in the church, and

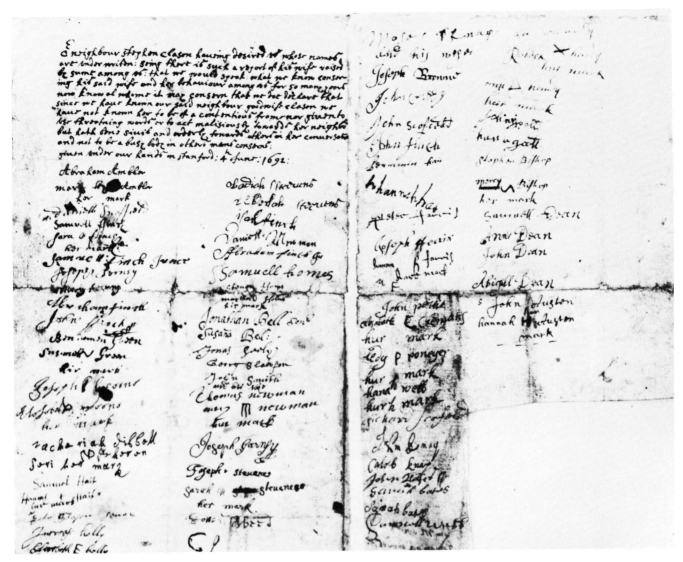

that, just as the bell was raised, a rope broke and a parishioner, John Holmes, lay dead. But this building rapidly proved inadequate, too. Seats were rearranged and galleries added. Finally in 1702 the town voted to build a third edifice, 50 feet square, and covered with cedar shingles. No provision was made for a bell; the beating of a drum again summoned the faithful to meetings.

As meeting houses rose and fell, agitation on the question of seating the meeting remained constant. The town meeting allocated pews to families on the basis of "dignity, age, and estate." The decisions were not easy. In 1673 a special committee composed of Law, Bell, and William Newman, was set up for the sole purpose of seating the women. Customarily Waterburys, Webbs, Hoyts, Davenports, and members of other first families of the village filled the front pews.

The community's pastor, John Bishop, became increasingly querulous as his ministry lengthened. Like other Congregational clergy, he sorrowfully noted a general decline in religion. He was personally sorely disappointed that not one of his eight sons took up his vocation. Just two years prior to his death, he became engulfed in the witchcraft mania which drifted down from Salem, Massachusetts, in 1692 and settled on Stamford like a poisonous cloud. Following charges of the practice of witchcraft by hysterical young girls, 19 women and one man of Salem were put to death.

In May, 1692, an unstable, 17-year-old servant, Katharine Branch, who was subject to seizures, accused Elizabeth Clauson (or Clawson) of Stamford, Mercy Disborough of Compo (Westport), and four women of Fairfield of consorting with the Devil and inflicting fainting fits and torments on her. The accused were all respectable goodwives.

Though the four Fairfield women were never brought to trial, Clauson and Disborough fared ill at first. A committee of women found suspicious "excrescences" on Disborough through which the Devil might have entered into her. When both women were bound and thrown on water, each floated "like a cork." It was asserted that the pure water had rejected the evil bodies of the witches. While the women were confined to the Fairfield County jail, Bishop and the Reverend Thomas Hanford of Norwalk prayed with Katharine Branch and urged her to name all her tormentors.

A special Court of Oyer and Terminer, set up by the legislature and held in Fairfield, made a preliminary investigation and handed down an indictment against both women. The court held that Clauson had had "familiarity with Satan . . . and afflicted and done harm to the bodies and estates . . . of his Majesty's subjects . . . and . . . deservest to dye."

At the jury trial which followed, a clutch of witnesses supported the credibility of Katharine Branch while others vouched for the innocence of the accused. Forty-eight men and 28 women of Stamford braved the atmosphere of intimidation and signed a petition to affirm the good character of their neighbor, Elizabeth Clauson. The jury failed to reach a verdict and was dismissed, but the women remained in jail.

During the fall of 1692, the mood shifted; reason returned. A group of ministers met in Hartford in October and denounced all the proceedings. A reconvened court now found Clauson innocent and Disborough guilty. The Governor, Robert Treat, unhappy with the outcome and confronted with a new memorial on behalf of Disborough,

appointed a committee of three notables, Samuel Wyllys, William Pitkin, and Nathaniel Stanley, to review the whole affair. In May, 1693, the report of the blue-ribbon committee asserted that the evidence was not valid, granted a full reprieve to the two accused, and strongly recommended that witchcraft trials be permanently abolished.

After the year of turmoil, the end of the matter must have brought enormous relief to the divided village. The minister was undoubtedly disheartened. In September, 1692, Bishop asked the town meeting for an assistant. By November the assembly had called on the Reverend John Davenport to make trial of the Stamford pulpit. The outcome was mutual satisfaction. With the death of Bishop in 1694, Davenport took over as spiritual leader.

John Davenport was the grandson and namesake of the founder of New Haven and inherited the stern Calvinist creed and habit of command of his grandfather. Educated at Yale and later a trustee of his alma mater, fluent in Greek, Latin, and Hebrew, he was a glittering ornament in the town, region, and even colony. His fellow ministers of Fairfield County called on him to act as spokesman; he delivered the election sermon in Hartford in 1703; and he was instrumental in devising the Saybrook Platform of 1708, which set up a system of associations of ministers and consociations of Congregational churches in Connecticut along county lines.

Davenport possessed a sharp acquisitive instinct as well. While his original salary as a fulltime minister had been £100 annually, he left an estate appraised at over £10,000 and including 5,000 acres. He married twice and sired nine children. Each of his two sons by his second wife, Abraham and James, became a celebrated figure in his own way.

The death of Davenport in February, 1731, signaled more than a change of ministers. His passing coincided with a growing restlessness, and released pent-up centrifugal forces. Both the union of the town and the church and the reign of the single church—conditions which had existed for 90 years—came to an end within months of Davenport's passing.

Since 1641 the town meetings in Stamford had made all decisions on issues pertaining to the Congregational Church. Early in the 18th century, however, the General Assembly made lay societies responsible for the properties and affairs of churches. Immediately after the old minister's death, the First Society was organized. It kept its own books and elected its own officials, frequently the same individuals who filled the corresponding town posts.

Because of shifts in Connecticut policy, the town meeting lost control of the common schools when it lost technical control of the church. Stamford had its share of "dame schools," where boys and girls learned their letters from a hornbook in a goodwife's kitchen. The early Connecticut and New Haven codes, however, had both placed the responsibility for the further instruction of boys on the towns. In Stamford the meetings had responded to the charge sporadically. The first schoolmaster, Richard Mills, was hired in 1657. Like his successors, he remained in his post only a short time. When plans were made to tear down the first meeting house, the town voted in 1671 to use the timbers for a one-room schoolhouse 10 or 12 feet square. A stove was introduced in 1685; and a new schoolhouse was built in 1699. In 1706 the meeting appointed a school committee, the first standing committee in its history.

When Connecticut authorized the establishment of lay societies, it placed the common schools under them. The First Society assumed overall responsibility for education in 1731 and formed a school committee. As neighborhoods developed, more one-room schools, school districts, and district school committees were organized. In 1732 there were five; by 1776 there were 25. Despite problems with funding and a high rate of teacher turnover, the system assured a decent level of literacy for males. It did little more.

The break in the union of town and church was accompanied by the end of the reign of the single Congregational Church over the 80-square-mile parish. With the death of Davenport, the husbandmen and their wives, living in the outlying areas, evinced a sudden and strong determination to form separate parishes.

In May, 1731, petitioners from northeast Stamford joined petitioners from northwest Norwalk and asked the General Assembly for permission to form the Canaan Society. In July the legislature approved. Three years later a group from southeast Stamford and western Norwalk also petitioned for parish privileges. This time opposition from Stamford was more intense, but Middlesex parish was set off in October, 1737. Early in the next century Canaan Parish evolved into the town of New Canaan, and Middlesex Parish, into the town of Darien.

Other separation attempts were successful in ecclesiastical, if not political, terms. Forty-eight men in northwest Stamford and northeast Greenwich asked the General Assembly to form a congregation in 1731 and received permission to establish the Stanwich parish the next year. In 1733 parishioners in the Woodpecker Ridge section, six miles north of the Old Meeting House, secured the right to hold winter services. Only in 1780 did they obtain permission to form the North Stamford Congregational Church. Neither Stanwich nor North Stamford seceded from the town of Stamford, however.

By the late 1730s, with four Congregational pulpits where there had been only one a few years earlier, discourse was lively and controversy endemic. In both Canaan and Stanwich parishes, a series of ministers quarreled with deacons, elders, and parishioners during the remainder of the Colonial era. In Middlesex, however, there was uncommon calm. The settlement there of the Reverend Moses Mather in 1744

presidency of Yale College, his alma mater, and named a Fellow. Literary, erudite, owner of a fine classical and theological library, he employed a lively style and sardonic wit to attack ideological critics from the pulpit and in writing.

All Connecticut Congregational ministers of the 1730s, 1740s, and later decades had need of strength. They faced two challenges unprecedented in the history of the established faith: the Great Awakening and the rise of the Church of

ushered in a leader as commanding in style and as fiery in conviction as he was impeccable in family credentials. A religious conservative, he became an uncompromising and vociferous political patriot. He served for 62 years, until his death in 1806 at the age of 88.

At the First Society, Davenport was succeeded by another Yale graduate, the Reverend Ebenezer Wright, who maintained a low profile during his 15-year tenure. After his unexpected death in 1746, the congregation chose Noah Welles, who shared Mather's blend of theological conservatism and political liberalism. He was considered for the

England.

The Great Awakening, which began in the Connecticut Valley in 1734-1735 and reached its climax in 1740-1742, was an evangelical crusade that touched every section, class, and denomination. Fiery preachers such as George Whitefield and Jonathan Edwards called on men and women to abandon rote church-going and to make a public commitment to Christ. In Connecticut it divided Congregationalists into New Lights, who supported enthusiasm, and Old Lights, who clung to tradition. Stamford's churches remained staunchly Old Light, although Wright complained of secret meetings in private homes and disorderly behavior on the Lord's Day.

Yet Stamford was the home of James Davenport, the most intemperate of New Lights. A son of the Reverend John Davenport and a brother of Abraham Davenport, both pillars of orthodoxy, the Reverend James Davenport underwent a conversion in 1740 that led him to abandon his Long Island pulpit and to take to the streets of Connecticut towns from Branford to Stonington to bring his hearers to redemption. A contemporary has left a harrowing description of his behavior:

By a violent straining of His lungs, and the most extravagant wreathings of his Body . . . [he] creates Laughter and Indignation . . . occasions great meltings, screamings, cryin swoonin and Fits; you would be apt to think that he was a madman just broke from his Chains had you seen him . . . with a large Mob at his Heels, singing all the Way through the Streets . . . with his Hands extended, his Head thrown back, and his Eyes staring up to Heaven.

Davenport denounced the "unconverted" ministers of New Haven and called on the people of New London to gather their finery and false writings and burn them in a huge bonfire. Yet he made no attempt to awaken his native town. Eventually Connecticut passed an Anti-Itineracy Law in 1742 which effectively barred preaching by ministers without settled pulpits. And James Davenport ultimately suffered a change of heart and died at the age of 40. He was, surely, one of the most troubled sons ever reared in Puritan Stamford.

In the very year that the Great Awakening began to abate, 1742, the Society of St. John's Church, Church of England, made its appearance on the Stamford documentary record. The rise of the Church of England in Connecticut

The Old Newfield School, built in 1731, saw the education of countless Stamford youngsters in its time. The building, on Old Newfield Avenue, stood for two centuries.

was a heavy burden for the Congregational clergy to bear. They knew that their ancestors had left this church, with its bishops and rituals, at great cost. They were especially shocked to discover that the adherents of Episcopacy were not newly arrived British immigrants, reared in the old faith, but American-born converts, who had deliberately abandoned Congregationalism.

The success of Anglicanism in Connecticut dated from 1722, when seven Congregational ministers in New Haven, led by the rector of Yale, the Reverend Timothy Cutler, proclaimed that the Congregational form of ordination was in error and that the Church of England rite was valid. Fourteen years earlier, in 1708, Connecticut, pressed by the Crown, had reluctantly allowed "sober dissenters"— other than Roman Catholics—the right to worship. After the Yale conversions so many ministers and laymen followed the path of Cutler that, by the time of the Revolution, Connecticut counted more members of the Church of England than any colony where Anglicanism had not been established. Yet despite urgent pleas, the hierarchy in England refused to send a bishop to America and placed all American Anglican societies under its missionary arm.

The Episcopal movement made its greatest inroads in the western part of the colony, precisely where the impact of the Great Awakening had been weakest. In 1742 the St. John's Society succeeded in securing from a reluctant Stamford town meeting a small piece of ground, surrounded by ledge rock and swamp, at the eastern end of the Country Road. The first church, built in 1744, was destroyed by lightning and fire, but a second edifice was in place by 1747.

For John Lloyd, a wealthy merchant, Obadiah Seely, a large landowner, and other St. John parishioners, a building

Right: This house on Old Long Ridge Road was built circa 1749 for Jacob White. Later the residence of George Lounsbury, the house was occupied by Joshua Logan after World War II.

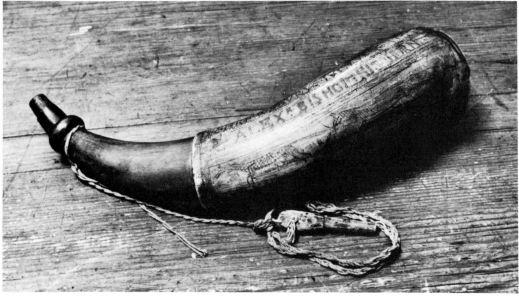

Left: One of the more intriguing 18th-century items in the Stamford Historical Society's collection is this one, inscribed, "Alexander Bishop, his horn, July 3rd, 1747."

and an occasional visit by a priest were not enough. To secure a resident minister, St. John's Society offered to pay the costs of a trip to England for a candidate who wished to secure ordination at the hands of a bishop. The offer was accepted by the Reverend Ebenezer Dibble, a Danbury native who had graduated from Yale in 1734 but who, after more than a decade, had not been able to settle into a Congregational pulpit. In Anglicanism Dibble found fulfillment. Returning from England in 1748 an ordained priest, he threw himself into work for the church. Indefatigable, enthusiastic, gentle, he remained faithful to his mission through war and revolution

and personal tragedy until he died 51 years later. His letters to the missionary headquarters brimmed with news of baptisms, catechisms, communions, and conversions. Responsible for a parish that extended from Sharon to Horseneck (Greenwich), he conducted as many as three services in different villages on the same Sunday. His followers came from a wide variety of backgrounds and included a number of free blacks and slaves. By the time of the Revolution he numbered 220 heads of families from Stamford and Greenwich in his flock.

Unlike the established clergy, Dibble, with his wife and seven children, was almost completely dependent on London for his income. The St. John's Society, however, found a magnanimous patron in St. George Talbot, an Anglican from Rye, New York, who admired Dibble and donated a sum totaling £600 to the church, as well as a bell, a silver tankard, and a salver. The money enabled John Lloyd, acting for the vestry, to purchase a 22-acre tract of land just north of the North Field, to serve as the glebe lands of the church. The area now borders on Franklin Street and is the site of St. Andrew's, an Episcopal church consecrated in 1861.

Around the middle of the 18th century, the Stamford community, while inbred and parochial, may have commanded as impressive an array of spiritual and intellectual talent as it has ever possessed. The trio of Mather, Welles, and Dibble was formidable. As the wars between England and France drew to a close and as the rift between England and her American colonies widened, each of the ministers, along with his parishioners, confronted a more complicated world. After 1755 the days of Stamford as an island community, largely concerned only with internal economic and religious issues, were rapidly coming to an end.

III THE CRISIS
OF THE REVOLUTION

Artist Delos Palmer painted the mural in the Old Town Hall of which this is a detail. It depicts Abraham Davenport on the famous "Dark Day" of 1780. Photograph by Norma David.

For every community from New Hampshire to Georgia, no matter how insular, the years between 1756 and 1790 were portentous: France lost virtually all her North American empire to her old adversary, Great Britain; Britain lost a substantial portion of her Atlantic imperium to the upstart United States of America; and the United States transformed itself from a loose confederation into a sovereign nation.

Stamford made only a marginal contribution to the French and Indian War, the final imperial war, fought from 1756 to 1763 on territory largely west of the Hudson. Four area militia companies were called up in 1758. On the night of July 8, some 500 recruits under the command of Captain David Waterbury of Stamford participated in an ill-planned assault on Fort Ticonderoga. Waterbury noted in his Orderly Book that seven men on his muster roll died and that 400 disappeared from the ranks during the abortive attack. By November the companies had returned home.

As in other New England towns, the war proved a boon to local businessmen. Purchases by British forces increased profits for the Lloyds, Davenports, and other entrepreneurs. Beginning on November 30, 1757, the town supplied billets, bedding, firewood, and candles for four months to 250 men of Colonel Fraser's Highland Battalion and to 17 women and 9 children who accompanied them. The community had invited the unit and was handsomely compensated for its hospitality.

Soon after victory over France, the British government, swamped with debt, significantly altered its policies on imperial taxation and trade regulation. Colonial leaders found the innovations outrageous and illegal. Each new duty, regulation, and oversight committee, whether on sugar, stamps, or tea, appeared worse than the one before. Led by such figures as Benjamin Franklin, Thomas Jefferson, John Adams, and George Washington, the colonists began to rethink the relationship of the colonies to the mother country. Within a period of 13 years, the process of appraisal and the British response to it led to continental congresses and petitions, to embargoes and street demonstrations, and ultimately to revolution.

From early spring, 1774, to July 4, 1776, frictions between Patriots and Tories in Stamford mounted along fault lines established years earlier. The fiercest critics of Britain tended to be Congregationalists; the staunchest apologists, Anglicans. Patriots increasingly suspected a British plot to thwart Congregationalism, home rule, and colonial growth. The passage of the five "Intolerable Acts" between March and June of 1774 confirmed their worst fears.

The statutes were enacted to punish

A MAP of the COLONIES of CONNECTICUT and RHODE ISLAND, Divided into Counties & Townships, from the best Authorities By Tho. Kitchin Geog.r

This 1758 map by British geographer Thomas Kitchin is the first printed map primarily of Connecticut now extant, and the information it provides on township boundaries is not found on any earlier maps still in existence. Courtesy, Library of Congress

Boston for the dumping of East India Company tea into its harbor. The notorious Boston Tea Party of December, 1773, followed a new Parliamentary order on tea imports. The first act of 1774 closed the Port of Boston. Another edict rescinded the Massachusetts charter and severely curtailed town meetings in the colony. Two other decrees dealt with the trials of officials and quartering of troops. A final statute placed the new territory west of the Appalachians under the Province of Quebec. The Patriot faction in Stamford and Connecticut argued that British dominion, once successful in Massachusetts, would move to abrogate the Connecticut charter and town meetings and that British interests, once in control of the frontier, would stifle colonial expansion. Placing the western lands under a Catholic province was an egregious insult. Following the lead of the

first Continental Congress and other New England towns, the Stamford town meeting, on October 7, 1774, set up a committee to collect subscriptions for besieged Boston and firmly resolved that:

The inhabitants of this town, sensibly affected with the distresses to which the town of Boston and province of Massachusetts Bay are subject by several unconstitutional acts of the British Parliament and also viewing the Quebec bill whereby the Roman Catholic religion is established over a great part of His Majesty's extensive continent of America as an attempt not barely to destroy our civil liberties but as an open declaration that our religious privileges, which our Fathers fled their native country to enjoy, are very soon to be abolished . . . join with our sister towns to assert our just rights and oppose every design of a corrupt ministry to enslave America . . .

Patriot opinion was steadfastly bolstered by the Old Light Congregational establishment. In a sermon in December, 1765, Welles denounced the Stamp Act, and he supported the Patriot side ardently at every opportunity. However, while visiting British prisoners in his capacity as chaplain, he contracted "jailhouse fever" and died suddenly on December 31, 1776. His post as minister of the First Society was not filled until 1781. But in neighboring Middlesex, Mather continued his fiery Patriot rhetoric and, indeed, excoriated Britain and her American sympathizers ever more shrilly. Mather is credited with writing the influential tract, published anonymously in Hartford in 1775, entitled *America's Appeal to the Impartial World. Wherein the Rights of the Americans as Men, British Subjects, and as Colonists . . . are Considered. . . .*

At the side of the ministers was the Honorable Abraham Davenport, son of the late Reverend John Davenport. Even at a time when deference to a prominent family was common in New England towns, the accumulation of offices, as well as acreage, by Davenport was remarkable. He held a dazzling array of posts simultaneously from the mid-1740s to his death in 1789 in his 74th year. On the local level he served as a selectman for 31 years, moderator of town meetings, town treasurer, and member of every important committee. On the colony level, he was an elected deputy from 1747 to 1766, and served as clerk of the House 13 times and speaker four times. Throughout the Revolutionary period he was a member of the Council of Assistants and the powerful Council of Safety. That Davenport was part of the inner circle of Governor Jonathan Trumbull undoubtedly gave Stamford a distinct voice in state affairs during the period.

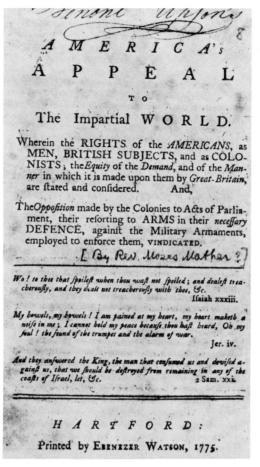

Although its authorship is not absolutely certain, "America's Appeal to the Impartial World . . ." was probably written by Stamford minister and ardent Patriot Moses Mather. Published in Hartford in 1775, the broadside was as influential in shaping public sentiment as it was impassioned. Courtesy, Beinecke Rare Book and Manuscript Library, Yale University

Davenport also filled the posts of justice of the peace for Fairfield County, judge of the Fairfield County Court, judge of probate of Stamford, and judge of the special Maritime Court of Fairfield County. In addition he was deacon of the First Church, member of the First Society Committee, and a colonel in the militia.

Davenport's political and ecclesiastical responsibilities did not curtail his passion to possess land. In delivering the eulogy for his wife's cousin, Dr. Timothy Dwight, president of Yale, noted that "Colonel Davenport acquired property with diligence and preserved it with frugality." Building on a base of about 650 acres inherited from his father, Davenport left a record of 119 land acquisitions in Stamford alone during his lifetime. He was a founding member of the Susquehanna Company, organized in

1753, to establish the right of Connecticut to a portion of Pennsylvania. In 1775 he was by far the wealthiest property owner in Stamford. During the War of Independence he was able to increase his holdings appreciably in his position as judge of the Probate Court, which ordered confiscations of Loyalist estates, and judge of the Maritime Court, which condemned prizes taken at sea. Along with his sons, John and James, and his brother, Silas, he acquired a significant portion of the confiscated farms.

Beyond his wealth and power, Davenport left a legacy to history. The episode known as "The Dark Day" revealed a part of his character. On May 19, 1780, the day turned so dark at noon in Hartford that members of the House of Representatives fell on their knees and clamored for adjournment. But Speaker Davenport rose to his feet and declared: "I am against adjournment. The Day of Judgment is either approaching, or it is not. If it is not, there is no cause for adjournment. If it is, I choose to be found doing my duty. I wish, therefore, that candles may be brought." Candles were produced, and the House continued in session. As the poet John Greenleaf Whittier later declaimed, Davenport had stood "A witness to the ages as they pass,/ That simple duty hath no place for fear."

In opposition to the Patriot establishment were the local Loyalists, or Tories. The Reverend E.B. Huntington, who published a history of Stamford in 1868, estimated the number of adult male Loyalists at 60. More recent observers have put the figure at 117 or 131. Though the definition of who constituted a Tory is not clear, all scholars have found Stamford and western Fairfield County hotbeds of Loyalism.

Reasons for attachment to the Crown were undoubtedly diverse. Class

background, however, appears to have played an insignificant role, since the majority of Loyalists, like the majority of Patriots, were middle-class farmers. Most Tories seemingly preferred reform to rebellion and shared a deep attachment to King and Empire, at least during the first years of the war. The critical factors were probably allegiance to the Church of England and to a pro-British kinship-and-neighborhood network.

During 1775 and the first half of 1776, Fyler Dibble, a hot-tempered young lawyer who was the son of the Anglican minister, was the ringleader in a desperate effort to halt the drift toward independence. In January, 1775, with the

The Honorable Abraham Davenport (son of Stamford's John Davenport and great-grandson of one of the founders of New Haven) is one of the most remarkable figures in Stamford history. Lawyer, politician, and landowner, Davenport was also very influential throughout Connecticut, especially during the Revolution. This portrait is by noted Connecticut painter Ralph Earl. Photograph by Joseph Szaszfai. Gift of Mrs. Harriet C. Davenport. Courtesy, Yale University Art Gallery

help of another militia captain, he tried to stop the passage of barrels of gunpowder out of Stamford by reporting their location to the deputy customs collector. Though he was questioned and supposedly repented, he did not convert. In pamphlets and speeches he urged non-cooperation in the anti-British boycott decreed by the Continental Congress.

Dibble's efforts proved futile, as did similar endeavors by other Loyalists. According to one newspaper story, Sylvanus Whitney was caught selling "forbidden" tea in June, 1775. In a variation on the Boston Tea Party, a Stamford crowd first hung the offensive package of tea on a gallows, specially erected at Main and Bank streets, and then burned it in a public bonfire.

With the adoption of the Declaration of Independence, Loyalists confronted agonizing decisions. Families and neighborhoods were sundered. In the northeast corner now known as Springdale, for example, 16 landowners opted for Loyalism and 11 for the Patriot side. (Three left no record of allegiance). Almost all the families in the first category were Anglican and related to the patriarch proprietor Obadiah Seely. As lines hardened, some adherents in each camp resorted to tactics of insult, harassment, plunder, and even whipping. Following the legislative mandate to confiscate the properties of departed Loyalists, a little over 1,000 acres, or about 1.5 percent of the town's area, was sold at auction.

The range of Loyalist response was wide. The Reverend Ebenezer Dibble himself, and perhaps the majority of his congregation, remained outwardly neutral and were not molested. Other British sympathizers, while apparently quiet, refused to serve when called up by the militia or hid reluctant draftees—or, worse, aided the enemy by furnishing arms or providing secret intelligence and guidance to hostile raiding parties. As late as August, 1781, a committee of the General Assembly identified 16 active "inimicals" in Stamford.

During the first year of the war, some 40 householders, including Samuel Jarvis, the longtime town clerk, whose family had been roughly treated, departed for British-held Long Island. Many later moved to friendly New York City and finally, at the close of hostilities, took ship to New Brunswick, where the British government allotted them grants of land.

Some young men openly joined the King's service. In October, 1777, the Selectmen petitioned the General Assembly for a reduction in Stamford's militia quota on the grounds that over 100 men had "gone over to the enemy." A few, such as Samuel Crissy and Nathan Munday, quickly regretted their decisions and returned. Others, such as John Morehouse and Benjamin Betts, later claimed they had been enticed or abducted. But Joseph Hoyt 5th, son of a Patriot hero, voluntarily boarded the *Asia* on the first day of 1776 and unabashedly solicited recruits for George III. Fyler Dibble left for Long Island, too, and joined a British regiment, but he and his wife and family suffered the trials of Job. Despite repeated moves they were turned out of their homes and stripped of possessions and clothes four times and ultimately migrated to St. John's, New Brunswick. Once there, however, Dibble confronted more misfortune, the possibility of long imprisonment for debt. One day in March, 1784, while the family was at tea, he took a razor and slit his throat.

The Tory problem, though perhaps the most painful, was only one of the dilemmas posed for Stamford during the War of Independence. In coping with the war, the traditional town meeting mechanism worked well. When the state required that each freeman take an Oath of Fidelity, 288 men stepped forward on September 16, 1777, and swore fealty, although only 101 names had been registered on the 1777 freemen list. At the town meeting held on January 12, 1778, each article of the Articles of Confederation was unanimously approved.

For each new function assigned to communities by the Continental Congress or the General Assembly, the town meeting established a special purpose committee and, when necessary, levied a special rate. The system was effective, because plain farmers were willing to serve and to pay taxes despite the costs in time and money. There were committees to enforce the embargo, to assist the commissary with clothing and provisions, to inspect supplies, to assist families of Continental servicemen, to monitor dangerous persons, to procure recruits through hiring or the draft, and as late as February, 1782, to organize a town guard. Membership ranged from one to 18 and rotated annually. In addition, from 1779 to 1790, in response to the scourge of smallpox, the town set up a "hospital" on the village outskirts to "carry on innoculations," first under Dr. James Cogswell, then under Dr. John Wilson.

Life in Stamford during the Revolution was recaptured by participants in Bicentennial festivities held at Fort Stamford in 1976. Photograph by Tom Ryan.

The number of Stamford men who served as soldiers may have been about 420, but it is not possible to arrive at a precise figure. Continental, state, and local jurisdictions each raised contingents; one branch sometimes temporarily co-opted the units of another; and individuals enlisted in different services or repeatedly in the same service. Approximately 165 men saw Continental service; over 200 served only in the militia. The number under arms peaked during the years 1775 to 1777 and 1780 to 1782, when peril from British forces seemed at its worst. Official archives record the deaths of at least 22 in field,

volunteered for the 5th Connecticut Regiment under Colonel David Waterbury, opposed the adoption of the regiment by the Continental Army, organized in May, 1775. Sent on the ill-fated and miserable campaign to take Canada under General Richard Montgomery, significant numbers deserted in October and November. Similarly local soldiers, who enlisted in the 7th Regiment of Colonel Charles Webb, resented absorption by the Continental Army and departed from the Boston camps without leave.

A month after the resolution for independence, raw militia were thrown

A skirmish between Patriots and Redcoats was reenacted during the Bicentennial celebration at Fort Stamford. Photograph by Tom Ryan.

hospital, and prison.

Many local enlistees were not initially prepared for armed confrontation away from home and left the service precipitously during 1775 and 1776. The 33 men from Stamford and Greenwich who marched to Boston after the Lexington alarm, under veteran militia captain Joseph Hoyt, returned in eight days when they found the city not in danger. Many Stamford-area men, who

against the British professionals at the Battle of Long Island. The 9th Connecticut Regiment of Colonel John Mead, drawn from the Stamford area, was unready. In the chaos that followed the retreat across the East River to Harlem Heights, only 74 of the original 600 men remained with their unit. Beginning in 1777, however, as leaders and men gained in discipline, skill, and experience, such episodes were rare.

Both Waterbury and Webb carried on. Each was a prosperous, popular Stamford landowner, well into his fifties, who had served frequently as selectman and deputy. Though denied a Continental commission, the stubbornly patriotic Waterbury was appointed a brigadier-general by the General Assembly in June, 1776. Among other responsibilities he supervised naval construction near Fort Ticonderoga and was second in command to General Benedict Arnold at the disastrous battle of Valcour Bay. Captured, exchanged, and placed on parole for three years, he took charge of constructing a fort in his home country in 1781. Webb, commissioned a Continental colonel in 1776, led his regiment in battle at White Plains, Trenton, and Princeton, suffered a disability, and was discharged early in 1778. His son, Charles Webb, Jr., was less fortunate: he was killed by a gunboat in the Sound.

Younger men showed fine mettle, too. Both Stephen Betts, who enlisted at age 18 in 1775 and served for the duration, and William Brown, who joined as a boy of 16 and left a man of 22, were part of a group of 20 who attacked a redoubt (stronghold) at the opening of the Battle of Yorktown in October, 1781. Betts was commander and Brown standard-bearer of the high-risk maneuver, dubbed "the Forlorn Hope." For courage Betts was breveted major, and Brown received the Badge of Merit, predecessor of the Order of the Purple Heart.

At home geography placed Stamford on the frontier once more. From the beginning of hostilities, the British controlled New York City, and much of Long Island and Westchester County. Royal forces also dominated Newport, Rhode Island, from December, 1776, to October, 1779, and crippled commerce in

southern New England waters. With provisions of all kinds at a premium for both sides, Stamford lay at the center of a web of schemes and plots and of incursions and raids, by sea and land, by regulars and irregulars during all the nine years of fighting.

The Revolution provided unprecedented opportunities for gain in supplying livestock and such commodities as flour and firewood to either side. The most profitable mode was by sea. Although the General Assembly early banned trading with the enemy and export of essential materials from Connecticut, instituted price and wage controls, and pursued an erratic monetary policy, trade was brisk up and down and across the Sound. Along with legitimate exchange, smuggling and collusion flourished. When the French alliance of 1778 failed to bring the war to a swift conclusion, the atmosphere of intrigue and edginess along both banks of the sound grew heavier.

The line between privateering—encouraged by the state—and piracy was a thin one. The adventures of the whaleboats, commissioned as privateers, remain almost as shrouded in fog as the coves in which they hid. Peculiar to the western region, they were reputedly 20 to 30 feet long, sharpened at both ends, equipped with 4 to 20 oars and a sail, sometimes armed with a swivel cannon, and manned by a captain and six to eight crewmen. About 30 such vessels were berthed in Stamford, and itinerant craft also anchored in nearly sheltered creeks. One intrepid whaleboat captain, Ebenezer Jones, was credited with boarding and capturing a royal sloop-of-war in Oyster Bay by pretending that he led an official inspection party. Others may have taken direct part in military operations.

Raids by regular forces on western Fairfield County towns were a constant threat. Landings and incursions by the

enemy took place all around Stamford, though the town itself was not invaded. General William Tryon led three major assaults: on Danbury and Ridgefield in April, 1777, where Stamford's General David Wooster was mortally wounded; on Horseneck (Greenwich) in April, 1779, where the ride of General Israel Putnam became a legend; and on Fairfield and Norwalk, as well as New Haven, in July, 1779, where each town was put to the torch. In companies and even as individuals, area militia, under Colonel John Mead and other commands, were kept busy coping with these and dozens of other engagements. Many fought valiantly.

American forces retaliated against British invasions with offensive operations across the Sound designed to collect or destroy stockpiles of provisions and to capture prisoners for purposes of exchange. Major (later Colonel) Benjamin Tallmadge used Shippan Point as a staging area for the first successful counter-attack on Lloyd's Neck. On September 5, 1779, his hundred Light Dragoons attacked a force of 500, took 100 prisoners, and returned to Stamford without a single casualty. Until December, 1782, he returned repeatedly and secretly to the Point to launch raids on the Island, perhaps sometimes with the assistance of whaleboatmen.

Beside the attacks and counterattacks of the regular troops, the depradations of the irregulars were a chronic source of anxiety. Bands of "cowboys" and "skinners," such as DeLancey's Corps from Westchester, made overland forays and drove off horses, cattle, oxen, hogs, and sheep. Sometimes they entered homes and took clothing, utensils, jewelry, and whatever else was portable. After 1779 episodes of pillage multiplied. Between 1776 and 1779 only 17 Stamford householders requested tax abatements on the grounds of damages suffered from

This woodcut, believed to be the work of Henry Dawkins, first appeared during the Revolution, on a proclamation issued by Governor Jonathan Trumbull in 1777. Fittingly, for the state and the time it was issued, it shows items relating to sea trade and instruments of war.

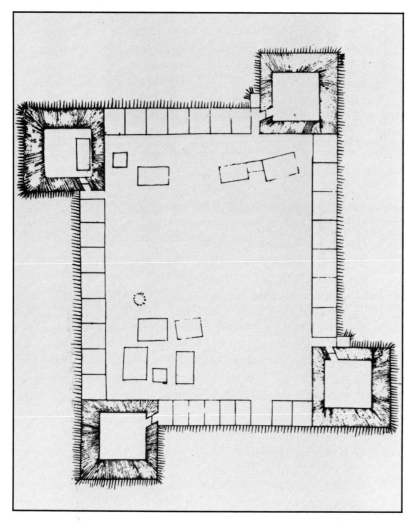

This is the plan of Fort Stamford, designed by Colonel Rufus Putnam, the architect of West Point. David Waterbury supervised construction of the fort between September and November, 1781, and it remained an important defense against the British for the rest of the war. The fort, now a national monument, is on Westover Road, a mile south of the Merritt Parkway.

raids by strangers. Between 1780 and 1782, the number of claimants rose to 172.

Loyalists who had stayed home (and, presumably, their Patriot counterparts) also engaged in rustling livestock. Doughty Thaddeus Hoyt lay in wait for and captured his Tory neighbor, Samuel Lockwood, in the very act of rounding up his cattle. Gideon Weed was not so lucky. Only 19 years of age, he was left in temporary charge of a Middlesex militia company on August 2, 1781. He spied a Tory gang near the schoolhouse and lined up his men to face them. He was fatally shot while standing between two of his brothers.

Worse than raids for gain were raids for

revenge. At Lloyd's Neck and other points, Loyalist refugees sought retribution for acts of harassment and confiscation. Moses Mather of Middlesex, whose anti-Tory tirades were unceasing, was a prime target. On July 29, 1779, eight men, including five former parishioners, ransacked his home. Along with four of his sons, he was taken to New York and kept in prison for over a month. His home was again looted on March 19, 1781. Four months later, after he had delivered a barbed sermon on treasonous Tories, about 40 men silently crossed the Sound at night in seven boats and hid in a swamp. The next day, Sunday, July 22, 1781, they surrounded the meeting house during the afternoon service. Captain Frost, an ex-neighbor, demanded and secured surrender. The invaders lined up the 50 adult male parishioners in pairs, tied them arm to arm, and placed Mather at their head. After appropriating horses and jewelry, they marched their prisoners to the boats and crossed back to Lloyd's Neck. Twenty-four captives were returned on parole, but 26 were taken by brig to the execrable Provost Prison in New York City. On December 27, the 19 survivors of the ordeal, including Mather, were exchanged and returned home.

The outrage committed against the Middlesex minister and congregation reinforced deep fears of further British assault. During the summer of 1781 Connecticut and Continental strategists considered the erection of a chain of forts from the Sound to the Hudson. On August 31, Governor Trumbull and the Council of Safety, prompted by Waterbury and probably Davenport, authorized Waterbury "to erect some small fortifications to prevent a surprise attack from enemy's horse . . . and to make choice of a strong woody ground." Waterbury immediately set to work to build Fort Stamford on a ridge above the

Mianus River, on the western border about three miles north of the Sound. Colonel Rufus Putnam, one of the architects of West Point, prepared the plan for a 135-by-165-foot earthwork fort, with a redoubt, measuring 30 feet square in the interior, at each corner. According to Waterbury's Orderly Book, construction began on October 4; heavy work was completed by early November; and the garrison, initially numbering some 700 militiamen, served as an effective deterrent against regulars and raiders in the western zone.

Even after the surrender of Cornwallis at Yorktown on October 19, 1781, both the General Assembly and the Continental command considered the Stamford region, as well as much of the Northeast, vulnerable. When the terms of Waterbury's troops expired in February, 1782, an apprehensive Major General William Heath sent Major Hugh Maxwell and 300 Continentals to man Fort Stamford temporarily. Two months later

Colonel Samuel Canfield and a new contingent of 300 state militia arrived and stayed for the duration. In November, 1782, negotiators in Paris agreed to preliminary articles of peace. In April, 1783, the Continental Congress proclaimed a cessation of hostilities, and Fort Stamford was permanently decommissioned. On September 3, the final peace treaty was signed.

With the Treaty of Paris, the war with Britain ended. But the "civil war" between Patriots and Loyalists that had wracked the community for nearly a decade took longer to subside. Memories of loss nurtured an attitude of repugnance and intolerance toward former Loyalists on the part of some Patriots. On January 2, 1782, thirty-seven Stamford and Greenwich residents signed a petition cautioning the General Assembly against efforts to allow Tories who had served in the British forces to return home. As late as December 8, 1783, the Stamford town meeting again warned such

Moses Mather's anti-Loyalist sentiments were well-known throughout the Revolution and they made him a target of harassment three times between 1779 and 1781. His parsonage, shown here, was ransacked twice. After the first attack, Mather was taken to New York and imprisoned by the British for more than a month. After the third, at the meeting house, he and 25 other men were taken to Provost Prison in New York for five months, during which time six died.

Major John Davenport (son of Abraham) and his wife, Mary, as painted by Ralph Earl. Photograph by Joseph Szaszfai. Gift of Mrs. Harriet C. Davenport. Courtesy, Yale University Art Gallery

"unwholesome" persons out of town. Nevertheless the state government, impelled by concerns for civil peace and economic reconstruction, moved quickly to restore calm and stability. At the May, 1783, session the General Assembly repealed the principal anti-Tory pieces of legislation, except for the confiscation measures.

For the new nation facing peace after triumph in war, the new political order began shakily. Under the Articles of Confederation the states retained sovereign powers while the Confederation functioned largely as a debating forum. The system proved so weak and divisive in peacetime that the very survival of the United States was threatened. Rescue came with the drafting of the Constitution of 1787, which gave sovereign power to the federal government while retaining significant

roles for the states. For the small state of Connecticut, the framework established by the Constitution offered clear political, financial, and commercial advantages. After the General Assembly ordered the towns to choose delegates to a special ratifying convention, a majority of the Stamford town meeting selected John and James Davenport, sons of the late community leader, as their deputies. Connecticut became the fourth state to ratify when the delegates at the Hartford convention of January 4, 1788, approved the Constitution by a vote of more than three to one. The Davenport brothers, along with every representative of Fairfield County, voted yes.

After years of turmoil generated by war and civil strife, Stamford swiftly and gladly fell into place as a link in the chain of communities that made up the new federal republic.

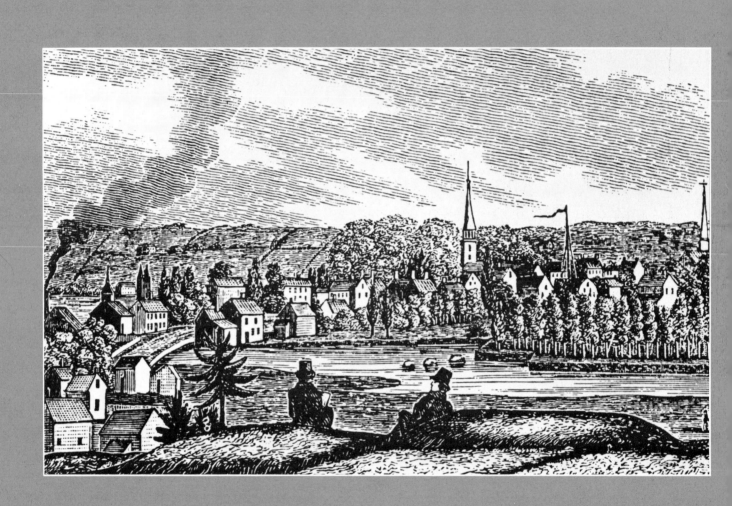

IV OLD TOWN IN THE NEW REPUBLIC

With the Constitution in place the towns and villages of America could rely on a durable national framework. Between 1791 and 1843 the old community of Stamford strove to adapt to the dynamic economic currents and political pressures of the new republic.

Stamford in 1790 was an agricultural and market town of 4,051 inhabitants. It had grown 11 percent since 1774. The residents were largely farmers who raised potatoes, wheat, corn, rye, and oats, as well as livestock, and exported their surpluses (particularly potatoes) to the ready market of New York. The typical family, which included five children, was descended from early settlers. As late as 1831, over one-third of the town registry list was made up of Scofields, Smiths, Lockwoods, Weeds, Hoyts, and Junes. The black minority included 46 slaves and 27 free persons—about 1.5 percent of the population, a figure that remained virtually unchanged until 1900.

Farms were scattered over the town's 80 square miles. In 1800 a total of 77 families, or about 10 percent of the residents, lived in the central area surrounding today's Atlantic Square. At this point the east-west Country Road, or Main Street, intersected the north-south thoroughfare now known as Atlantic and Bedford streets. To the north of Main Street, a short wide avenue called Broad Street connected Atlantic Street to the Rippowam River. Several lanes, guarded by gates, led south from the Country Road to landings on the Sound. Four general stores sufficed to handle the local demand for drygoods, groceries, and spirits. Sarah Munday also kept a stock of candy available for the children. Webb's Tavern and Leeds' Tavern offered refreshment to both residents and travelers on the stages between New York and New Haven. When George Washington breakfasted at Webb's Tavern while on tour in 1789, he found it a "tolerable good house." Country folk also exchanged neighborhood news in outlying gathering places such as Shippan, the Cove, Bangall, Long Ridge, or Canaan, where they could find a general store, a sawmill, a gristmill, a school, and sometimes a church.

Over the course of the first four decades of the 19th century, changes in the economy of Stamford were modest and most clearly evident in respect to transportation. The first shock of the new for some residents came with the publication of the plans of the Connecticut Turnpike Company. The Stamford town meeting had voted in 1805 to petition the General Assembly to deny the company, led by John Davenport, Jr., and associates the right to build a turnpike. The following year, however, the Assembly granted the corporation a charter to build a toll road between Fairfield and Byram.

There was little dispute on the need

1791–1843

Webb's Tavern, on Bank Street, was a Stamford landmark not only during the 18th century—George Washington breakfasted here in 1789—but well into the next century also. It stood until 1868.

for a new thoroughfare or on the size of the revenues to be reaped at the four gates proposed for the route. Virtually every coach traveler who journeyed between Boston and New York City dreaded the rocky and hilly portion of the Boston Post Road that traversed Stamford. The Connecticut Turnpike Company, however, revealed in 1806 that, in accordance with the recommendation of the Connecticut Road Commission, it proposed to build the highway straight through the center of the village and to divide the oldest community burying ground. Fury erupted. Appeals failed. When the corporation began carefully to move graves to Park Place, captains Isaac Lockwood and Thaddeus Hoyt and others resisted. After the first day of grading operations in the cemetery, citizens with ox teams worked all night to set huge rocks before both entrances. The Turnpike Company removed the rocks the next day, but the

men and animals returned the following night. After three nights, state officials intervened with threats of legal action and brought the resistance to an end. The turnpike was eventually completed, but the outraged Lockwood and Hoyt avoided the "desecrated" portion of the road ever after.

While the turnpike remained the only overland artery through Stamford until the coming of the railroad, access to transportation by water steadily improved. In 1833 excavation began on a ship canal linking the east branch of the Rippowam River to a point 10 rods (55 yards) south of Atlantic Square. Alfred Bishop, a native son who had migrated to New Jersey to farm and had subsequently turned to canal construction, guided the undertaking. His company dug the channel, along what is now Canal Street, and erected a bulkhead and two warehouses at a cost of $7,000.

The federal government designated

Stamford an official port of entry, and a lively West Indian, as well as domestic, freight trade developed in the second quarter of the 19th century. The local newspaper reported that $45,513 was collected in duties between 1823 and 1845. While a pink, the *Blossom*, of 70 tons, was built in Stamford in 1690, the first and largest full-rigged vessel constructed in the harbor was built in 1832 or 1833. Little is known about it except that its principal builder, Captain Shadrach Hoyt, committed suicide when the ship was almost ready to put to sea. In the mid-1840s five or six Stamford-based brigs and barks plied the Caribbean, and 12 or 14 brigs or schooners were active in the coasting trade. Unfortunately the silt which collected in the harbor and the failure to secure federal funds for dredging (prior to 1886) eventually limited local water-borne commerce.

In contrast, seagoing passenger traffic between Stamford and New York flourished during most of the 19th century. It took approximately 10 hours to make the trip under sail. When the Stamford Steamboat Company, organized in 1825 by James Stephens and Peter Smith, announced that the *Oliver Wolcott* would make three regular trips a week to New York, the service was instantly popular. Imitators soon followed. The fare averaged 50 cents, and the voyage usually involved several ports of call. Cornelius Vanderbilt, owner of the *Citizen*, which steamed between Port Chester and New York, tried in 1830 to eliminate the competition by cutting the fare in half. To the relief of the other captains he soon lost interest and sold the *Citizen* the following year. The local newspaper editor commented acidly that, "The proprietor of Long Island Sound has relinquished that part of it lying between New York and Bridgeport." Direct Stamford-New York service was instituted

Construction of the Connecticut Turnpike was seen as a mixed blessing by Stamford residents in 1806, when it was learned that the highway would go through the middle of town and the oldest burying ground. Resistance proved useless. These gravestone fragments, unearthed only a few years ago near Cascade Road, are all that remain of many of the tablets from the pre-1806 period.

For those who have wondered how Canal Street got its name, this 1851 map clearly shows Stamford's ship canal, completed by Alfred Bishop in 1833. Until it was eclipsed by the coming of the railroad in 1848, the canal was a major factor in promoting commerce. Sloops, towed by horses, glided into town and unloaded at two warehouses near Atlantic Square.

in 1852. Despite recurrent problems with fires, the *Stamford,* the *Shippan,* and other vessels each carried as many as 500 passengers to the metropolis in the 1860s and 1870s during the height of the traffic and for decades after the coming of the railroad.

Manufacturing enterprises remained small and closely linked to the needs of an agricultural population during the years between 1791 and 1843. From the beginning of settlement, gristmills and sawmills proliferated, and mills which produced rolled iron, tinware, wire, machinery, and furnaces emerged along the Rippowam River. In small shops, often in homes, woolen cloth, hats, shoes, carriages, cabinets, and barrels were turned out. The Census of 1840 listed blacksmiths, saddlers, carpenters, masons, silversmiths, and a dozen attorneys and physicians. During the half-

Alfred Hoyt, who served as a state representative in 1864, 1865, and 1869, was active in the West Indies trade. With Captain William Lockwood, Hoyt built the Julia Ann *and imported pineapples and other goods.*

century following independence, the only large-scale enterprise established in Stamford was flour-milling. According to the *Gazeteer* published by Pease and Niles in 1819, the Cove Mills complex of John William Holly was the largest flour mill in Connecticut.

Commercial, agricultural, and allied activity was sufficient, however, to generate local wealth. When editor William H. Holly in 1837 drew the first detailed map of central Stamford that has survived, he counted 169 buildings, including 61 stores and shops, 4 iron manufactories, and the Town House. The Stage House, an impressive hostelry midway between New York and New Haven, was the designated site of the United States Postal Service for the exchange of horses and handling of passengers and mail. There were several

elegant mansions, including the homes of Lieutenant Governor Charles Hawley (designed by Thomas P. Dixon), of John Davenport (at which Lafayette was received during a tour in 1824), and of George E. Waring (which was elaborately "Gothicized" a few years later).

The community's economy was dynamic enough to stimulate a public meeting in March, 1834, to establish a town bank. The result was the drafting of a petition to the General Assembly. In the May, 1834, session, the Assembly granted a charter to the First Stamford National Bank and Trust Company and named Charles Hawley, Thaddeus Betts, Joshua Ferris, John Bell, Jr., and John W. Leeds as commissioners. In return for the charter privilege, the bank was obliged to pay Wesleyan University $5,000 in two installments. In June 2,000 shares of stock, at $50 each, were offered to the public and sold within five hours. After a short period during which business was transacted in the home of Isaac Quintard, the grocery store of John Leeds on Main Street was transformed into a bank and used for the next 50 years. Despite the Panic of 1837, the First Stamford Bank, under the direction of Charles Hawley, Theodore Davenport, and others, survived nicely.

Farmers, merchants, and other groups in Stamford who depended on domestic exports, however, did suffer from the severe depression which followed. Local trade had already been reduced by the completion in 1825 of the Erie Canal, which brought products directly from the Great Lakes region into New York City. When the cholera epidemic of 1832, the fires of 1835 and 1839, and the bank failures of 1837 seriously weakened the economy of New York City, the economy of Stamford was further chilled. Revival began only in 1843 with improvements at the national level.

In contrast to the relative stability of

the economy, politics in the half-century following adoption of the Constitution were lively, even dramatic. In the bracing atmosphere of the early republic, community and state institutions inherited from the Colonial past were challenged and, in some cases, permanently altered.

Three movements modified Stamford's government structure between 1800 and 1830. The first blow to the status quo came from the Canaan Society. Established in 1731, Canaan Parish, which included about 1,500 inhabitants, was divided between two towns. Two-thirds lay in Norwalk, one-third in Stamford. In 1796 the 274 families of the

parish petitioned the General Assembly for incorporation as the Town of New Canaan. The principal argument of the petitioners was that the distances from their homes to the center of Norwalk or Stamford, which sometimes equalled 9 to 12 miles, prevented them from fulfilling their duties as freemen. Although Stamford appointed an agent to argue against the secession, the Assembly granted the petition in May, 1801.

The second blow came from the east. The Middlesex Society, established in 1737, had been a hotbed of Patriot-versus-Loyalist fury during the Revolution. Peace and the passage of time, however, had brought a degree of

miles of land, the area it occupies today.

The effect of the loss of the two parishes on the community was deepened by the migration of sons and daughters to more attractive lands in northwestern Connecticut, Vermont, upstate New York, Ohio, and other points west. In 1810, after the departure of New Canaan, the population reached 4,440, an increase of only 389 over the figure 20 years earlier. In 1820, after the departure of Darien, the number fell to 3,284. The population climbed slowly to 3,707 in 1830, but in the midst of a depression, shrank to 3,516 in 1840.

The final change in the local system of government arose from the reluctance of the majority of farmers to expand political responsibilities beyond the traditional concerns of the rural population. The town meetings dealt only with essential issues. Between 1798 and 1856 public school affairs, following state guidelines, developed on district committees, elected by the freemen in each district, and school societies, composed of representatives from the district committees and members elected at large. (At times there were 15 or more school districts, most served by one-room schoolhouses.) In the town meetings debates and decisions revolved around repair of roads, ringing of swine, and conduct of lawsuits. Many legal battles concerned efforts to compel other towns to take responsibility for paupers. In 1839 David Waterbury petitioned the town meeting for compensation "for the loss of cows in consequence of eating pickles thrown from the poorhouse" and was awarded $50.

In general the freemen succeeded in controlling expenditures. During the years between 1824 and 1842 the budget stood between $900 and $1,700, with the exception of one year: in 1830 the freemen agreed to spend $2,945, which included $999 to cover the cost of

John William Holly, a descendant of one of Stamford's earliest settlers, built a complex of mills on Cove Island. In the 1830s and 1840s Henry J. Sanford purchased the Holly home and mills and launched the Stamford Manufacturing Company. This 1842 pencil sketch shows the East and West mills at either end and Holly's home between them.

tranquility to the parish of 1,126 inhabitants. In 1804 the freemen petitioned the General Assembly for incorporation as the Town of Darien. During the next six years, Stamford regularly voted to oppose the excision in town meetings. The real obstacle, however, was confusion over the eastern boundary of the parish and the objection of Norwalk to further "mutilation." At length, in 1820, Thaddeus Bell, who lived in Middlesex and who served as a representative from Stamford, persuaded the Assembly to establish the Town of Darien entirely on territory that had been part of Stamford. As a consequence, Stamford itself was reduced to 38 square constructing a modest, wooden, two-story Town House. Located in Atlantic Square, the building served as the community's center for 37 years before being sold for use as a private home.

The growth of the core of the village, a three-quarter-mile enclave abutting the harbor and river, made the cautious and thrifty farmers increasingly uncomfortable. By 1830 the area where 633 people lived contained 68 dwellings, 4 churches, 11 stores and shops, a public school, 5 private schools, the Town House, a printing office, a flour mill, a tannery, and 3 iron-rolling mills. Clearly demands would soon arise at the town meetings for funds for the prevention of fire, control of traffic, and a range of new services for the sector.

Other Connecticut towns had already devised ways to relieve the town meetings of municipal responsibilities. The solution was to create a borough, a structure derived from medieval England, as a government-within-a-government. In Stamford the 633 core inhabitants would remain town residents, but would be subject to an additional tax and government. In 1830 David Holly and others, responding to the town consensus, successfully petitioned the General Assembly for the creation of the Borough of Stamford. A new and additional governing body, the Board of Warden and Burgesses, was established. The seven-member board met frequently, made practical decisions on policies, and proposed ordinances and mill rates. The borough budget, subject to approval by the borough meeting, varied between $150 and $160 annually during the next decade. Extended to cover a 1.5-mile area in 1854 and given additional powers by Special Acts, the borough managed the emerging "downtown" of Stamford for 63 years.

Changes in forms of government tell only part of the story of politics in Stamford after independence. The impulse to dissent that had been manifest during the Revolution did not disappear in the new nation but took different forms. In Connecticut the Federalist Party of Hamilton and Adams was allied to the Congregational clergy and elite families such as the Davenports. In 1798, the year of the notorious and short-lived Alien and Sedition Acts, which were designed to repress criticism of the Federalists, community leaders including Captain Isaac Lockwood, George Mills, and other followers of Jefferson and Madison met secretly to form a Democratic-Republican Society. In New Haven and Norwalk the opposition organized similar partisan clubs, which eventually coalesced and emerged openly as the Democratic-Republican Party. Lockwood went on to serve 24 terms as selectman and 16 times as moderator; Mills served five terms in the Assembly and four times as selectman. (Lockwood's later militant opposition to the turnpike may have been partially inspired by his partisan opposition to the Federalist Davenports.)

The Democratic-Republican group perhaps muted opposition in the community to the prosecution of the War of 1812, which was strongly denounced by leading Connecticut Federalists at the Hartford Convention in 1814. Two local companies of militia were raised for a few days in September, 1813, when English ships appeared off Shippan Point. A third company of infantry was also called up during the last two months of that year. In his *History of Stamford* Huntington listed 29 individuals who volunteered. Several served in the defense of New London; Reuben Dibble and William W. Lounsbury were taken prisoner; and Captain William W. Skiddy was a midshipman aboard the *Hornet* when it participated in the defeat of the *Penguin* in the South Atlantic at the end of 1814.

Huntington also commented that several wealthy townsmen got their start in business by engaging in wartime privateering.

After the close of the war in 1815, resentment against the Federalist establishment in Connecticut and in Stamford mounted. When independence had been declared, Connecticut had chosen to retain the Charter of 1662 as its state constitution and, along with the Colonial document, a religious tax and special privileges for the Congregational churches. (Except for Rhode Island, every other state drafted a new state constitution.) The opposition of the members of St. John's Episcopal Church in Stamford, a large minority in the town, to the Connecticut Charter was reinforced by the rise of a variety of dissenting churches around the turn of the century.

Promoted by local adherents and supported by networks in neighboring towns and counties, four new denominations erected houses of worship. In 1773, four years after the baptism of Ebenezer Ferris by Elder Gano in New York, Ferris and others formed a Stamford Baptist church. A meeting house was erected in Bangall near the site on which Fort Stamford was later constructed. The church attracted numerous former Congregationalists from Fairfield and Westchester counties. In June, 1790, a second Baptist church was raised on River Street near the Broad Street Bridge. Meanwhile the Methodists established a Fairfield-Westchester circuit, the oldest in New England, in 1788 and first held services in the home of Isaac Reed. In April, 1814, the town meeting authorized the selectmen to give a 99-year lease to the Methodist Society for a piece of ground near the old cemetery which some called a "mudhole in the Commons." Nevertheless a church was erected there within the year, and a

second edifice was dedicated in 1844. The Society of Friends, or Quakers, who had numbered adherents among the earliest settlers, built a small square meeting house in 1811. Finally, 14 Universalists of the Long Ridge section, who had held monthly meetings in homes for years, organized a formal church in 1833 which built an imposing Gothic meeting house in the center of town 12 years later.

The diverse denominations joined the political opposition in criticizing the antiquated state charter and pressing for a constitution which would finally separate church and state. Stamford overwhelmingly supported the Tolerationist coalition of Episcopalians, Dissenters, and Republicans in the gubernatorial elections of 1816, 1817, and 1818. A landslide Tolerationist victory in the state in 1818 paved the way for the calling of a Constitutional Convention in Hartford in late August. Stamford was represented by James Stevens, an ardent Republican lawyer, who had served in the Assembly continuously since 1804 (and who went on to serve a term in Congress). Stevens was a member of the drafting committee and advocated radical reforms. Convinced that the finished document was too conservative, he and John Weed, Jr., the other Stamford representative, voted against the new constitution in the convention. Stamford freemen, however, gave the document their firm approval by a vote of 107 to 51.

During the decades following 1818, when Jacksonian Democrats lustily battled Whigs, the founding of a weekly newspaper provided a lively outlet for community opinions. On April 8, 1829, the *Stamford Intelligencer*, a four-page weekly printed on a hand press, appeared. Its first editor and publisher, Albert Hanford, a printer from Norwalk, promised that it would be "strictly

The Grand Union Hotel, which played a role in the "Miller Excitement" of 1842-1843, opened amidst much celebration by the "Millerites" in May, 1844. Designed by architect Thomas P. Dixon, who had to resort to some creative tactics to oversee the construction, the hotel was a prominent Stamford landmark for nearly 80 years. This photograph was taken in 1892.

Republican." Hanford was succeeded briefly by an Alexander Hamilton, about whom little is known.

Beginning in February, 1830, the journal came under the editorship of William H. "Will Hen" Holly (the designer of the 1837 map). A man who functioned as the town's voice during the next four decades, Holly was a seventh-generation Stamford native possessed of the kind of political acumen, zest for controversy, and ready wit that made him a natural community leader. He enlivened caucus and convention meetings, served frequently as moderator of town meetings, and was a member of every important local board. He was repeatedly elected judge of probate and, though without formal legal training, reportedly confounded attorneys with his detailed knowledge of the common law.

Except for periods in 1839-1840 and 1841-1843, the paper remained under Holly's stewardship until 1848. He shifted party allegiance and changed the paper's title several times but gave partisans ample space in letters and columns. Holly began his editorship as a Whig, became

an ardent supporter of Jackson and Van Buren, and returned to the Whig fold with the Panic of 1837. This mercurial figure then actively supported "Tippicanoe and Tyler too" in 1840. The newspaper, which was not always regular in publication, was called at various times *The Sentinel, The Democratic Sentinel, The Farmer's Advocate, The Stamford Sentinel and Fairfield County Democrat, The Farmer's and Mechanic's Advocate,* and finally *The Stamford Advocate.* Because of illness Holly sold the *Advocate* in 1848 to editor Edgar Hoyt and his partner, Andrew J. Smith. As the Civil War approached, the paper settled in firmly under the banner of the new Republican Party.

During his editorial tenure Holly inveighed against intemperance, gambling, lottery subscriptions, and other practices and strongly defended the Masonic Order which had supported a lodge in Stamford since 1763. In 1830 the rise of an anti-Masonic movement and the virulent fulminations of the Reverend Joel Mann of Bridgeport on the secret philanthropic society produced outrage in the press. When a pair of roving "lecturers" hired a hall in Stamford to "expose" the fraternity, the defenders of Masonry fired a cannon at the building and hanged the men in effigy. The two agitators departed hurriedly by a rear door.

The zest of the Jacksonian age for controversy showed itself in the furor over the cause of a young woman, Martha Blackwell Miller. Married in 1834 at the age of 17 to Charles F. Miller of New York, she fled to Stamford late in 1842 to escape her husband. The irrepressible Holly denounced Miller as a philanderer, a "brutal and unfeeling wretch," and "a vile monster." He reviled the Millerites, who reputedly included members of the Locofocos, or workingman's wing, of the Democratic Party. Albert Seely, proprietor of the Stage House, and a coterie of young men joined "Will Hen" in rallying to the defense of the appealing young woman, whom they saw as a greatly injured innocent. Undaunted, the husband, armed with pistol and fast horses, made several futile attempts to find his wife. On January 25, 1843, he finally spied her at a window of the Stage House. He seized her instantly and, with the help of a friend, drove her, screaming and disheveled, at breakneck speed through the streets of Stamford and back to New York.

The affair was not over, however. In revenge against Seely, the triumphant Millerites organized a joint-stock company to build a rival hotel opposite the Stage House. They engaged Thomas P. Dixon, architect and master-builder, to design and oversee the project. Seely responded by securing a warrant against Dixon. The intrepid architect outwitted Seely by perching in inaccessible alcoves and shouting instructions to the workmen through a tin trumpet. The Miller faction celebrated the completion of the Grand

Union Hotel with a lavish banquet in May, 1844. Yet their victory, too, was partial. The following spring the General Assembly, by a vote of 135 to 31, granted a divorce decree to Martha Miller.

High-spirited public demonstrations were numerous in the 1830s and 1840s. "The Miller Excitement" was only one example of the release of community energies and perhaps unusual in the degree of contentiousness evoked. Almost any event could serve as an excuse for a village gathering—a Whig or Democratic rally, a carriage race, a band concert, even the downfall of King Charles X in France. The bicentennial of the founding of Stamford in 1841, however, was marked by a decorous evening service in the Congregational Church and an impressive historical address by the Reverend J.D. Alvord.

The most ebullient occasions of all were the celebrations of the Glorious Fourth. Festivities began at dawn with the ringing of church bells and continued through the day and night. The celebration on the Green included prayers by the clergy, orations by the politicians, musical renditions by the 30-piece brass band, refreshments distributed to the children, and the reading of the Declaration of Independence by William Holly. A lively parade and lavish fireworks completed the patriotic festival. To observe the holiday in 1844, the town meeting appropriated $130, about half to cover the outlay for gunpowder and gunners.

After 50 years under the Constitution, the Stamford of the early 1840s emerged as a lively community that shared in the democratic and egalitarian spirit of the age. It remained a village still, homogeneous and parochial. The transformation from village to city began in the middle of the decade and has not yet ceased.

V THE IRISH, THE IRON HORSE, AND THE CIVIL WAR

First Lieutenant (later Captain) Charles A. Hobby of Company B was one of six brothers who fought in the Civil War; one brother, Horace, died in 1866 from the effects of two years in six Confederate prison camps. According to Stamford's Soldiers Memorial, by E.B. Huntington, Charles "made one of our best captains—considerate, careful, yet fearless and ready to share any danger to which he called his command." Captured in Florida, in May, 1864, he was released six months later. Captain Hobby died in 1890.

In the late 1840s the potato fields of Ireland were yielding only starvation; railroad tracks were spreading, binding American towns; and, slowly but inexorably, tensions between Northern and Southern states were escalating dangerously. None of these events began in Stamford; yet all of them permanently altered the homogeneous and insular character of the town.

The tragedy of the Irish famines of 1845, 1846, and 1848 drove millions across the seas. Some of the refugees found their way from New York to Stamford, particularly after the opening of the railroad in 1848. The local census of 1850 counted 173 males born in Ireland; the census of 1870 counted 622, or about one-fourth of the adult male population. The community, which seemed to have reached a plateau of 3,516 in 1840, jumped to 5,000 in 1850, to 7,185 in 1860, and to 9,700 in 1870. The local editor dubbed the increases of the 1840s and 1850s "the largest access of outside population which the village has hitherto received."

For the refugees an immediate issue was housing. Multi-unit dwellings had already appeared in Stamford. Venturesome builders, such as George A. Hoyt, proprietor of Hoytville, and George W.A. Jenkins responded by constructing wooden tenements, often with kitchens in the basements and rooms to lease upstairs. Hoytville, or the South End, turned into an Irish enclave. After the laying of track and opening of the railroad switchyard in 1848, rowhouses mushroomed on the east side of Atlantic Street along Cottage, Pacific, and Meadow streets. The neighborhood was popularly known as "Dublin." A similar sector, labeled "Kerrytown," arose immediately to the west of the Rippowam along Broad Street.

An equally powerful concern of the newcomers was employment. Initially, as in other towns, the men from Erin found work as laborers, the women as domestics. Only a handful had the means to undertake farming or to open their own enterprises. Fortunately, with the end of the depression that lasted from 1837 to 1843 Stamford underwent a measure of expansion in manufacturing just at the time of the heavy migration. In 1844 Henry J. Sanford bought the Cove Mills, the largest flour mills in Connecticut, from the Hollys and converted them into the Stamford Manufacturing Company. This new corporation imported tropical woods from South America and produced extracts used for dyes, drugs, and licorice paste. The highly successful firm, whose net

1844–1868

worth increased from $125,000 in 1855 to $1 million in 1867, invigorated the local economy. The Iron Works on Stillwater Road in 1850 employed 28 men of Irish origin; the Phoenix Carriage Company on Gay Street, the Harding Woollen Mills on the river, other shops and factories, and the railroad provided opportunities, too. Later in the 19th century, Yale & Towne, which at first preferred workers of English background, became a prime employer of Irish-Americans.

The most enduring legacy of the Irish influx was the establishment of the Roman Catholic Church. Services were held as early as 1842 in the home of Patrick Drew with the help of visiting priests. Following the Irish settlement, the Reverend John Brady took up

Above: The Stamford Manufacturing Company, which rose on the site of the old Holly gristmill at the Cove in 1844, imported tropical woods from South America and the Caribbean and manufactured many products, including dyes, quinine and other drugs, and paints.

arrived in 1868, he found the church building inadequate and the ground low and marshy. He was able to purchase a site on Atlantic Street from Andrew J. Bell for $12,500 and to approve a design for a Gothic structure of gray stone and granite trim. The first services in St. John's Roman Catholic Church were held in the basement in 1875, two years after the death of Father Fagan. Under Father William H. Rogers and contractor John Ennis, the impressive structure was completed and dedicated in 1886. By then approximately 4,000 Irish-Americans lived in Stamford.

The Irish were the first significant non-Yankee, non-Protestant minority to settle in the community. Longtime residents had little real understanding of the ravages of the Great Hunger and were apprehensive about the sheer numbers, the desperate economic plight, and the Catholic loyalties of the immigrants. Resentment focused on the rise in the number of taverns and on the signs of drinking and fighting in the streets. At one point the freemen at a town meeting threatened to post the names of all intoxicated persons on an old whipping post. Newspapers equated the "sons of Erin" with brawny, untutored laborers at best, and with drunkards, cursing street brawlers, and criminals at worst. The borough, to the end, distinguished between "Americans" and "Irish" in its records of arrests. Some private

Above, right: This display of items from the Stamford Manufacturing Company includes a fustic log and a ball of the hard quebracho wood (both used to make dyes). Close inspection of the log reveals the words, "Stamford dye-wood Cove Mills." Photograph by Don Piper.

permanent residence in the Cove area. The first church, a one-story frame building, 40 feet by 60 feet, was erected on Meadow Street in 1850. Successive priests enlarged the edifice and opened a small Catholic school with lay teachers on Meadow Street in 1860. Ten years later the Sisters of Mercy moved into a convent and took charge of the school. When the dynamic Father John Fagan

institutions made similar distinctions.

Anti-foreign and anti-Catholic sentiments surfaced throughout Connecticut. During the stormy and confused politics of the mid-1850s, William T. Minor—Stamford native and resident, Yale graduate, lawyer and judge, state representative and senator—was nominated for the post of governor by the Know-Nothing Party, a secret order hostile to immigrants and Catholics. In 1855 Free Soil, Democratic, Temperance, Whig, and Know-Nothing groups all supported candidates for governor. In 1856 the new Republican Party fielded a candidate, too. No individual secured a popular majority in either year. Coalitions in the General Assembly chose Minor as governor both times.

The two-year administration of Minor was notable for its anti-Catholic record. The legislature passed an act which mandated that all Catholic Church property be held in the name of individual congregations and not by bishops or the hierarchy. The Assembly also drafted an amendment to the Connecticut constitution which added a literacy requirement to the franchise and which was approved by the voters in the fall. The naturalization process was made more difficult. Finally, though he had to fire an adjutant general, Minor ordered

Left: William T. Minor, a former judge and state legislator, and the candidate of the Know-Nothing Party, became governor of Connecticut in 1855 and 1856 thanks to coalition votes. Minor's administration concerned itself with legislating ownership of Catholic church property, impeding the naturalization process for immigrants, and disbanding militia units made up of foreign-born men.

Although Catholic services were held in Stamford in the early 1840s, this small, one-story building on Meadow (later Hawthorne) Street provided Stamford's Catholics, whose numbers dramatically increased as the Irish arrived, with their first real church building in 1850.

the dissolution of the six militia companies which were composed of foreign-born men.

With the raid on Harper's Ferry, however, the issues of slavery and disunion overwhelmed nativism in Connecticut, and the Know-Nothing Party disappeared before the end of the 1850s. The Irish remained, and within a generation became a distinct force in local and state politics. In 1861, under the pressures of war, Governor William A. Buckingham restored the Irish militia units.

The New Haven Railroad, which brought the Irish immigrants to Stamford, brought much more. Schemes to attract the "iron horse" to the coast had been bruited for years. Since 1844 the resourceful Albert Seely had run a stagecoach each morning to White Plains, where rail connections to New York could be made. The town meeting endorsed Seely's proposal for extending the Housatonic Railroad along the southwestern coast in 1845. In the end the New York and New Haven Railroad, chartered in 1844, won the prize. Its directors, skilled in the ways of the Connecticut General Assembly, secured the right of way, put down tracks, and opened the line to service at the close of 1848. The *Advocate* graphically described the scene when the first locomotive, with passenger and freight cars attached, came through Stamford:

Animals of every description went careening round the fields, sniffing the air in terror, and bipeds of every size, condition, and color set off at full run for the railroad depot. In a few minutes the cause of all the commotion appeared in the shape of a locomotive puffing off its steam, and screaming with its so-called whistle at a terrible rate.

Similar alarms arose on the opening of the Cos Cob Bridge a few days later.

Nevertheless, by 1849 the New Haven was operating three trains daily between New York and Stamford. The number increased steadily. When the New Canaan branch line opened in 1866, the neighborhoods of Glenbrook and Springdale expanded rapidly. After much political manipulation, consolidation with the older Hartford and New Haven Railroad and establishment of the New York, New Haven & Hartford Railroad followed in 1872.

Regular and frequent train service encouraged the arrival of a new breed, the affluent commuter who lived in Stamford and worked in New York. Perhaps the most celebrated example of

Annie Picker, daughter of Irish immigrants, had several careers including hatter, dressmaker, and clerk at Yale & Towne. Her accomplishments were quite remarkable for her time and background

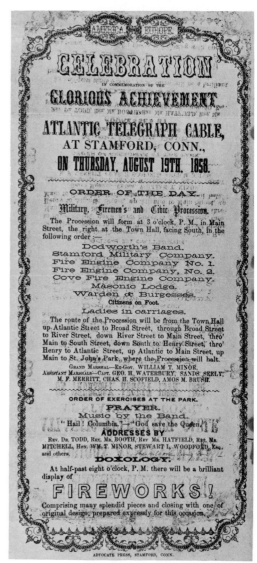

Right: Coincident with the transportation revolution of the mid-19th century was the revolution in communications. This poster announces the celebration of Stamford's link with an amazing achievement: a telegraph cable between the United States and Europe.

The arrival of the railroad at the end of 1848 caused quite a stir in Stamford, but when this photograph of the depot was made, in the late 1860s, a passenger could board one of the 13 trains per day headed toward either New Haven or New York.

that era was Truman Smith, a well-known lawyer from Litchfield County and former Whig Connecticut Representative, United States Congressman, and United States Senator. He resigned from the Senate when he moved his legal practice to New York City and took up residence in Stamford in 1854, where he remained until his death 30 years later and where he added considerable luster. He was appointed a judge of the Court of Arbitration in 1862, under the terms of the treaty with Britain, and subsequently a judge of the Court of Claims, established after the Civil War.

A large number of the commuters had been members of Presbyterian churches in New York. For awhile Presbyterians and Congregationalists, both followers of Calvinist principles, worshipped together. In 1853, however, Presbyterian loyalists decided to form a separate church and erect a separate edifice. The First Presbyterian Society of Stamford was organized and accepted by the Third

Selling shares made the completion of railroads, such as the New Canaan, possible in the 1800s. This certificate, issued to Charles Quintard in 1867, was for six shares at $50 per share.

Wilton, Betts came back to Stamford in 1844 to guide the flourishing Betts Academy on Strawberry Hill. Between 1850 and 1855, four more private schools for boys and for girls, boarding and day, opened, and after the Civil War another three institutions were established.

The most outstanding of the educators was Catharine Aiken, a Quaker teacher from Cape Cod who, in 1855, became the first principal of the Stamford Female Seminary and remained in the post for 41 years. In books and articles she expounded a system of mind training based on intense concentration. Ultimately 3,000 young women, some from as far away as South Carolina and Wisconsin, passed under her tutelage. In 1867 she hired young Georges Clemenceau to teach French and horseback riding. The future prime minister of France fell in love with a young American student, Mary Plummer, of a prominent New York family. Miss Aiken helped to arrange the nuptials, performed by Mayor A. Oakley Hall of New York in 1869, and remained a friend of Madame Clemenceau even after the

Presbytery of New York; the Reverend J. Leonard Corning arrived as Stated Supply; and a frame church, 44 feet by 72 feet, with a spire rising to 135 feet, was erected on Broad Street.

The ease of access provided by the railroad for New York families also encouraged the appearance of a clutch of private schools. As early as 1838, James Betts had established an academy for boys. After a brief return to his native

The opening of branch lines in the 1860s and 1870s stimulated the growth of neighborhoods such as Glenbrook. By the time this photograph was taken, Glenbrook had enjoyed train service for 26 years.

Catharine Aiken, a veritable Stamford institution for nearly 50 years, was the first principal of the Stamford Female Academy, later known as the Aiken School. This photograph depicts the school and many of its young ladies, in crinolines, circa 1867. It was during this time that young Georges Clemenceau, later prime minister of France, taught horseback riding at the school and fell in love with and married one of the students.

couple separated.

The return of prosperity in 1844 and the arrival of the railroad in 1848 produced a minor boom in building and in community spirit. By 1866 there were 33 named streets—triple the number of 30 years earlier. Isaac Quintard and Albert Seely constructed the first brick stores downtown. Around 1850 Thomas P. Dixon, architect of the Union House and of St. John's Episcopal Church, completed his last local building, the Concert Hall. Nathaniel E. Adams built a handsome Center School on Broad Street in 1852. (The first graded school attracted the largest number of common-school students by far and dispensed with tuition charges within a few years.) Adams also opened a host of new streets north of Broad and erected several multi-unit dwellings. Two telegraph companies, the first savings bank, and a number of insurance companies opened offices in the late 1840s and 1850s. Most of the major religious denominations in town erected handsome new buildings during the period.

After a devastating fire swept through

Main Street in 1861, brick became a more common medium of construction. Seely's Hall, the favorite site for community festivities, Hoyt's Hall, several stores, the new Center School of 1867, and the new railroad depot of that year were all built of brick.

The annual Fourth of July festivities, agricultural fairs, and parades, dominated by the oom-pah-pah of the Stamford Brass Band, continued to build community spirit. During the summer months hundreds boarded horse-drawn carriages for Shippan Point. At one picnic and clambake hosted by Philander Daskam in 1845, some 500 celebrants turned out.

The expansion in population, business, and construction in the decades following 1844 raised political problems for the Borough even as Special Acts enlarged the area to 1.5 square miles and added to the powers of the Board of Warden and Burgesses. Fire remained the prime concern. In 1844 the Borough purchased the *Rippowam*, a gooseneck engine operated by manpower, and authorized the formation of Rippowam Engine

Company #1, composed of 30 volunteers. The next year an engine house was built in back of the Town Hall. Ten years later Fire Engine Company #2, a second company of 30 men, was formed to man the *Stamford*, a second engine, and was assigned headquarters on Gay Street. The two groups competed lustily with each other at parades, in racing to the scenes of blazes, and in generating streams of water across the spire of the new Congregational Church. The Fire Department, set up in 1857, attempted to curb the ebullience of the comrades in the interest of effectiveness.

Despite complaints about street gangs and public drunkenness, the borough made no attempt to establish a police department. The burgesses relied on part-time regular and special constables and policemen paid on a fee-for-service or per-diem basis. Only in 1866, after gaining permission from the General Assembly, did the burgesses establish a "lockup." When Horace Scofield, the town tax collector, absconded with $3,000 in public tax money in 1855 and boarded a train for California with his wife and family, the county sheriff hastily called the Chicago police and secured Scofield's apprehension.

Construction, repair, and maintenance of sidewalks and streets took up much of the time of Borough boards. A year after Edgar Hoyt, editor of the *Advocate*, put on a demonstration of gas lighting at an agricultural fair in 1853, the Stamford Gas-Light Company was formed. Borough houses and shops were brightened, and the cautious board signed a contract for the illumination of some downtown streets. The burgesses carefully monitored the installation and repair of lamps. In December, 1867, because of the incidence of "furious driving," they repealed the eight-mile-per-hour speed limit and substituted a six-mile-per-hour limit.

Parks were a new urban concern in the late 1850s. Stamford acquired its first park, the vest-pocket Central Park, almost by accident. After the Congregational Church built a new edifice on Atlantic and Bank streets in 1858, it auctioned off the old church and property across from the Town Hall. Edward Hewes (or Hughes) of Greenwich bought the complex for $5,000 in 1859. The Phoenix Carriage Company purchased and removed the old building, and somehow the rumor spread that the first person who fenced the empty plot could claim it. Rival parties appeared with picks and shovels, and ludicrous scenes and lawsuits followed. Hewes, however, remained the rightful proprietor. After a group of nearby residents and businessmen raised a private fund to recompense the owner, the deed to the plot was conveyed to the Borough. The Central Park of 1859 is today's

Architect Gage Inslee designed the fifth edifice of the First Congregational Church, which was completed in 1858. It stood until 1911.

Veterans' Park. Two years later the newly landscaped and lavish grounds of the 40-acre Woodland Cemetery, perched above the sea, were also opened to the public.

While accounts of local fires and petty scandals took up space in the *Advocate,* national issues were also discussed in the journal and by the freemen and their families. The election of 1844, which pitted Polk against Clay, was fought with intensity and briefly produced an opposition newspaper, the *Democratic Banner.* Clay carried Stamford easily, by a vote of 484 to 268, but not the nation. The local press, faithfully Whig, denounced "Polk's" Mexican War of 1846-1848 as a slaveowners' ploy designed to admit more pro-slavery states into the Union.

The war was fought by professionals.

On the list of the attorney general of Connecticut, only a handful of regular Army soldiers claimed Stamford as their home town. Two privates, George Sherwood of the Infantry and George R. Weed of the Dragoons, died in the service.

Just as the Revolution had riven the community in two, the slavery question produced deep and agonizing division. Benjamin Daskam, a "station master" on the Underground Railroad, hid fugitive blacks and led them on their way north to freedom. But others were caught between the claims of conscience and the fear of disunion. In the 1860 election, after a heated campaign enlivened by torchlight parades of the "Wide-Awakes," bands of young Republican partisans, some 627 freemen voted for Lincoln and

Edward Quintard's stone residence, built in 1867, was one of the most impressive homes in Stamford during the period. Located on Clark's Hill, it now belongs to St. Basil's College on Glenbrook Road.

500 for a combination of his opponents.

When the shots rang out over Fort Sumter, however, doubts evaporated. Thirty young men, led by Theodore Miller and Theodore Delacroix, responded to Lincoln's first call for volunteers in April of 1861. At a mass meeting that followed, $4,500 was pledged to the Union cause. Following stirring speeches, plans were laid to erect a 150-foot flagpole in the town center and to raise the flag on the following Fourth of July.

During the first year of war, when hopes for an early victory were high, three volunteer companies attracted men from Stamford. Rifle Company F of the Third Connecticut Regiment of Volunteers, under Captain Albert Stevens, included 39 men from the community. Mustered in May for three months, it served through the dark days of the first battle of Bull Run. Although Union forces were badly beaten there, many of the recruits re-enlisted. Company D of the 6th Connecticut Regiment, under Captain Lorenzo Meeker, began with 84 Stamford men and eventually included 107 from the town. The regiment left Connecticut at the end of August and served in grim battles in Virginia and on the coast of the Carolinas. Company G of the 10th Connecticut Regiment, under Captain A.G. Brady, recruited 18 men from Stamford at first and added 17 more. It suffered heavy casualties at the battle of Kingston Bridge.

In mid-summer of 1862, when "Father Abraham" called for 300,000 more recruits, a crowded meeting in Seely's Hall raised $3,000. The community launched an all-out campaign to fill the rosters of Company A, under Captain Frank R. Leeds, and Company B, under Captain Cyrus D. Jones, of the new 28th Connecticut Regiment. On September 2 the town meeting promised a bonus of

$100 to each nine-month volunteer and set aside the afternoon for the drive. All stores were closed; every church bell was rung; and women and children gathered on the Green to inspire the crusade. Altogether 203 men responded to the call. It was Stamford's "hour of exultation."

Since the town was heavily represented among the officers and men of the 28th, Stamford was selected to donate the regimental colors. The regiment was mustered in New Haven in November, 1862, and put aboard ships which steamed through Atlantic and Gulf storms to reach the Mississippi River. The men participated in the victorious assault on Port Hudson in the summer of 1863. After the crucial battle, survivors again took ship, moved north on the Mississippi to Cairo, Illinois, and then boarded trains for the trip home to Connecticut.

By the time of the October, 1862, draft, Stamford had raised 537 men and was only six men short of its quota. After that date no more volunteer companies were raised in town, although individuals continued to join Connecticut and New York regiments. Seventy-eight men rendered service in the Union Navy as well.

Just six years after the close of hostilities, the Reverend Elijah E. Huntington listed the names of 512 veterans in his *Stamford Soldiers' Memorial*. About 30 years later, the publisher E.T. W. Gillespie estimated that between 750 and 800 Stamford men—more than 10 percent of the population—had served in the war. Huntington also included 122 obituaries of Stamford-connected servicemen. Charles Durand, of Company B of the 28th, died at the hands of Southern sharpshooters during the first few minutes of the Fort Hudson battle. Morris Carroll of Company G of the 10th, aged 19, refused to have his shattered hands amputated and died in hospital. John Buttry of Company B of the 17th, may have expired in the foul Confederate prison in Andersonville, Georgia. Horace P. Hobby, of Company D of the 6th, one of six brothers who fought, never recovered from his army and prison experiences and died soon after his discharge.

The latter part of 1862 and the months of 1863, following the slaughter at Antietam, Fredericksburg, Kingston Bridge, and Chancellorsville, were among the Union's darkest hours. During this time the local peace movement gained strength; the notorious Ohio Copperhead, Clarence Vallandigham, spoke in Stamford. In the April, 1864, gubernatorial elections, the pro-Union Republican incumbent, William Buckingham, garnered 555 votes in the community, while his pro-peace Democratic opponent, Thomas Seymour, collected 551 votes. By November's Presidential election, however, perhaps because of the efforts of the postmaster and Republican leader, Theodore Daskam, Abraham Lincoln secured 622 votes to McClellan's 586 in Stamford.

Despite the periods of gloom, public financial support for the young men never wavered. A resounding resolution of the town meeting of April 29, 1861, called for "restoring to our government the forts, arsenals, and property which have been stolen and are now held by traitors" and for "lifting the Stars and Stripes of our national flag, now being trailed in the dust by rebels and secessionists, to their proper places. . .over a land dedicated to Freedom by our sires of '76." A special rate of 1.5 mills was voted to support the families of volunteers and encourage enlistment. The town granted $3 a week to each wife and widowed mother of a soldier and $1 a week to each child under 15 years of age. The

$100 bounty paid to servicemen in 1861 was raised to $300 in 1863. Following the introduction of national conscription, the town meeting, in the interests of fairness, voted in August, 1863, to give the same sum of $300 to each draftee who wished to use it to procure a substitute. A few private citizens, such as Alfred Hoyt and William Skiddy, proudly contributed $300 each to hire enlistees as well. Altogether, through tax assessments and bond issues, the town expended some $76,000 during the war. Years later, when 42 men claimed that they had not received the $100 bounty promised in 1864 for re-enlistment, the town awarded the sum of $247.90 to each man to cover the original amount plus interest.

Beside the official allocations, private individuals and groups made fiscal and other contributions. In addition to the monies pledged at the mass public meetings of the early years, $1,700 was donated to the United States Christian Commission, and $1,000 was raised for the benefit of the loyal poor of East Tennessee in 1864. Several Stamford men subscribed funds for the establishment of Fitch's Home in Darien in that year. At first the institution sheltered disabled soldiers of the region; later it cared for orphans and destitute

Left: Dr. Walter Keeler Scofield was an assistant surgeon in the Navy during the Civil War, serving in hospitals in Boston, New York, Norfolk, Key West, Pensacola, and New Orleans. He witnessed the bombardment of Fort Sumter, the capture of Appalachiola, and the blockades of Galveston and Mobile. Dr. Scofield survived the war and was practicing in Boston as of 1869.

Right: Fitch's Home For Soldiers was chartered in 1864 in anticipation of the need by the Civil War veterans of the area for care. It was named for its founder, Benjamin Fitch, who contributed more than $100,000 toward its support. Its trustees discovered, however, that veterans did not need such an institution, so they decided to make it a home and school for the orphaned and destitute children of dead or disabled soldiers. From Harper's Weekly, March 17, 1866. Courtesy, Ferguson Library

FITCH'S HOME FOR SOLDIERS AND ORPHANS AT DARIEN, CONNECTICUT.—[SKETCHED BY STANLEY FOX.]

SOLDIERS' AND ORPHANS' HOME AT DARIEN.

WE illustrate on this page the Home for Disabled Soldiers and the Orphan Children of such as have died in military service in defense of the country, which, by the munificence of Mr. BENJAMIN FITCH, has been erected at Darien, Con-

necticut. From the beginning of the war Mr. FITCH has been interested in the cause for which our two millions of patriot soldiers have so bravely fought. At the first outbreak of rebellion, too old and infirm himself to shoulder the musket, and appreciating the tender anxiety of those who by going to the field must leave behind them wives and children, whom they might be leaving forever, Mr.

FITCH'S HOME—SCHOOL-ROOM.

"THE RETURNED SOLDIER."

FITCH'S HOME—DINING-ROOM.

children of veterans.

No group contributed more ardently to the Union cause than the Ladies' Soldiers' Aid Society. Led by Mary Ann Dickenson Smith (Mrs. Truman Smith), Catharine Aiken, and several women formerly active in church affairs, it enrolled 114 members in June, 1861, and 142 within the first year. In cooperation with the United States Sanitary Commission and similar societies in other towns, the Stamford women raised a sum between $6,000 and $7,000 and prepared and collected food, clothing, and hospital supplies. They sent items ranging from bandages and shirts to jellies to soldiers in the field, to the nearest military hospital on David's Island, to Dorothea Dix in Washington, and to New Haven for transshipment. Women met trains at the depot and fed and nursed wounded soldiers on board.

In letters to the *Advocate* at the time and for years afterward, soldiers, members of the Sanitary Commission, and veterans expressed heartfelt gratitude for the provisions and comforts. The culmination of the Society's patriotic activities was a

three-day Sanitary Fair held at Seely's Hall in July, 1864. Despite—or perhaps because of—the years of suffering, the fair raised $3,500. Old divisions and hostilities tended to melt in the common effort.

After the long nightmare of war, joy erupted with the news of the surrender at Appomattox on April 9, 1865. But elation changed to sorrow only six days later when word was received that Abraham Lincoln had been assassinated. No cloud, however, could dim the celebration of the Fourth of July of 1865; the display was labeled the "most elaborate" in the history of the town.

The Stamford of the late 1860s was not the Stamford of the mid-1840s. With the arrival of the Irish, the day of ethnic homogeneity had gone forever. With the arrival of the railroad, the day of village insularity had passed permanently. The Civil War exacted a terrible price in men and in money. But it also left the community more tightly knit by the shared experience and readier to face the challenges of industrialization which lay ahead.

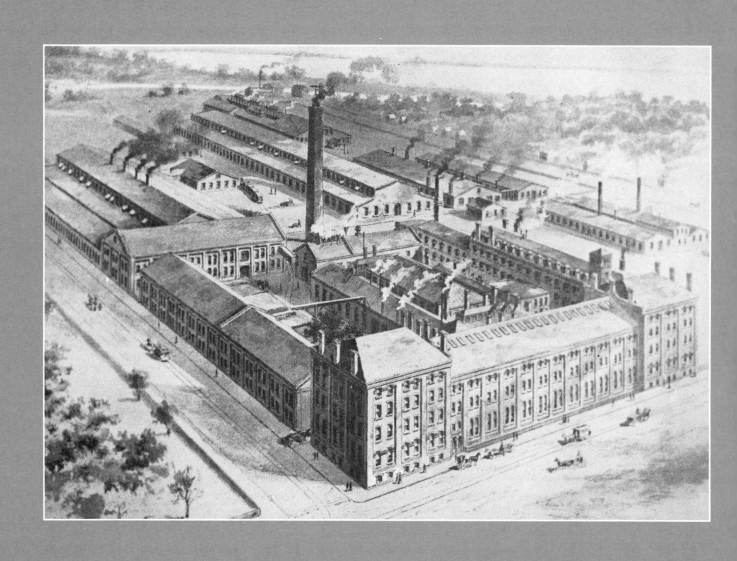

VI EMERGENCE OF THE COMPANY TOWN

Young Henry Robinson Towne brought the Industrial Revolution to Stamford. With the aid of 30 workers, he began the manufacture of Yale locks and keys in March, 1869, in a shop located between the canal and the railroad tracks in Hoytville. The Yale lock and key rapidly became internationally known. Hardly a facet of community life escaped the influence of Yale & Towne and of its dynamic president over the next quarter-century. The period can be enclosed as if in parentheses by his sudden arrival and even more sudden departure.

Henry R. Towne was the only surviving son of John Henry Towne, a wealthy engineer and entrepreneur who had built gas utilities, railroad systems, and iron works and whose bequest later established the Towne Scientific School at the University of Pennsylvania. During the Civil War young Towne left engineering studies at the University of Pennsylvania to oversee installation of steam engines in Union warships. Aged 21 at the close of hostilities, he studied for a time in Germany and France and returned home, eager to make his mark.

A mutual friend introduced Towne to Linus Yale, Jr., an inventor, portrait painter, and proprietor of a small lock factory in Shelburne, Massachusetts. Yale had created a design for a pin-tumbler lock and slim, flat key which were vastly superior in safety and convenience to the bulky security contrivances of the day.

Towne quickly grasped the technical advantages and commercial possibilities of the invention. With generous aid from the senior Towne, the two young men formed the Yale Lock Company in October, 1868. The sole tangible asset of the corporation, owned by the two families, was the patent for the pin-tumbler lock.

The partners decided to move the Yale plant from Massachusetts to Stamford primarily because of Stamford's rail, canal, and harbor facilities and pool of craftsmen. Unfortunately Linus Yale died on Christmas Day, 1868. Towne unhesitatingly pushed forward with the plan to open the lock factory in Hoytville. He purchased a mansion on Atlantic Street for his bride and moved to Stamford. Following his father's death in 1875, Henry R. Towne became sole owner of the company. In 1883 the corporation was reorganized as the Yale & Towne Manufacturing Company, and some shares were sold on the open market. Towne remained president until 1915 and served as chairman of the board until his death in 1924.

Despite the severe depression of 1873-1879, the success of the new firm never faltered. By 1881 the company employed 250 workers and met a monthly payroll of $12,500. Eleven years later it employed 1,000 men and women in a community that numbered under 16,000, and paid out $60,000 in wages monthly. Under

1869–1893

Towne's astute leadership, the corporation secured tight control of other patents and expanded in Stamford and elsewhere into the manufacture of post-office lock boxes, bank locks, ornamental bronzes, builders' hardware, and materials-handling equipment. By 1892 Yale & Towne shops and foundries occupied a 21-acre complex lying between Pacific Street and the canal, Market Avenue and Henry Street.

Direction of every aspect of the enterprise remained firmly in Towne's hands. Wearing a distinctive skull cap, he was a familiar figure on the shop floor. At an anniversary celebration in 1938, Schuyler Merritt, formerly secretary and treasurer of the corporation and a Congressman from Connecticut for 20 years, recalled, "despite his gentle manner, there was never any doubt that Mr. Towne was the head of the business. His word was law."

Towne was an ardent believer in the principles of Scientific Management advocated by his good friend Frederick J. Taylor. He also developed his own

policies of industrial paternalism. He promoted a mutual benefit society and a works hospital, in-house publications and entertainments, a subscription library, and, after World War I, a package of home-building loans, stock-purchase plans, and anniversary premiums. In the 1880s he experimented unsuccessfully with a gain-sharing scheme. He established an apprentice school in 1908 which combined classroom instruction and shop experience and provided an avenue of education and mobility for over 400 young men during its 35 years of existence. In his will Towne left 6,000 Yale & Towne shares to establish a Service Building for employees.

What the authoritarian Towne would not countenance was any sharing of decisions with his growing army of workers. Like so many other industrialists, he loathed unions. He deemed strikes "intolerable oppression by organized labor." While wage levels at Yale & Towne were comparable with wage levels elsewhere at the end of the 19th century—adult males earned

between $2.25 and $4 a day—workers did nourish grievances. Yet, as the century closed, there was only one attempt at a strike.

After a brief visit by Samuel Gompers, president of the American Federation of Labor, to Hoytville in the spring of 1890, the molders at Yale & Towne demanded the rehiring of one of their number who had washed up 10 minutes before the 6 p.m. closing whistle and who had been fired. Towne refused to yield on the issue of wash-up time during factory hours. Twenty-eight molders, considered the elite of the plant, went on strike on June 27. Towne responded first by locking out the molders and hiring substitutes from New York, and then by closing the entire works on July 16.

Within a month opinion in the company town, spurred by hostile sermons and editorials, turned against the

The "Gilded Age" seems a very appropriate description of the time when looking at the decorating style of the affluent. The dining room seen here was in the Franklin Wardwell home on Elm Street.

The prosperity of Stamford in the late 19th century is perhaps best illustrated by the homes of some of its leading residents. This house, photographed circa 1890, was owned by Charles E. Dingee. Formerly the home of J.M. Sheffield, a toolmaker, the house was on Pond Road (now Weed Avenue).

strikers. Despite a brief appearance by Gompers, who urged resistance "to the bitter end," a committee of chain-workers petitioned Towne to reopen the plant on August 15. As each worker lined up to return on the following day, he signed a document (often called a "yellow-dog contract" by labor), which prohibited him from joining any organization of which management disapproved. The company refused outright to hire 22 of the original 28 molders and several other militant former employees.

The growth and success of Yale & Towne were the catalysts which transformed Stamford into a bustling, small industrial city, one of the many that dotted the Connecticut landscape during the period, which Mark Twain wryly labeled the "Gilded Age." The rhythm of community life quickened visibly after the depression of the 1870s. The population rose from 9,714 in 1870 to 11,297 in 1880 to 15,700 in 1890. With the aid of federal appropriations, a lighthouse was erected in the harbor, and dredging operations began in 1886. Two

commercial banks and one savings bank were added to the commercial bank and the savings bank established earlier. The Stamford Manufacturing Company remained the only large-scale manufacturing enterprise beside Yale & Towne, but a number of small factories, producing shoes, hats, woolens, shirts, carriages, wallpaper, and stoves, appeared and disappeared.

Stamford acquired an urban look. Streets expanded in almost every direction. The *Directory of 1889* listed 185 by name. In the central area arose a score of multi-story commercial buildings and "blocks" of adjoining buildings of brick and brownstone. The state constructed an imposing armory near the railroad station in 1884. Several of the 18 churches erected parsonages and chapels. Near the shore wealthy New Yorkers erected vacation houses, and on the hills appeared elaborate Victorian mansions in French Empire and Queen Anne styles. The publisher E.T.W. Gillespie issued a huge, glossy volume, *Picturesque Stamford*, in 1893 and filled it with photographs of

Henry Towne built "Rockland" on Atlantic Street around 1875 and lived in it until his sudden departure in 1892. Incorporating several styles, the Queen Anne house was pictured in an 1890 Scientific American *issue which featured American architects and builders. Serving for a time as the Rockland Hotel, the building fell victim to an arsonist in 1970.*

spacious homes and serious men.

Urban amenities appeared downtown as well. Each service was supplied by a private corporation composed of prominent local figures, under a contract negotiated with the Board of Warden and Burgesses. In 1871, after years of delay, the Stamford Water Company piped clear water from Trinity Lake, an amalgamation of three ponds in North Stamford, into downtown stores, offices, and homes. Illumination of the streets by electricity was delayed by the opposition of the Stamford Gas-Light Company which had provided borough lighting since 1854. For four years beginning in 1886 the borough contracted with two corporations. Finally, pressed by Walton Ferguson, the two utilities were merged into the Stamford Gas and Electric Light Company in 1893. A Horse Railroad Company began trolley service in the mid-1880s, though it subsequently became enmeshed in legal disputes. Towne launched a Stamford-Norwalk Telephone Company in 1880 and quickly sold it to the Connecticut Telephone Company. The borough sector, at least, boasted all the conveniences of the modern city.

Fourth-of-July and traditional public festivities continued to flourish, along with some 75 volunteer societies ranging from the YMCA and a post of the Grand Army of the Republic to the Orden Germania and the Oolah Pleasure Club. A $10,000 bequest by wealthy bachelor lawyer and civic leader John Day Ferguson made possible the fulfillment of a century-old community goal: the establishment of a public library. The Ferguson Library opened its doors in 1882 in rented quarters on Atlantic Street and moved to its own building, a frame house opposite St. John's on Atlantic Street, seven years later.

Industrialization and urbanization brought jobs, growth, and comforts to

Stamford. But they also raised grave problems that demanded political attention. Towne, Ferguson, Merritt, W.W. Skiddy, (the president of the Stamford Manufacturing Company), and other notables frequently advocated expansion of government services and

The Shady Side, operated by the Stamford Freight Company, was a handsome vessel which began carrying both passengers and freight across Long Island Sound in 1886.

The Stamford News *began publication in 1886; its publisher-editor was George W. Sawter.*

found themselves at odds with freemen and board members, who were concerned to hold down costs and at times suspicious of the motives of elite figures. Yet the issues were so compelling that, in the end, both town and borough government implemented an unprecedented number of programs during the Gilded Age.

At the conclusion of the Civil War, Stamford electors fell firmly into the Republican column. Beginning in 1876, with the waxing of depression and waning of wartime emotions, the two parties competed on almost equal terms. Locally the GOP and the Democrats differed little on issues. Partisan energies were directed primarily toward securing offices in an almost unending series of elections and were displayed in a continual round of committees, caucuses, and conventions, parades, barbecues, and spectacles. Party organizations were managed mainly by a handful of lawyers who were masters of oratory and parliamentary tactics and frequently

formed bipartisan partnerships. The weekly *Advocate*, which became the property of the Gillespie family in 1867, remained staunchly Republican. But it faced a series of competitors, notably *The Stamford Herald,* which tilted toward the Democrats. The *Advocate* alone endured, and launched a daily paper in 1892.

The major controversies of the 1870s—a town house, the schools, the poor, and prohibition—fell on the town meeting agenda. Since selling its modest Town House in 1867, Stamford had lacked a town hall. James H. Olmstead, a flamboyant Democratic attorney, sparked the drive to erect a proper municipal building. Critics cited costs and hinted at chicanery. Almost every proposal that involved outlays evoked similar protests. Eventually the freemen agreed to the proposal and to a $100,000 bond issue to finance it. By 1871 a handsome, three-story, brick Town House stood at the corner of Atlantic and Main streets. On the first floor were stores and businesses;

on the second a courthouse and offices; on the third, an auditorium for political, cultural, and recreational gatherings. On the Fourth of July a graceful fountain began to play in the Green in front of the building, and a clock tower was added later. Undeniably the Town Hall was an object of civic pride.

The struggle over school consolidation raised the subtle issue of ethnic loyalties as well as the open question of costs. In Stamford in 1872, a child attended one of 15 town district schools, one of 4 joint district schools, or one of 6 private schools, including a small Catholic school. Only the Center School was graded; most of the country schools were staffed by a single teacher. The Second District, or Green School, which served Dublin, was scandalously overcrowded and had seats for only half the children of the neighborhood. Ferguson, the Republican lawyer Samuel Fessenden, and Protestant clergymen, as well as the state educational leadership, supported

Left: A century ago it was much more common than it is today for a city, even a small one, to have more than one newspaper. In the late 1800s, Stamford had three weeklies. The Stamford Advocate, launched in 1829, was acquired in 1867 by the Gillespie family. Seen here are Edward T.W. (in doorway with arms folded), Richard H. (at right), and Richard, Jr. (at left). Frank Weed is at right in the doorway.

Right: The photographer in the foreground wasn't the only one taking pictures of the handsome Town Hall and Atlantic Square during the festivities of 1892.

the centralization of all the district schools and boards under a common board as the most effective way to upgrade the quality of education. Father John Fagan, the priest of St. John's Parish, and Irish-American parents were unwilling to relinquish Dublin's voice in the curriculum and neighborhood's control of the Green School Board. They were supported by Democratic lawyers Olmstead and Galen A. Carter, Jr.

For two years debate was fierce. Finally, late in the evening of the annual town meeting of 1872, after six hours of oratory, Ferguson's pleas for universal schooling and Fessenden's eloquence won the day. Consolidation passed by a vote of 235 to 220. A single school committee, the nine-man Board of School Visitors, went to work enthusiastically to reorganize the system, though five years passed before a new schoolhouse arose in Dublin.

Educating the young was a straightforward challenge; handling the poor was a thornier problem for Stamford, as it was for other communities. Paupers were commonly perceived as individuals with character faults whose care was best left to the ministrations of church and private fraternal societies. The most extreme and chronic cases were placed on the Outdoor Poor Account or in the Poor House erected on Scofieldtown Road. Conventional community solutions to the problem of poverty, however, foundered during times of severe crisis. In the depression of the mid-1870s, the Ladies' Henry Street Benevolent Society and similar organizations distributed food, fuel, and clothing to families in want. But the greater challenge came from great numbers of tramps who scrambled off the New Haven freight cars and spread fear among the householders. Newspapers estimated the number at between 1,000 and 8,000 a year. During the desperate winter of 1875-1876, the town meeting established a workhouse to deter

The school attached to St. John's Catholic Church was one of six private educational institutions in Stamford late in the 19th century. The 1885 graduating class is seen here with an unidentified nun.

stopovers by vagrants. Tramps were bedded overnight on blanketless planks and required to crush stones the next morning. Quarry laborers and workhouse neighbors objected angrily. Towne suggested a movable, wooden workhouse which could be carted around to stony locations. The proposal was approved but, with the return of better times, abandoned.

When depression hit again in 1893, the town was two-thirds larger than it had been 20 years earlier and the number of victims greater. Working-class families, who lived near the tracks and canal, suffered particularly. The Reverend Samuel Scoville, the ebullient Congregational minister, organized a band of seven energetic, affluent women into the Society for the Prevention and Cure of Pauperism. They visited about half of the 110 cases on the Outdoor Poor

rolls of 1893 and found shocking housing and sanitary conditions. In their report they recommended establishing an inspector of housing, a conservator for alcoholics, and a home in the country for juveniles. The community was not ready for such innovations, however, and responded to the exigency along more traditional lines. A host of private relief agencies gave out food, medicine, and coal to those in want. In addition the Greyrock Land Company and the Borough hired unemployed men to break stone, and the Stamford Civic League operated the Stage Street Lodging House, where transients could pay for board by chopping wood.

The sufferings of the depression of the 1870s also renewed agitation to suppress intoxication and the local liquor traffic. In the late 1860s Oliver Hoyt, a leather merchant, and the Reverend J. Smith

Dodge, a Unitarian minister, had formed a temperance society, and Father Fagan had organized the St. Patrick's Roman Catholic Total Abstinence Society. After 1873 alcoholism and alcohol dealers were held responsible for poverty, joblessness, vice, delinquency, and crime. A mass meeting in April, 1874, launched the Temperance League of Stamford. It proposed to supplement the efforts of female praying bands with investigations of saloons, especially in Dublin, open on the Sabbath or selling to juveniles. During the cruel winter of 1875-1876, the Reverend J.M. Buckley, a fiery Methodist preacher, claimed that one legal liquor-dispensing establishment existed for every 62 males in town. Others counted some 65 licensed and nonlicensed outlets. Michael Kenealy, son of an Irish immigrant grocer, and Father William Rogers joined fellow attorneys and clergymen in denouncing rum and rum sellers. The campaign was successful. Somewhat to its own surprise, the town meeting of 1877, by a tally of 865 to 441, voted to deny all licenses to sell liquor within Stamford.

The temperance forces were jubilant. Women formed a Stamford chapter of the Women's Christian Temperance Union in 1878. Enforcement, however, proved difficult. Discovery of liquor sales depended on informers, and the residents did not prove forthcoming. In his zeal to prosecute violators of the ban, Buckley hired three New York undercover detectives, who relied on entrapment. Sometimes they lured "respectable" citizens into their nets. The community was outraged and moreover found that public drunkenness had not diminished. After three years of prohibition, the town, by a vote of 959 to 567, restored liquor licensing in 1880.

Stamford did not try to ban liquor again in the century, not even during the hard times of the 1890s, despite pressures

The Reverend Samuel Scoville, minister of the Congregational Church from 1879 to 1899, spearheaded the formation of the Society for the Prevention and Cure of Pauperism in the depressed 1890s.

by the WCTU chapter and Sunday raids on illegally open Dublin saloons led by Scoville. Indeed, one of the most prosperous establishments in the community was John H. Lee's "Silver Dollar Cafe," which opened on Main Street in March, 1892. The saloon achieved regional notoriety for its flashy brass spittoons, electric lights, and floor inlaid with silver and gold pieces.

The prosperous 1880s placed different issues on the political table. New inventions and methodologies raised questions about fire control, road building, and sewage disposal that the Borough had to address. The two volunteer companies of the Borough Fire Department suffered from poor organization and discipline and used manually operated machines. Beginning in 1872 Towne, who consistently urged the adoption of the most advanced technology available, proposed the purchase of a steam engine and warned of the perils of fire in crowded areas. His pleas were rebuffed until lightning struck

These four men were all of Stamford's post office employees in the mid-1880s.

the steeple of the Presbyterian Church in August, 1882. Hundreds of volunteers failed to build up enough water pressure to prevent demolition of the building. Only the arrival of a steam fire engine from Norwalk prevented the blaze from spreading. The lesson was obvious. In September the freemen voted overwhelmingly to purchase a "steamer," and two years later they approved a plan to reorganize and professionalize the fire department.

By the 1880s Stamford was advertising itself as a modern city and delightful resort. Yet its streets of packed earth turned into notorious pools of mud after every rainstorm. The *Advocate* launched a crusade for the purchase of a steam road-roller and the paving of the most-used steets in August, 1886. Disputes erupted

immediately: over the costs of such a machine (about $5,000); over what kind of pavement was best (gravel, brick, or asphalt); and over which streets should be selected for improvement. At a heated Special Meeting in June, 1889, when the warden threatened to arrest nonresidents who voted, the borough freemen gave their consent to the purchase of a road-roller and a $5,000 bond issue. Later they agreed to the borrowing of an additional $15,000 to pay contractors to operate the machine and stipulated that "preference" be given to Stamford labor.

The question of sewage disposal plagued the borough longer and more profoundly than any other issue. Residents were beginning to suspect that the absence of a sewer system was in part responsible for Stamford's shockingly high mortality rates from typhoid, diptheria, measles, and scarlet fever. Because of the smallpox menace, the town had established a Board of Health in 1854, but its impact was limited. During some months in the years between 1889 and 1893 Stamford death rates were the highest in the state and took an appalling toll of the children in Dublin, Kerrytown, and the Cottage-Pacific Street triangle. In the latter sector residents lived next to a reeking, stagnant pool formed by the damming up of the upper portion of the canal in 1868.

Many citizens still believed that "miasmas" or vapors from the impacted earth caused infections. It was difficult for sanitation experts to convince the community of the need for a comprehensive costly sewer system to carry off waste and water. Beginning in 1871, after the introduction of piped water, downtown proprietors proposed a spate of resolutions to secure a city sewer system. In 1880 Towne entered the fray. For some time he had been in correspondence with George E. Waring, Jr., a civil engineer from nearby Pound Ridge who had already gained fame as the designer of a waste-disposal system for Memphis, Tennessee, which had aided in controlling a massive yellow fever epidemic. (He would go on to achieve national celebrity for his sanitary and street-cleaning reforms in Havana and New York.) Waring developed a plan for Stamford that he deemed efficient and economical. It called for the separation of household sewage from other wastes, the disposal of this sewage through a system of narrow pipes, and the daily flushing of the pipes into Wescott's Cove by special pumps. It also called for the disposal of surface water into the harbor by the force of gravity alone.

In September, 1880, Towne assembled a Committee of 40, composed of almost every major property holder in the borough, which commissioned a report by Waring. The detailed account of the disposal plan appeared in the *Advocate* on November 5. The meeting of Borough freemen the following week greeted the report with harsh skepticism.

A bitter five-year battle followed. Charges provoked counter-charges, and every parliamentary delaying tactic was utilized. Among the diehard opponents of the Waring scheme was John Ennis, who questioned the motives behind and costs of the plan and advocated a simple gravity scheme. Irish-born, a Civil War veteran, resident of Stamford since 1880, and proprietor of a bathing pavilion in Shippan, Ennis was a dedicated swimmer, skater, and "pedestrian," an early proponent of physical fitness for both sexes, and an irascible contender.

After five years Towne won the first round. In November, 1885, by a tally of 393 to 82, the Borough freemen agreed to implement Waring's plan and voted a $25,000 assessment and a $100,000 bond issue. Unfortunately the construction was plagued by labor troubles and the design by grave technical flaws. Pumps and pipes proved grossly inadequate; death rates soared; odors were sickening. Critics, such as Ennis, pointed to leakages and blamed "sewer gas" for the typhoid and diptheria epidemics. In vain Towne argued that the disposal system should be extended. Unexpectedly he found himself the object of resentment and anger.

The Towne-Ennis feud continued in various forms in the early 1890s. On balance the community was the loser. In August, 1891, Ennis, Dr. Charles Rowell (a homeopathic physician), Fessenden, and others proposed that the town purchase 40 acres in Shippan Point for the sum of $60,000 to establish a shorefront park. Ennis owned two-thirds of the property. The community did not officially own any open space except for a few small squares. Park advocates argued that 12,000 Stamford inhabitants, including children, lived in the crowded downtown area and would benefit from a healthful, recreational, cultural facility close to nature and the sea. Though public opinion seemed overwhelmingly to favor the notion at first, opponents, such as Towne and Olmstead, secured delay after delay at town meetings and suggested a series of alternate sites. By the end of 1892 they succeeded in scuttling the whole idea. Stamford lost an opportunity to create a park at Shippan Point permanently.

The year 1891, so fraught with issues, was also the year of the 250th anniversary of the founding of Stamford. Serious planning for the event only began in the summer. A consensus quickly emerged to postpone festivities to the fall of 1892. In January of that year, a Committee of 50, composed of community notables, proposed that the town erect a memorial monument on the Green as part of the celebration. The committee recommended a design, created by John Rogers, a Stamford native and well-known sculptor, which consisted of two large, central, bronze figures, a Puritan man and an Indian woman, and two smaller figures, on the side, a Revolutionary volunteer and a Civil War soldier. Towne, a descendant of Salem forebears, was passionately committed to the sculpture. The Committee suggested that $13,500 be raised by tax levy and $20,000 by private pledges.

By mid-1892 success seemed assured. Donations reached $20,000, the largest single sum ever raised in Stamford from private sources. It was not widely known that the major portion of the money had come from John Clason, the judge of probate and former state representative, a farmer, and a bachelor who had insisted on anonymity. Nevertheless, at a special town meeting held in May, denunciations were vehement. Ennis, Rowell, and others criticized not only the expense but also the design which, they contended, slighted the war veteran and elevated the Puritan.

Underlying the protest was a new factor, born of apprehension over the waves of epidemics and perhaps resentment over the interventions of Towne. A conviction, quietly discussed and deeply felt, emerged: such a large amount of money would be far more wisely spent on a desperately needed hospital. The town meeting temporized and appointed new committees.

Within two months Clason and the Committee of 50 resolved to reallocate the fund to provide for a community hospital. For some reason Towne was not informed of the decision. He was told of the shift in plans at a joint meeting of committees in July, 1892. Astonished, frustrated, and furious, he embarked immediately on a trip abroad. When he returned, he took up residence in New York. Stamford lost its pre-eminent citizen permanently.

The departure of the industrialist was hardly noticed during the elaborate celebrations which took place from October 16 to October 20, 1892. Elation and pride filled the bedecked streets. The program included special church services, an exhibition of antiquities, literary exercises, choral and band concerts, a parade of hundreds of school children, a procession of thousands of marchers with splendid floats and fire companies in full regalia, open house by three warships of the U.S. Navy, and stunning rocket displays.

The anniversary festivities underscored what many were well aware of: Stamford had become a city. Four-fifths of the population lived in one-fifth of the downtown area and required urban services and urban governance. The town meeting system, with administration in

Stamford native John Rogers created this model for a memorial monument to be placed on the Green during the city's 250th anniversary festivities. Henry Towne was enthusiastic about the statue, and donations seemed to ensure its completion. However, as time went by, the Committee of 50 and the major donor, John Clason, decided that the money would be better spent on a hospital. When Towne learned of the decision, his fury at not having been consulted led him to leave Stamford forever.

the hands of part-time selectmen, was cherished but amateurish and rurally oriented. The Board of Warden and Burgesses was efficient but had charge of a small enclave only and was composed largely of Yankee businessmen and professionals. After decades of discussion, the time seemed ripe for the establishment of a municipal government, made up of a full-time mayor and a ward-based common council. Such a structure would supply a chief executive who would stand for the interests of the whole community, would make room for minority representation, and might resolve urban dilemmas with less acrimony and more alacrity.

The city-making process was necessarily fraught with controversy. Glenbrook, an eastern neighborhood, insisted on exclusion. Each party, as well as intra-party factions, jockeyed for advantage. Ordinary taxpayers and the General Assembly kept a watchful eye. Four different charter drafts were prepared between the fall of 1892 and the spring of 1893, three by borough committees and the last by State's Attorney Samuel Fessenden, a former and future representative, at the request of the legislature. In the final document the city boundaries included all the area below Bull's Head with the exception of Glenbrook and a rural strip on the west. The Charter established the office of mayor and a nine-member Common Council, composed of one councilman chosen at large and two councilmen elected from each of four wards. Standard municipal powers were granted to the body.

All voters within the future city limits were eligible to vote on the adoption of the City Charter at public meeting. It passed by 215 to 168 at 12:23 a.m. on May 17. By Special Act of the General Assembly, the City of Stamford came into existence in July, 1893. Residents within the city were hereafter subject to the jurisdiction of both the city and town of Stamford; residents outside the city limits were subject to town jurisdiction only. The pattern endured for 56 years.

The popular ballot and the Assembly act of May, 1893, made Stamford—with its Yale & Towne base, its pattern of development, and its problems— juridically what it had been culturally for many years: a small urban-industrial complex, "The Lock City."

VII EXPANSION OF THE INDUSTRIAL CITY

The Mechaley brothers, seen here in a 1904 Cadillac, operated a garage on Summer Street from 1898 to 1923, the services of which are described on their sign. Joseph Mechaley, on the left, designed and manufactured the Stamobile about this time, but unfortunately it was not a success; there are not even any known pictures of the auto named for its creator's hometown.

"Only a nucleus of the population of Stamford today can survey for itself the tremendous changes which have taken place in the town during the last generation," wrote Stamford historian Herbert F. Sherwood in 1930. Within his memory Stamford had become a prosperous small city with an expanding downtown and more diverse population. Horses and buggies had disappeared from city streets, and new businesses and services added to the feeling that Stamford was a very different place than it had been only a few decades earlier.

Downtown, large commerical, industrial, and public buildings were replacing the small frame and brick structures of earlier eras. Banks, theaters, civic buildings, schools, hotels, library, post office, hospital, and armory were all located there, many designed by leading New York and Boston architects. On Atlantic Street the five-story Weed's Hall, constructed in 1888, had a rare cast-iron front and Classical Revival elements. The *Stamford Advocate* building of 1894 resembled a Neo-Italian Renaissance palazzo and made clear the important place of a daily newspaper in the community. Several bank buildings in the form of Greek and Roman temples were, according to a 1912 *Advocate* article, designed "to convey an impression of solidity that inspires confidence."

Among the new early 20th-century

structures of lasting importance to the city and its residents were the Town Hall, Ferguson Library, and the Stamford Theater. After the 33-year-old Town Hall burned in a spectacular evening fire thought to have been started by a faulty gas jet in February, 1904, town fathers rebuilt a fireproof Beaux Arts structure on the same Atlantic Square site, the most convenient and important in the city. In 1911 the red brick Georgian-style Ferguson Library building was completed on the corner of Broad and Bedford streets, a key location and one that the library would occupy permanently. Enterprising businesswoman Emily Wakeman Hartley built the Stamford Theater on Atlantic Street in 1914 to encourage pre-Broadway tryouts of new plays in Stamford. Opening with *On Trial,* a new play written by Elmer Rice and produced by George M. Cohan and Sam Harris, the theater was an immediate success. Other well-known Broadway playwrights and producers previewed their works there, and a stock company was in residence between 1922 and 1927. In the 1930s it became a movie theater and, in the 1980s, the keystone for the new Stamford Center for the Arts.

Ever-more-numerous factories occupied land near the harbor, railroad, and downtown areas where workers lived. By 1921 the South End plant of Yale & Towne covered a 25-acre site bounded by

1894–1928

Gutzon Borglum was a resident of Stamford for many years, designing the huge national monuments that would be carved at Mount Rushmore and Stone Mountain in his Wire Mill Road studio. A friend of Theodore Roosevelt, Borglum also played a vigorous role in local politics.

Sailing became a popular recreational activity early in the 20th century. This happy group enjoyed an excursion on Long Island Sound in May, 1915.

Pacific, Henry, Canal, and Market streets. Factories located nearby included the Blickensderfer Typewriter Company, Schleicher & Sons Piano Company, and Lincrusta-Walton Wallpaper Company. In 1919 the old buildings of the Stamford Manufacturing Company at the more distant Cove Island burned to the ground and were not replaced.

Crowded tenements and older buildings in the central city housed Stamford's ever-growing immigrant population. The two-family houses, frame bungalows, and Queen Anne-style dwellings lining residential streets within walking distance of the city center reflected the taste and increasing prosperity of the expanding middle class. Springdale and Glenbrook, north and east of the city, offered attractive suburban homesites at reasonable prices. Affluent business and professional families built large, comfortable homes in Shippan Point, Revonah Manor, and other new residential developments outside the congested city center. Large estates and summer homes of wealthy and prominent persons were scattered on Strawberry, Palmer, and Noroton hills as well as in rural North Stamford. Country villages in the northern ridges, once thriving agricultural centers, became suburban neighborhoods after farming ceased to be a factor in the local economy.

Among those moving to Stamford were the noted sculptor Gutzon Borglum and his wife, classical scholar Mary Montgomery Borglum. Much to the concern of their neighbors, during World War I the Borglums used "Borgland," their large estate on Wire Mill Road, as a military camp for Czechoslovakians recruited and trained in America before their assignment to European battlefields. After the war, in his Wire Mill Road studio, Gutzon Borglum designed the colossal national monuments he later carved in granite at Stone Mountain,

Georgia, and at Mount Rushmore, South Dakota.

Like the Borglums, others chose to live in pleasant surroundings far from the crowded city after new and more efficient means of transportation reduced travel time between home and work. During the 1890s the bicycle and horse-drawn trolley were popular and inexpensive alternatives to horse and carriage. Then, about 1900, the first automobiles appeared on Stamford streets. That year an *Advocate* headline announced: "Dealers in Bicycles Will Probably Add Horseless Carriages to Their Stock in Trade, Though the Popularity of the Former Shows No Sign of Waning Here." Locally, early Stanley Steamers and Locomobiles had to compete with the Stamobile, a car designed and manufactured in Stamford by bicycle dealer Joseph Mechaley. Although Mechaley entered his car in the first automobile show in New York, popularity of the Stamobile quickly waned.

The popularity of trolleys was more long-lasting, however, especially after the Shippan Railroad and other lines were converted to electricity. The new electrified service began on July 4, 1894, just in time to transport thousands of local residents to the city's most popular shore resort at Shippan for the traditional Independence Day celebration. Electrification of other lines and expansion of service followed purchase of the financially troubled Stamford Street Railroad by the New York, New Haven & Hartford Railroad in 1895.

All trolley lines met at Atlantic Square, hub of the new public transportation system and focal point of downtown life. Trolleys ran at 10-to 30-minute intervals, and for the standard fare of five cents passengers could ride to Bull's Head, Springdale, Noroton, the Cove, Shippan Point, the South End, or Greenwich. By 1905 mergers had resulted

After the turn of the century, developers and the Chamber of Commerce promoted Stamford as a delightful place to live. These photographs showing residents of Shippan playing tennis, sailing, and swimming were part of a volume produced for the Shippan Point Land Company. Photographs by Brown & Dawson. Courtesy, James Murphy

in a regional system with 50 miles of track and the possibility of traveling by trolley to either New York City or New Haven in about four hours.

More flexible motor buses eventually replaced trolleys on city streets. Although the first bus lines to Stamford Hospital, Noroton, and Strawberry Hill ran along routes not served by trolleys, by 1927 buses had replaced trolleys on most lines. The final local trolley run took place on November 12, 1933.

Travel by train also improved after four-tracking of the New Haven line permitted introduction of express trains in 1893. Twin passenger stations were built on either side of the tracks in 1895, and electrification of lines in 1907 further speeded up travel and eliminated the grimy smoke and soot from steam engines. By 1913, eighty trains a day were making the 50-minute trip between Stamford and New York and increasing the city's popularity as a suburb and summer resort for New Yorkers, who could continue their journey by boarding a trolley at the Stamford railroad station plaza.

Trains also brought many new immigrant groups to Stamford after 1890. Political, economic, religious, and social pressures had driven them from the farms, villages, and ghettos of southern and eastern Europe. Economic opportunity attracted them to Stamford. During the peak years of immigration between 1900 and 1910, Stamford was one of the fastest-growing cities in Connecticut. While the population of the state increased 23 percent during the decade, the population of Stamford grew from 18,838 to 28,836, an increase of 53 percent. By 1910 a third of Stamford's residents were foreign-born. Although federal acts restricted immigration during the 1920s, at least 1,000 newcomers came to Stamford each year until 1930.

Left: Leonard B. Gaylor patented his design for this high-wheel safety bicycle on October 2, 1883, and manufactured it in Stamford until 1892. The unusual bicycle had the larger wheel in the front, rather than the rear, giving the rider better balance.

Right: One of the first automobiles to appear in Stamford was the Stanley Steamer; and one of the first owners was druggist Wilbur Lewis, pictured here with his new "horseless carriage."

Late-19th-century enthusiasm for the bicycle is well expressed in this 1892 view of Mrs. Amy Peckham and fellow members of a bicycle club, seen here at an abandoned mill site.

Arriving alone or in family groups, newcomers were met in New York by relatives, friends, or even people they did not know who directed them to Stamford. From the train station it was only a short walk to most of the city's ethnic neighborhoods where immigrants hoped to live among people of similar backgrounds, receive assistance in finding jobs, learn English, and gradually adjust to a new life. Franciszka Podrazik (later Frances Parker), one of the first Polish immigrants to settle in Stamford, became assistant immigration officer for the Stamford district. Twice a week she traveled to Ellis Island to aid immigrating Poles and to direct them to Stamford. She was affectionately known as "Grandma Parker" for her important role in welcoming and assisting Poles who settled in "Polska Ziemia" (Polish Land), the Polish community in Waterside and the South End.

Although many immigrants went to the Cove to live and find work in mills and factories, it was along bustling Pacific Street that members of every ethnic and racial group could be found living, working, and shopping. Immigrant families lived in small, crowded rooms above groceries, bakeries, meat and fish markets, restaurants, saloons, Chinese laundries, barber shops, hardware stores, tailor shops, shoemakers' shops, and even undertakers.

Near Main Street, where Pacific Street began, native-born Americans and earlier immigrants lived side by side with newcomers. Jewish and Italian families occupied buildings and entire blocks in the Pacific-Canal-State Street area. In 1910, for example, 42 members of 8 Italian and Jewish households occupied the rooms above a confectionary. More than 50 years later a former resident still remembered, "We were just as close to our Italian neighbors as our Jewish ones. . . . We were bound to each other by need and by respect."

Immigrant groups developed sub-communities containing elements of the life and culture left behind. Like their Irish predecessors, Germans, Poles, Italians, Slavs, and others organized

Decoration Day, 1898, brought everybody out, either to watch the parade, or to be a part of it. Seen here are members of the Tomasso Campanella Society, led by Lelio Donatelli (in front of the two flags) at the intersection of Main Street and Summer Street Extension. The first Italian organization in Stamford, the society was organized in 1894 and was devoted to the general welfare and education of Italian-born Stamford residents.

fraternal, benevolent, and mutual aid societies to provide assistance and sociability. Athletic, educational, and cultural organizations became focal points for community life. The German Turner Liedertafel, a choral society, was the forerunner of the German-American Cultural Club, while the Italian Social Institute and other Italian organizations merged to form the Stamford Italian Center.

Organizing a church, synagogue, or parish and constructing a sanctuary were pressing matters for most immigrant groups. Protestants from Germany and Scandinavia formed religious societies, held church services when a pastor was found, and built churches after they had accumulated adequate funds. Members of the Russian Orthodox faith organized in 1904 and met in private homes until they were able to build St. Mary's Russian

Orthodox Church on Pacific Street in 1916. The first Greek Orthodox community in Connecticut was founded in 1905 by Greeks living in Stamford's South End. They used St. Luke's Pacific Street Chapel until 1917, the year they completed the Church of the Annunciation nearby. A splinter group formed the Church of the Archangels in the late 1920s.

Jewish families incorporated Agudath

Sholom Synagogue in 1889 and conducted religious services in members' homes or stores until 1904, when they laid the cornerstone for an orthodox synagogue on Greyrock Place. The synagogue and the Hebrew Institute, chartered in 1916, constituted the religious, educational, cultural, and social center for Stamford's Lithuanian, Polish, and Russian Jews until the 1920s, when a group withdrew to form the conservative

Immigrant groups were quick to adapt to American life, which in the late 19th and early 20th centuries meant, among other things, forming societies and clubs. This group, photographed in the 1920s, is the Third Ward Italian American Republican Club.

Left: Eddie, Eve, and Joe Gildin were photographed together for a special occasion in 1915: their mother was afraid that Eddie, at left, who was a sickly child, might not live much longer. Happily, he survived his childhood and is still living. From the Barbara Hotz exhibit, "Pacific Street," 1983

Right: Dr. Jacob Nemointin, born in Vitebsk, Russia, came to the United States as a young man and trained as a physician in New York before settling in Stamford early in the 20th century. For more than 50 years he was the dedicated physician of Stamford's immigrant community; his wife, Frances, was very active in community affairs. Their young son, Bernard, followed in his parents' footsteps, becoming both a physician and a community leader. Courtesy, Bernard Nemointin

Right: These children posed on busy Pacific Street around 1920. At the time, Pacific Street was, in the words of one former resident, a "marvelous example of the melting pot called America." From the Barbara Hotz exhibit, "Pacific Street," 1983

Temple Beth El. The Hebrew Institute was also the nucleus of the Stamford Jewish Center, founded in 1928.

The process of creating separate ethnic parishes was difficult for Roman Catholic immigrants, who found the Irish in firm control of St. John's, the only Catholic Church in Stamford. Uncomfortable there because of differences in language and customs, each ethnic group hoped eventually to break away to establish a separate parish. In 1903 Polish Catholics successfully organized the Holy Name of Jesus Church as Stamford's second Roman

Catholic parish. Two years later they built a church, rectory, and classrooms at South and Atlantic streets. As St. John's grew larger, St. Mary's parish was formed in 1907 for Catholics living in eastern Stamford. Only in the 1920s were other parishes established: Sacred Heart for Italian-speaking Catholics in 1923, St. Vladimir's Ukranian Catholic Church in 1928, and St. Benedict's Slovak-American Roman Catholic Church in 1930.

Immigrants sometimes encountered prejudice and discrimination from native-born residents because of their religion, language, or customs. Nativist groups encouraged patriotism and the preservation of traditional American values. To speed up assimilation of immigrants, more sympathetic groups

Although Agudath Sholom was incorporated in 1889, it wasn't until 1904 that work began on this synagogue on Greyrock Place. After it was destroyed by fire in 1932, a new synagogue was erected on Grove Street, and in the 1960s the congregation built a new sanctuary on Strawberry Hill Avenue.

developed pioneer Americanization and social service programs. Beginning in 1904 the Daughters of the American Revolution sponsored lectures, in Italian, on citizenship and adult-education classes as well as special services for foreign-born women. St. John's Episcopal parish founded Neighborhood House in 1922 as a meeting place, information center, and clearinghouse for new immigrants.

The immigrants' urgent need for employment often meant taking any jobs available. Depending on their skills, they could earn from 75 cents to $3 for a 10- to 12-hour day. Unskilled men became gardeners, drivers, or manual laborers.

Those with skills worked in the building trades, on the railroad, at a foundry, machine shop, ironworks, or in specialized factories. Enterprising immigrants who started at the bottom in the retail trades or as peddlers sometimes owned their own small businesses after a few years. Few first-generation immigrants, however, entered white-collar or professional fields, seemingly the preserve of the native-born.

To contribute to family income, boys and girls typically left school between the ages of 14 and 16. Young men took jobs as trainees in offices, shops, or factories. After 1908, some attended the Yale &

Polish residents of Stamford organized Holy Name of Jesus parish in 1903, as Stamford's second Roman Catholic parish. The cornerstone for their church on Pulaski Street was laid on August 24, 1925.

Towne apprenticeship school. Young women often worked several years before marriage as domestic servants or in factories making chocolate candy, paper boxes, straw hats, shoes, suspenders, or shirtwaists. Married women assisted in family businesses; washed, ironed, or sewed for others; or, like many Pacific Street residents, kept boarders in their own cramped quarters.

Stamford's black population, like its foreign-born population, expanded after 1900, increasing from 275 persons in 1900 to 2,138 in 1930. Blacks from the South, particularly the Carolinas, came to Stamford to work in wire mills, foundries, and factories. For the unskilled, however, the only jobs open were in manual labor and domestic

service. Blacks shared with European immigrants the problems of adapting to new social, economic, and political situations, complicated by prejudice and racial discrimination.

Living primarily in the West Side and South End, blacks organized their own small sub-community. In 1888 the Wells and Doswell families and others founded the Union Baptist Church, the first black church in Fairfield County. In the 1890s the congregation bought property on Adams Avenue and built a sanctuary there. Under the leadership of the Reverend C.P. Cole, a black Methodist mission was founded on Pacific Street in 1895. It became, in 1904, the Bethel African Methodist Episcopal (A.M.E.) Church. By the 1930s, Stamford's black community had organized two other missions, as well as political, social, and athletic groups.

The abundant supply of labor was a major factor enabling Stamford firms to expand and prosper. Between 1900 and 1910 the number of manufacturing establishments increased from 49 to 86, the size of the industrial labor force nearly doubled, and the value of products manufactured increased by 123 percent— the largest gain in any Connecticut city during that decade. As employers prospered, workers began to organize trade unions and make demands for a shorter work week and increased pay. During 1916, for example, the 13 labor unions in Stamford held 6 strikes.

The work force at Yale & Towne, still Stamford's principal employer, expanded by 600 percent between 1892 and 1916. That year, because of munitions manufacture, the number of employees reached an all-time peak of 6,500. According to company records, between 1898 and 1918 the worldwide sale of their products also increased sixfold, reaching $76 million in 1918. After the War, Yale & Towne, still under the direction of founder Henry R. Towne, claimed to be the world's largest producer of locks, latches, padlocks, and chain blocks, and one of the largest producers of builders' hardware, door closers, and electric hoists. For 40 years Yale & Towne also furnished all lock boxes for U.S. post offices.

Although Stamford was still known as "The Lock City," other entrepreneurs and inventors were establishing highly specialized manufacturing firms in Stamford. In 1892, in a little shop behind his Bedford Street residence, inventor George C. Blickensderfer developed a small, inexpensive, portable typewriter with type set in a revolving interchangeable cylinder, similar to those in use today. Soon after he and his

brother William set up a manufacturing business, their "Blick" became the world's best-selling typewriter, and their Stamford firm the world's largest typewriter manufacturer. With export business cut off by World War I, ingenious George Blickensderfer invented a belt-loading device for machine guns and secured enough orders to keep the business going. The firm closed soon after the untimely death of George Blickensderfer in 1917. That same year Walter H. Bowes moved his Universal Stamping Machine Company from New York to an empty factory at Walnut and Pacific streets. In 1919 he merged his postage-stamping firm with the postage meter company of Chicago inventor Arthur H. Pitney to form the Pitney Bowes Company. Their postage meters combined the most desirable features of both inventions and within a few years brought about a revolution in postal service.

To govern more effectively the rapidly growing city, a new city charter was adopted in 1894. It modernized municipal government and gave Irish wards and political leaders a larger voice in local politics. Thereafter Republicans and Democrats alternated control of city government, and in April, 1897, prominent Democrat William T.H. Bohannan, an Irish-born attorney known as "Billy Bo," was elected mayor, marking the full acceptance of the Irish in local politics. Conservative Republicans continued to retain control of town meetings, resisting change, and tightly controlling spending in areas within their jurisdiction.

Progressive Democrat Homer S. Cummings, dashing young attorney and gifted orator, served three terms as mayor after the turn of the century. He advocated, without success, public ownership of utilities and consolidation of town and city governments. He did secure biennial elections for city officials, improvement of streets and some public services, and creation of a Board of Appropriations, a forerunner of the Board of Finance. Through Cummings' efforts the city bought land on Long Island Sound for a shorefront park, called at first Halloween Park and many years later renamed for its sponsor. In 1909 attorneys Cummings and Charles O. Lockwood founded the Stamford law firm bearing their names. Homer Cummings also held key posts in the national Democratic Party, and in 1933 Franklin D. Roosevelt appointed Cummings U.S. Attorney General, a position he would hold for six years.

City elections were particularly colorful during the years when Dr. Charles D. Rowell, homeopathic physician and one of Stamford's most experienced

politicians, led a splinter group called the "Citizen's Party." Rowell was elected mayor in 1910, the only third-party candidate ever to hold that office. When Rowell ran again in 1912, during the Progressive era, the election became one of the most spirited in Stamford history. Rowell feuded publicly with Gutzon Borglum, who led the state and local Progressive Party campaigns for his old friend, Bull Moose Presidential candidate Teddy Roosevelt. Borglum spoke on streetcorners and at factory gates. During one torchlight parade his donkey wore an elephant head on his tail end to appear as a symbol for both major parties.

Campaigns of local Socialists also added to the excitement in 1912. Philanthropist-reformer James Graham Phelps Stokes and his wife Rose Pastor,

One of the manifestations of Stamford's industrial ingenuity before the turn of the century was the typewriter designed by George Blickensderfer. The first lightweight, portable typewriter to use a printwheel design, the "Blick" was for a time the world's best-selling typewriting machine. This model No. 8 was manufactured in 1907.

foreign-born cigar maker and daughter of a rabbi, both ran for office. Stokes hoped to be a mayoral candidate, but the Stokes residence on Caritas Island in Long Island Sound was declared outside the city limits, so he ran for the Connecticut General Assembly instead. Rose Stokes was a candidate for the Stamford School Committee, the only elective office open to a Connecticut woman at that time. Both were defeated. In 1912, Stamford elected Progressive Democrat Walter C. Austin as mayor.

Like city government, the public school system changed to meet the needs of a rapidly growing population. Stamford's first school superintendent, Everett C. Willard, introduced major reforms: free public night classes for working people, faculty with college degrees, standardization of texts and curriculum, and compulsory attendance to remedy the fact that on any school day up to half the students were absent. Traditionally, many students left school after completing the eighth grade, but by 1916 eighty percent were entering high school. Average daily attendance increased from 1,569 students in 1890 to 11,872 in 1929. To keep up with increased attendance, Willard instituted some half-day sessions and built new schools. These included the first separate Stamford High School on Forest Street, later converted to Burdick Middle School, and elementary schools in the densely populated immigrant neighborhoods of Waterside and the Cove. New schoolhouses were also built in Springdale, Belltown, Glenbrook, and North Stamford. The present Stamford High School building was constructed in 1928.

An important chapter in the history of private education came to an end when Stamford's two oldest private schools closed. The Betts Academy for boys on Strawberry Hill, which listed future

dramatist Eugene O'Neill on its student roster between 1902 and 1906, burned to the ground in 1908. William "Billy" Betts, son of the founder, decided not to rebuild. The Catharine Aiken School for girls on Walton Place, purchased in 1896 by Harriet Beecher Scoville Devan, grandniece of Harriet Beecher Stowe, closed in 1911. Financial difficulties at the school culminated in sale of the property to the Congregational Church as a site for their new sanctuary. The King School for boys and the Low-Heywood School for girls, both founded in the late 19th century, carried on the tradition of outstanding private education in Stamford.

Dedicated citizens founded organizations to provide community services such as a children's home, day nursery, home for the aged, visiting nurse service, and public hospital. After more than three years of planning and fund-raising, on May 7, 1896, Stamford Hospital, the city's first public hospital, opened its doors at "Rothenfels," an imposing three-story Victorian mansion at the foot of Noroton Hill. Everyone wanted to see the spotless white wards for

Catharine Aiken is seen conducting lessons outdoors for some of her students in the 1890s, shortly before she retired and sold the school to Harriet Beecher Scoville Devan. Unfortunately, it closed in 1911, just three years after the Betts Academy was destroyed by fire.

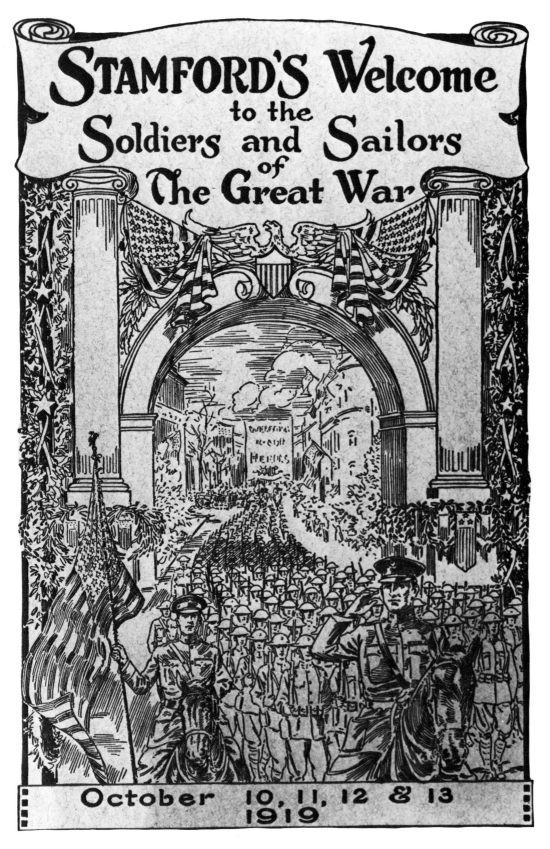

STAMFORD'S Welcome to the Soldiers and Sailors of The Great War

October 10, 11, 12 & 13 1919

In October, 1919, Stamford welcomed home the "Soldiers and Sailors of the Great War" with much fanfare, as this brochure indicates. Of the 2,637 Stamford men in the service during the war, 38 died; and one, Sergeant John Latham, was among only 90 of the 2 million Americans who served to receive the Congressional Medal of Honor for the heroism he demonstrated in France.

30 patients and operating room housed in a tower. Since affluent local residents continued to patronize New York hospitals, half of the 205 patients treated during the first year were foreign-born.

Railroad accidents, typhoid, and pneumonia were common causes for hospitalization in those days.

Pioneer women physicians Rosavelle Gardner Philip and Stella Quinby Root

Although some affluent residents began commuting from Stamford to New York in the mid-19th century, serious promotion of the idea is a 20th-century phenomenon. This booklet, featuring enticing color views of the city and its residential areas, was published by the Chamber of Commerce circa 1920.

SUBURBAN LIFE IN STAMFORD SCONNECTICUT

Published by
THE STAMFORD CHAMBER OF COMMERCE.

Engraved and Printed by
THE GILLESPIE BROS, INC.

Photographs Copyrighted by
PUBLISHERS PHOTO SERVICE, INC.

Photographs Colored by
LOUISE W. SNEAD

joined the medical staff, and a training school for nurses opened in 1901 under the direction of Daisy Caldwell Shields, who doubled as superintendent of nurses and hospital director. The hospital soon outgrew its quarters in the old mansion. Gifts and fund-raising financed construction of a brick, four-story, 100-bed hospital on West Broad Street in 1913. That original building is still an integral part of the large Stamford Hospital complex.

Major community, national, and international events captured public attention after 1915. Shortly after Stamford celebrated its 275th anniversary

STAMFORD EXPOSITION OF PROGRESS

"VISUALIZING OUR FUTURE"

HALLOWEEN PARK
MAY 28-JUNE 5

F.W.Brockett

in 1916 with a series of programs emphasizing history, ethnic diversity, and military preparedness, thousands of Stamford men and some women entered the military forces. At home foreign-born and native-born residents joined forces with equal zeal to support the war effort. Women registered for war work, and factories were converted to wartime production. Community groups such as the Red Cross and YMCA provided welfare and relief services, and local leaders conducted highly successful Liberty Loan drives to raise funds for the war.

No one who lived through the winter of 1917-1918 ever forgot the long record-breaking cold wave. An inadequate wartime supply of coal dropped to less than a day's supply at times after the harbor and Long Island Sound froze over. When dynamite blasts failed to open a channel for coal barges, coal arriving by rail was rationed in two-bushel lots. Schools and public buildings closed, pipes froze, unessential production and services

ceased, and families huddled together until the freeze ended in late February.

After the war, women won the right to vote and run for public office. Although several local women were candidates, beginning in 1920, none was elected until 1925, when Julia M. Emery of Glenbrook, wife of nationally known inventor and manufacturer Albert H. Emery, became the first Stamford woman to win a seat in the Connecticut General Assembly.

During the 1920s, efforts to reform municipal government continued, and in 1922 twenty-eight-year old Democrat Alfred N. Phillips, Jr., lively leader of a group of young politicians and grandson of the founder of Glenbrook's Phillips Chemical Company, was elected mayor on a reform platform. With the determination and energy that would be his hallmark, Phillips expanded municipal services, appointed a full-time health officer, and introduced the concepts of city planning and zoning.

While residents enjoyed the new social freedoms of the "Roaring Twenties," confident in their own and their city's future, civic leaders were concerned with maintaining the quality of life in their expanding and prosperous city. For the first time they were confronting the effects of unplanned growth. Public services were inadequate, and public health a major concern. Residents needed additional parks and recreational facilities. And their city's unity was threatened when both Shippan and North Stamford attempted, in 1927, to secede and become independent towns. Town leaders looked into urban planning and city leaders discussed charter reform. Both would become dominant issues in succeeding years, yet national and world events of the 1930s and 1940s would have an unforeseen effect on the development of Stamford and the lives of its people.

Stamford's business and civic leaders followed the early 20th-century method of city promotion with the "Stamford Exposition of Progress" in 1926. Little is known about the exposition itself; this reproduction of what must have been the poster appears on a small Chamber of Commerce brochure giving highlights of Stamford history and amenities as of that date.

VIII CONTRACTION AND CONSOLIDATION

Nearly 10,000 Stamford-area men and women served in World War II; their contribution was noted and celebrated here, as on many other occasions, by Mayor Charles E. Moore (at left microphone).

The stock market crash of 1929 and the Great Depression of the 1930s shattered the optimism and prosperity of a city on the threshold of planning for the future. Instead, Stamford turned its attention to maintaining the status quo. Only after postwar consolidation of city and town governments and a spurt of unanticipated growth did civic leaders once again consider the need to plan and control the development of their evolving community.

In 1926, during a period of unprecedented growth, the newly formed Town Plan Commission employed city planner Herbert S. Swan of New York to prepare a plan for Stamford. His farsighted and prophetic "Plan of a Metropolitan Suburb," published in 1929, attracted national attention for its analysis and solutions of the problems of a rapidly growing industrial suburb. Enthusiastically calling Stamford "a city of unlimited potential," Swan noted, "Without either knowing or paying any particular attention to the fact, Stamford is rapidly becoming one of the great cities of the country. . .due to its demands, its environment, and its opportunities. . . . Stamford is in a real sense a part of the New York metropolitan area," Swan continued, "yet in another sense, Stamford has an identity altogether its own."

Swan believed Stamford's destiny "depends almost exclusively upon how satisfactorily she adapts her plan to her environment." In the 10-year urban development program he outlined for Stamford, Swan placed a high priority on creating a network of highways to facilitate the flow of traffic through Stamford's maze of congested, narrow streets. "The street plan of Stamford," according to Swan, "is full of such little jokes and idiosyncrasies; it bubbles over with them; indeed, there is scarcely an intersection or a block that does not have its surprises in unexpected situations and novel experiences to the uninitiated driver."

Swan advised Stamford to acquire land for additional parks, playgrounds, and recreational areas along the 13-mile indented shoreline and the Rippowam and Mianus rivers, in his opinion the town's most valuable assets. He also recommended building a new railroad station and improving the grounds ("the ugliest in New England") as well as relocating town hall, library, and post office, together with civic auditorium and art museum, in a city center complex to be developed along the Mill River near Broad Street.

Finding Stamford "one of the few unzoned communities within the New York metropolitan area," Swan urged prompt adoption of uniform zoning regulations for city and town. Prophetically—and in vain—Swan warned in conlusion against waiting to

1929–1958

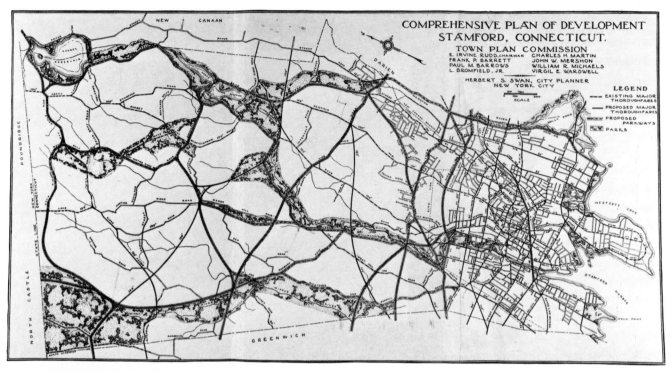

implement his plan until changes were unavoidable and land very costly to acquire. The crash of 1929, the Depression, and the war followed publication of the "Stamford Plan," and it was apparently forgotten.

During the Depression, however, one recommendation of the plan was carried out: construction of a major east-west

highway to relieve traffic on the historic Boston Post Road and to link Stamford with its neighbors as well as with the parkway system of Westchester County. After the first shovelful of dirt was turned on July 1, 1934, construction of the Merritt Parkway officially began. The parkway was named for venerable octogenarian Schuyler Merritt, who in 1934 was serving his eighth term in the U.S. House of Representatives. As chairman of the Parkway Commission and principal speaker at the groundbreaking ceremony, Merritt explained the goals of parkway planners: "We believe that it will be designed and built not alone or even primarily to afford rapid transit, but to be in itself an object of beauty and to tend to the rest and peace and satisfaction of those who inhabit the county and of those who pass through it."

Built by men who needed work during the Depression, the parkway was opened to traffic four years later, on June 29, 1938, by Connecticut Governor Wilbur Cross, flanked by Congressman Merritt

Above: Herbert S. Swan's "Plan of a Metropolitan Suburb," published in 1929, attracted considerable attention at the time for its sophisticated approach to solving the city's problems. As it happened, however, unanticipated events precluded adoption of the recommendations and it was put aside. Courtesy, Ferguson Library

Left: Schuyler Merritt, for whom Merritt Parkway was named, served nine terms in the U.S. House of Representatives between 1917 and 1936. Active in civic and business affairs in Stamford for most of his life, Merritt held the position of chairman of the board at both Yale & Towne and First Stamford Bank & Trust Company and was president of the Ferguson Library Association.

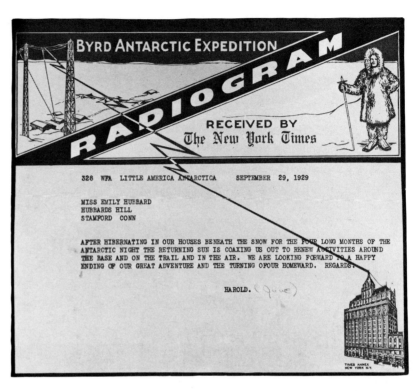

and U.S. Attorney General Homer S. Cummings. The Merritt Parkway received nationwide acclaim for its landscaping, well-planned approaches, and attractive bridges, each designed by a different architect.

During the early 1950s work began on a second major east-west toll highway running near the shore, parallel to the railroad and Boston Post Road. The Connecticut Turnpike was designed to link New York and New England and to carry the automobile and truck traffic then choking Connecticut shore towns on U.S. Route l. After the turnpike opened in 1956, it became a section of the interstate highway system extending from Maine to Florida.

Traffic congestion was a result of the rapid residential and industrial growth of Stamford. As newcomers steadily arrived to seek jobs in the city's prosperous economy, the population increased to 56,765 in 1930, a jump of 42 percent in a decade. According to city directories, in 1929 the industrial work force numbered 10,000 men and women, nearly one-fifth of the population. They

worked in 118 industrial establishments, manufacturing products valued at $40 million annually. The stock market crash, however, brought an abrupt end to industrial growth and with fewer jobs available during the 1930s, population growth also slowed, increasing only eight percent during the decade, to reach 61,326 inhabitants in 1940.

Stamford's heavy and durable goods and construction industries were hard hit by the Depression. By 1934 the number of industrial firms had declined by one-third and the value of goods manufactured locally was cut in half. The value of building permits dropped from $5 million during the boom year of 1929 to under $500,000 during 1934. As a result at least 1,000 workers lost their jobs and many others were laid off temporarily or took reductions in hours and wages.

Yale & Towne, still Stamford's largest employer, reached a turning point during 1931. After the firm transferred approximately 300 jobs from Stamford to other locations and removed executive

Above, left: The Crash of 1929 was forgotten, at least for a day, when Stamford residents greeted local hero Harold I. June on June 26, 1930. Lieutenant June earned his place in history thousands of miles from home—over the South Pole. June was a member of Rear Admiral Richard Byrd's first Antarctic expedition in 1928 and was at the controls when the crew flew over the pole in 1929. June was a much-decorated officer for his Antarctic trips and military service; a peak in Antarctica bears his name.

Above: Harold June sent this radiogram to Stamford native Emily Hubbard on September 29, 1929.

offices to New York City, the original facility at Stamford became another division of the corporation. President Walter C. Allen explained the move was due to "rapidly rising taxation in Stamford in recent years." To cut costs further, Yale & Towne reduced the pay of its executives. Nonetheless, by 1937, with sales off 50 percent or more, the company was losing money, and spokesmen began to talk about the high cost of labor in Stamford.

"The period 1929 to 1940 saw the rise and fall of many of Stamford's business houses and industries, all struggling to fight off the Depression," reported the *Advocate* in 1941. The Peoples National Bank was the only bank to fail, and its assets and liabilities were taken over in 1933 by the First National Bank & Trust Company with no loss to depositors. Several old firms, including Lyman Hoyt & Sons Furniture Company and Stollwerck Chocolate Company, closed their doors. New firms took over some facilities, providing jobs for unemployed workers. Borden Farms Products and Schavoir Rubber Company were two firms leasing empty factory buildings, and in 1934, one of the worst Depression years, Machlett Laboratories bought a Springdale factory and began manufacturing X-ray tubes there. Several businesses occupied the large Verran Company plant on West Main Street before the American Cyanamid Corporation leased the facility in 1935 for a research laboratory. Globe Slicing Machine Company and Clairol were among other firms moving to Stamford during the Depression.

Pitney Bowes gradually expanded its operations, and by 1940, when one of every five letters was metered mail, their Stamford work force had grown to over 500 employees. The electric dry-shaver industry was born in a Stamford loft during the Depression, where its

inventor, Colonel Jacob Schick, manufactured pencil sharpeners. By 1940 the Schick Dry Shaver Company employed nearly 1,000 workers in its Atlantic Street factory.

As unemployment increased during the 1930s, town selectmen were hard-pressed to provide adequate relief. In 1929 the town allocated $43,000, or about 4 percent of its budget, for relief and nearly $600,000, or 55 percent, for education. The town assisted 1,423 needy persons, more than twice the usual number, in 1930; and the following year selectmen described the growing problem: "The amount of money spent in this department during the past year is three times greater than during the ordinary year. . . . Many terribly pathetic cases have come to our attention . . . and we desire to express appreciation publicly to the untold number of people whom we know to be constantly helping their neighbors during this crisis." Escalating relief costs and declining tax revenues led the Town Board of Finance to cut the school budget by $200,000 in 1932. After 92 teachers lost their jobs, the Teachers Association unsuccessfully challenged the Board of Finance over the budget cut.

In response to the continuing crisis, First Selectman John T. Hanrahan hired New London social worker Elizabeth F. Hopson to organize a separate Town Welfare Department in 1933. To provide needed services, the welfare department, quickly growing to over 60 employees, worked closely with such voluntary groups as Family Welfare Service, Salvation Army, Catholic Welfare Bureau, and other affiliates of the Community Chest, itself organized during the Depression. Soon, however, town officials and civic leaders drew relief into the political arena. They scrutinized welfare expenditures, obtained the dismissal and replacement of the relief administrator, and instigated an investigation of shopkeepers who distributed commodities to persons on relief.

By late 1933 New Deal emergency relief programs began to provide public-works jobs for Stamford's unemployed men and women. The federal government paid two-thirds and Stamford one-third of annual relief costs, which reached $1 million. Each week from 427 to 1,011 individuals found work developing school grounds and playgrounds, painting public buildings, constructing an athletic field and stadium

in relief cases, but with 17 percent of the population receiving municipal funds, for the first time selectmen spent more money on relief than on education. High relief expenditures continued until the approach of World War II, the event credited with bringing the American economy out of the Depression.

Even before the Depression placed new demands on city government, political leaders recognized the need for charter revision. Republican William W. Graves, elected mayor in 1928 on a platform calling for revision, appointed a Charter

Many of the murals gracing America's public buildings were WPA projects of the 1930s. This detail is from a series at Stamford High School on Strawberry Hill Avenue; they were subsequently removed. Photograph by Dayton Snyder.

at Stamford High School, and renovating Town Hall. They widened roads and bridges and constructed storm sewers, curbs, gutters, and sidewalks. The federal government also provided funds for two low-cost housing projects in Stamford, 146-family Fairfield Court, constructed at Fairfield and Stillwater avenues in 1935, and Southfield Village, a 250-family project built on Selleck Avenue in 1939.

With New Deal programs in place by 1935, selectmen hoped to see a reduction

Revision Commission to study the forms of government suitable for the City of Stamford. Citizens weighed the pros and cons of the commission's recommendations: either a Strong-Mayor Charter with administrative powers concentrated in the hands of the mayor, or a Council-Manager Charter with an elected council and professional city manager. The *Advocate* announced the result of the May, 1932, referendum on the question: "Strong Mayor is Selected by a Majority of 2,178—Result is as Great a Surprise to Victorious Group as to Council-Manager Adherants."

The new charter, approved by the state legislature in 1933, provided for the election of a full-time, salaried mayor, a seven-member City Council, and a six-member Board of Finance who joined in passing appropriations. The council handled legislative matters, subject to the mayor's veto, and the mayor was completely responsible for the operation of the government. He also had power to appoint all other city officials, including the five commissioners who headed the departments of finance, health, law, safety, and services.

On January 1, 1935, Democrat Alfred N. Phillips, Jr., who had served two terms as mayor during the 1920s, took office as the first "strong mayor" of Stamford. He promised "to make Stamford a happier and more prosperous place in which to live. . .and to see that suffering in Stamford is abolished." An energetic and resourceful New Deal mayor, Phillips was in large part responsible for securing large federal works projects and increasing citizen participation in government.

Dissatisfaction with the new charter arose quickly, however. Some critics contended that the strong mayor had too much power and others pointed out that the dual structure of government, separating town and city for some functions and not for others, was an outmoded and inefficient way to govern a modern industrial city. In 1937 the Connecticut legislature passed a resolution calling for a commission to study the consolidation of town and city governments, considered by many the only rational way to govern Stamford. Further action was delayed by World War II.

In June, 1941, local attention was temporarily turned away from the

Depression and the war in Europe by a gala two-week celebration of Stamford's 300th anniversary. Planned by more than 200 citizens, festivities included pageants, balls, concerts by WPA bands, sports events, parades with historical floats and military and Civilian Defense marching units, and an exhibit of progress. On June 7, 1941, the *Advocate* commemorated the tercentenary with a 208-page edition featuring a comprehensive history of Stamford.

As war drew near, the shift to war production temporarily dislocated some workers. After the war began several local firms, including Electric Specialty Company, Stamford Rolling Mills, Yale & Towne, Pitney Bowes, Machlett Laboratories, and Norma-Hoffman Bearings shifted to war production. Short of workers, they recruited women and older men from the area and blacks from the South. By 1943, 40 percent of Pitney Bowes' workers were women, one of whom recalled that the majority were married and that those with children usually worked the 3 p.m.-to-11 p.m. shift. By 1944, 93 percent of industrial workers in the key munitions-making state of Connecticut were engaged in war

The devastating hurricane of September 21, 1938, killed one person, uprooted trees, and forced many families to evacuate the South End. According to the Advocate, *"The storm brought out many acts of heroism, and showed that despite the unexpectedness of the onslaught, Stamford was capable of cooperating to protect its own people." This photograph is of Bedford Street, looking south.*

production.

More than 9,500 men and women left Stamford to serve in the armed forces. Of these, 213 lost their lives. Civilians signed up as aircraft spotters and wardens, Civilian Defense leaders, and Red Cross workers. Despite wartime shortages, construction continued on 80-bed St. Joseph's Hospital on Strawberry Hill, and the city's second hospital opened in October, 1942, only a few months behind schedule.

As the end of the war approached in 1944, business and civic leaders organized the Stamford Postwar Planning Council, chaired by Kingsley Gillespie, scion of Stamford's newspaper publishing family. They discussed employment of returning veterans, absorption of displaced war workers, and orderly reconversion of local industries to peacetime production. Stamford's postwar plan, one of three receiving national recognition, served as a model for other Connecticut cities.

Implementation of the postwar plan was proceeding on schedule in the fall of 1945 when labor unrest, spreading throughout the country, erupted in

Stamford. Union and management at Yale & Towne could not agree on two union demands, the closed shop and substantial wage increases. When members of the International Association of Machinists, AFL, organized at Yale & Towne in 1942, called strikes at both the Stamford and Philadelphia plants on November 7, 1945, 2,500 of the 3,500 workers at Stamford walked out. They shut down the plant, and pickets barred company officials from entering the buildings. Management refused to give in on the open-shop issue or submit to any kind of compulsory arbitration, insisting on dealing directly with employees. Local and state police tried to maintain order, but by December "virtual siege conditions prevailed at Yale & Towne," according to newspaper accounts. Union members at other local plants passed resolutions of sympathy with the strikers, who also found widespread support within the community.

During the 21-week strike Mayor Charles E. Moore, local clergymen, Governor Raymond Baldwin, and conciliators of the U.S. Department of

Labor searched for a solution. Late in March, 1946, both sides agreed to enter collective bargaining in New York at the U.S. Conciliation Service. During 11 days and nights of continuous negotiating each side made compromises—more than either intended to—and finally one of the largest and most costly strikes in Connecticut history was settled. Striking union members at both Stamford and Philadelphia ratified a two-year contract calling for a wage increase of 12.5 cents an hour, compulsory irrevocable checkoff (deduction of union dues from paycheck), and improved vacation and paid holiday provisions. Recognizing that neither side had really won, the *Advocate* called the settlement "Peace Without Victory." After the strike Yale & Towne resumed production and sought orders lost to competition. In 1948 the firm began to reduce the size of its local work force, leaving only the Lock and Hardware Division in Stamford.

In another postwar development, the Charter Consolidation Inquiry Commission, formed before the war, reported back, recommending a single government for town and city. Nearly 40 years later, commission member Babette S. Ransohoff recalled the opposition to consolidation. "I was the only resident of the town on the charter commission who was in favor of it. The whole country area was against it. Even Town First Selectman Barrett who became its first mayor was against it." She explained one way the commission countered opposition and "why we ended up with two representatives from each district. Because the rural section had only six districts, we would have been so overwhelmed by the city, which was Democratic. . . So that's why we have a 40-member Board." Mrs. Ransohoff was a member of that new board, serving two terms as its clerk.

Despite strong opposition, voters

approved the Consolidated Charter in November, 1947. It took effect on April 15, 1949, ending separation of the 56-year-old city and 308-year-old town governments. The new charter provided for 66 elected officials: a mayor, 40-member Board of Representatives, 9-member Board of Education, 6-member Board of Finance, a town clerk, 2 registrars of voters, and 7 constables. The addition of 171 officials appointed by the mayor and approved by the Board of Representatives brought the total number of elected and appointed officials to 237.

The charter commission intentionally divided responsibility among mayor, Board of Representatives, and Board of Finance, according to commission member Ransohoff. Public administrator and charter critic Andrew D. Bender later called the government one with "few powers and many checks," pointing out that the mayor lacked clearly defined administrative power and had many limitations on his authority. No single individual was responsible for the overall operation of government. The system, however, provided citizens with many opportunities to serve on boards and commissions.

After the transition term of Republican Mayor George T. Barrett, Democrat Thomas F.J. Quigley served three terms as mayor. Quigley hired an executive aide, held monthly cabinet meetings, and tested the powers of the mayor to fix the tax rates under the new charter by filing lawsuits against both the Board of Finance and the Board of Representatives. He lost both suits. In 1951 the Board of Representatives created a five-member Urban Redevelopment Commission and in 1953 adopted the city's first Master Plan, an inevitable response to the changes in the city Herbert Swan had predicted many years earlier.

Rapid population increase and a

To meet the needs of consumers, new shopping centers with large parking areas sprang up outside the center of the city, including Ridgeway Center on Summer Street (1947), Bloomingdale's department store on Broad Street (1954), and Town and Country Center near Bull's Head (built in 1955 and demolished in 1983 to make way for a large hotel). As postwar shoppers increasingly patronized outlying stores, downtown merchants, like merchants in other American cities, expressed concern about the future of the central business district.

Like most other American cities, Stamford also needed additional churches and schools after the war. These institutions, as well, were placed in residential sections outside the city center. The architecture of two Bedford Street churches, inspired by medieval European sanctuaries, attracted widespread attention in the late 1950s. The design of the Greek Orthodox Church of the Archangels was based on 11th-century Byzantine architecture, while New York architect Wallace K. Harrison based his design of the new First Presbyterian Church on his firsthand study of German, French, and British Gothic cathedrals. Noting the unusual and symbolic shape of the modern structure Harrison created, parishioners dubbed it "the fish church."

To meet the educational needs of a diverse and expanding community, the city built several elementary schools during the 1950s, the Jewish Center opened a Bi-Cultural Day School, and Catholics constructed Stamford Catholic High School. In 1951 the University of Connecticut established a limited undergraduate program at Stamford High School for students living in the area. Ten years later the university expanded its programs and faculty and moved to its own spacious campus on Scofieldtown Road near the university's Bartlett

Stamford residents have been involved, directly or indirectly, in many wars since the city's founding, and World War II was no exception. Relief activity was just one of many contributions—and sacrifices—residents made during the war. Stamford's mayor during most of the war was Charles E. Moore, pictured at left. Next to him is Selectman George T. Barrett. Photograph by Leon Seaf.

building boom were among changes that followed World War II. The city gained more than 30,000 new residents between 1940 and 1960, when population reached 92,713 inhabitants, an increase of 50 percent in 20 years. Refugees from Germany and Hungary, migrating natives, and New York commuters moved into the crowded city center or new housing developments suddenly springing up on former farms and wooded hillsides. Waterfront property on Long Island Sound, the Mianus River, and North Stamford ponds attracted celebrities and performing artists from the musical and theatrical worlds, including Libby Holman, Gloria Vanderbilt and Leopold Stokowski, Ezio Pinza, Peggy Wood, Benny Goodman, and musicologist Deems Taylor. Joshua Logan wrote most of his popular postwar musical *South Pacific* at his home in Old Long Ridge Village.

St. Joseph's Hospital was organized in 1939 by the Most Reverend Maurice F. McAuliffe, bishop of the Catholic Diocese of Hartford, and completed in October, 1942. The hospital, originally built to accommodate 80 patients and expanded several times, is on land which belonged to the late Colonel Hugh Cooper on Strawberry Hill Avenue.

Arboretum. The Stamford Museum and Nature Center, founded in 1936 as a natural history museum and educational facility, moved in 1955 to the former Henri Bendel estate on High Ridge Road and there developed a farm, zoo, and nature center in addition to the museum, now housed in the estate's 40-room Tudor mansion. An observatory and the Ezio Pinza Theater completed the museum complex.

Stimulated by the Korean War, Stamford's economy experienced a short period of rapid growth before a major downturn occurred. Barnes Engineering, founded in 1952, was among the new firms in Stamford. When, in 1954, a slowdown in manufacturing was noted everywhere in Connecticut, a spokesman for the Connecticut Manufacturing Association called for a "grass-roots campaign" to preserve a favorable climate for industry in the state. After Schick Dry Shaver, in November, 1954, announced plans to move all operations to Lancaster, Pennsylvania, the Stamford Chamber of Commerce launched a study of the industrial potential of Stamford, focusing on how to hold existing industries and attract new ones.

Then in 1955, Yale & Towne moved its Lock and Hardware Division offices to White Plains, New York, and sold its South End Manufacturing plant, leasing back only one-third of the space. Company officials explained that the move was due to the inefficient layout and high cost of maintaining 81 separate buildings scattered over 27 acres, postwar labor strife, high utility costs, and high local and state taxes. When Yale & Towne, down to its last 450 employees, closed its doors in 1959, a long and important chapter in Stamford history came to an end.

Other manufacturers also moved out during the 1950s. They included Atlas Powder, Baer Brothers, Carboloy, Mt. Vernon Die Casting, Norma-Hoffman Bearings, and Tele-register. Only a few workers followed their jobs to new locations, and the local economy was not able to absorb all of its unemployed workers.

The city sought solutions to the undermining of its economic base. One problem recognized very early was the lack of industrially zoned land. If, however, small parcels of industrial property could be made available for light manufacturing or research and development facilities, the city reasoned, such firms might be induced to locate in Stamford. To make such land available, in 1953 the Urban Redevelopment Commission took, as its first activity, the East Meadows Industrial Project. A dozen acres of frequently flooded and blighted land off Harbor View Avenue, in the heart of the industrial district south of the railroad and turnpike, was successfully redeveloped for industrial use.

City fathers believed the city also needed to change its image, realizing that "The Lock City" was no longer appropriate as Stamford's motto. In 1958 they officially adopted the new slogan, "The Research City," in an effort to attract additional research and development firms. The research division of American Cyanamid and Clairol corporations and smaller local firms had been joined in 1955 by CBS Laboratories, which occupied a large facility on the former Barnes Sanitarium property on High Ridge Road.

During the 1950s Stamford thus took important steps toward a planned transformation of its economy, while planning for urban redevelopment represented its attempt to shape the environment to better meet the needs of the city and its residents. Together these two planning measures set the stage for the city's future development.

Downtown Stamford is now considerably busier than it was in the 1950s, when this picture was taken. West Park Place is seen here, behind the policeman; the former Methodist Church building is in the background.

Right: Sunday After Church, Stamford, Connecticut, *was painted circa 1850. Courtesy, George W. Samaha, Milan, Ohio*

Far right, top: The Town Hall was new when this turn-of-the-century post-card was made. Courtesy, Stamford Historical Society (SHS)

Far right, middle and bottom: Wilbur E. Lewis and H.J. Borgmann distributed these advertising cards in the late 1800s. (SHS)

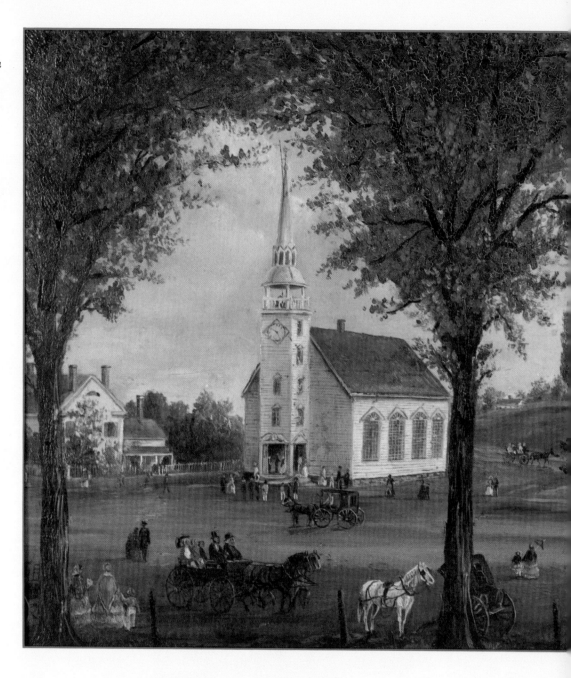

SOUVENIR VIEWS OF STAMFORD, CONN.

Town Hall.

COMPLIMENTS OF
WILBUR E. LEWIS,
DRUGGIST,
CORNER TOWN HALL,
Stamford, Conn.

Interior Home Furnishers

New, Antique and Reproductions

H. J. BORGMANN
INTERIOR DECORATOR
UPHOLSTERY & DRAPERY

60 SUMMER ST., STAMFORD, CONN.
Telephone

—MADE TO ORDER—
Draperies,
Curtains, Slip Covers
and Mattresses

Upholsterers

124

Right: Volunteer Patricia McLean demonstrates spinning techniques inside the Hoyt-Barnum House which contains many original elements, including the wide oak flooring.

Left, top: The inscription in the center of this friendship quilt, dated January 1, 1850, says that it was "presented to Miss Sarah A. Ayres by the friends whose names are here recorded and in the hope that down into the evening of her life it may prove a faithful remembrance of those friends of her early youth." (SHS)

Left, bottom: Adeline Scofield Briggs designed and stitched this appliqué tulip quilt in the late 1800s. (SHS)

Above: The Buxton-Lounsbury cemetery, in Turn-of-River, was used from 1792 to 1929 and contains some beautiful examples of early tombstone work.

Right: The Mianus River, which has some of the most rugged and heavily wooded land in the Stamford area along its banks, is a lovely reminder of what the area looked like to the original settlers.

Facing page: This breathtaking garden in North Stamford belongs to Ruth and James Levitan.

Reuben Nakian, an artist who is known internationally for his monumental sculpture, has lived and worked in Stamford since 1945. Many museums across the country, including the Chicago Institute of Art, Lincoln Center, the Whitney Museum, and the Smithsonian, have shown Nakian's work.

Above and left: The First Presbyterian Church of Stamford, designed by noted architect Wallace K. Harrison, is known as the "fish church" because of its exterior form. Dedicated in 1958, the church is admired for its unusual architecture and stained-glass windows by French artist Gabriel Loire.

With urban renewal, downtown Stamford was transformed during the 1970s and 1980s. The clock tower of the General Reinsurance building (left) was completed in 1984. Among the more than 20 Fortune 500 businesses headquartered in Stamford are Schweppes U.S.A., Ltd., on High Ridge Road (left, bottom) and General Telephone and Electronics (right).

Right: The Stamford Museum and Nature Center occupies the former Henri Bendel estate. The sleeping lion guards the entry and the three horses (facing page, bottom) are part of the neo-Italian Renaissance fountain at one end of the courtyard.

Below: This is a section of the gardens surrounding "Treetops," the mansion built for Libby Holman Reynolds, famed torch singer of the 1920s and widow of tobacco heir Zachary Smith Reynolds. Champion International purchased the property after Mrs. Reynolds' death and continues her tradition of inviting the public to view the extensive gardens every year during the daffodil season.

The Hoyt-Barnum House, built in 1699 by blacksmith Samuel Hoyt, is the oldest building still standing in Stamford. The Bedford Street house is owned by the Stamford Historical Society.

133

Above: Founded in 1880, the Ferguson Library moved into its building at Bedford and Broad streets in 1911. The white marble addition, completed in 1982, more than doubled the size of the library.

Right: One of the most imposing buildings in Stamford, St. Mary's Roman Catholic Church, on Elm Street, is reminiscent of France's Gothic cathedrals. The free-standing, all-masonry church was dedicated in 1908.

Facing page, top: This view of downtown Stamford was taken from the First Congregational Church.

Facing page, bottom: The Stamford Yacht Club, founded in the early 1890s, has contributed to the city's reputation as a boating center.

135

IX RENEWAL AND TRANSFORMATION

This view of downtown was taken from the east, near the intersection of Main and Elm streets. The white monument in the foreground is a war memorial to Stamford veterans from the French and Indian War through World War I.

"One need only look at Stamford's skyline and its downtown streets; at long last, there it is! The dream has become a reality," wrote Urban Redevelopment Commmission Chairman Edith Sherman in 1979, as she surveyed a revitalized city and booming business, service, and retail center. In 1960 Stamford had been a bedroom community with a faltering economy and rapidly deteriorating downtown. During the next 20 years, Stamford and southwest Fairfield County underwent a transformation that was unique in the state and nation, a phenomenon observers have called "the Stamford miracle."

During the last quarter-century Stamford has burst forth in terms of population, economic base, and demands on city government. Underlying the pace and impact of rapid change was the experience of extensive urban renewal. During the 1960s Stamford was the fastest-growing town in Connecticut and the state's only major city to gain population, increasing from 92,713 in 1960 to a peak of 108,798 in 1970. Proximity to New York, good transportation, and an attractive suburban setting were credited with drawing new residents. The postwar "baby boom" also contributed to rapid growth.

Regional planners predicted that the population would continue to grow rapidly and reach 125,000 to 135,000 inhabitants by 1980. Population, however, declined to 102,458 in 1980, a reduction of nearly 6 percent in 10 years and the first population decline since 1840. Explanations for the downturn included the scarcity of land for large-scale development, the high price of land and housing, and the decline in household size, due to a lower birth rate and an increase in one- and two-person households. Local officials and community leaders also cited undercounting of black and Spanish-speaking residents, many of whom would not speak with census enumerators. Estimates of the number uncounted exceeded 5,000, more than one of every five black or Hispanic residents.

In recent decades Stamford's population changed both numerically and in ethnic and racial characteristics. In 1970, 35.4 percent of the city's population was of first- or second-generation immigrant background, a slightly higher proportion than earlier. Recent immigrants have come not only from Europe but also from Asia, Central and South America, and the Caribbean. Most striking in terms of adaptation have been the large new groups of black, Spanish-speaking, and Haitian residents.

As blacks from the South and the West Indies came to Stamford between 1960 and 1980, the black population increased from 8.3 to 15 percent of the total. Newcomers found a well-organized black

1960–PRESENT

community with its own institutions, including churches, businesses, lodges, political and social clubs, and community centers. A major resource was the Yerwood Center, named in 1975 for its founder, Dr. Joyce Yerwood, a black physician and community leader who in 1937 began working with black youth in her own backyard and in 1939 organized Stamford's first black community center on West Main Street.

Community groups in Stamford, aware of the city's racial diversity and of the racial imbalance in the public schools, began to devise a plan to desegregate city schools in 1961. Their goal was to reflect the diversity of the school-age population in each school and to achieve equal educational opportunity for every child in the system. The Stamford Board of Education adopted the policy of giving every child "the opportunity to achieve his highest educational potential . . . regardless of race, color or creed, or economic status."

Beginning with the high schools, the Board of Education implemented the integration plan between 1961 and 1972. In response to increasing enrollment, the city built new schools in outlying areas and closed older, racially imbalanced inner-city schools. Subsequently the

School Board adjusted school district lines and, when necessary, cross-bused children to achieve a racial balance. Westover and Hart became magnet elementary schools, drawing children from all over the city to their special programs. Although public school enrollment peaked at 20,900 students in 1969, before the completion of the integration and school construction programs, the Board of Education continued to build new schools into the mid-1970s.

Both black and white residents participated in the Civil Rights Movement of the 1960s. Area clergymen and black leaders organized peaceful demonstrations, parades, rallies, and prayer meetings. Militant leaders also spoke in Stamford and used inflamatory rhetoric to call for direct action. There were, however, few disorderly incidents. John T. Brown, Jr., who later became executive director of the Committee on Training and Employment (CTE), a public agency funded to work with the city's disadvantaged population, recalled those meetings. "Many of the real protest meetings of the black community were held at the A.M.E. Church under the leadership of Reverend F. Lemoyne Whitlock," he said. "Some of the other ministers were more conservative in their approach and not willing to get out and speak on social issues, but Lemoyne Whitlock was willing to speak out and he did." Judge Robert L. Levister, a member of the mayor's Human Relations Council and the Stamford Board of Finance during the 1960s, also spoke out. He cited housing, education, jobs, politics, and white attitudes as the principal problems facing black residents of Stamford.

During the 1960s and 1970s, black residents moved into management, government, and education. Pitney Bowes, a pioneer in the employment of minorities, developed a program to bring more blacks into highly-skilled, office and managerial positions. For the first time black members were elected to the Board of Finance and the Board of Representatives. In 1969 Granville S. Roman became the first black to serve as a school principal; he was followed by Dr. Thelma King, who in 1975 became principal of Stamford High School. Black political leaders organized the Afro-American Democratic Club during the early 1970s. Their goal of "getting more political power for blacks and more blacks

Cuba, Colombia, Ecuador, and other Latin American countries came to Stamford to find work and a better place to live. They faced many of the same adjustment problems as other immigrant groups, complicated by a language barrier. Taking low-skilled manufacturing and service jobs at minimum pay, they were barred, in many cases, from advancement because they did not speak English or lacked immigration documents.

Hispanic immigrants had common problems and aspirations, geographical and social origins, language, and religion,

Physician Joyce U. Yer-wood (facing page), who came to Stamford in the 1930s with her husband, Dr. J. Lucian Carwin, has managed to combine an active professional life and work with black youngsters quite successfully for almost a half-century. Dr. Yer-wood founded the Negro Community Center soon after her arrival in Stam-ford; its successor is the Yerwood Center on West Main Street, where these children wait at the reception area. Courtesy, Yer-wood Center

into politics" was successful. By the late 1970s many members of the Black Caucus, founded as a social rather than political organization, held public office.

Like the black community, the Spanish-speaking community also grew in size during the 1960s and 1970s, increasing from .5 percent of Stamford's population in 1960 to 5.6 percent in 1980. Former residents of Puerto Rico,

but were divided in cultural and political terms. The Roman Catholic Church of Our Lady of Montserrat drew them together and with other organizations endeavored to assist Hispanics in adapting to a new life. In 1969 CTE sponsored the Spanish International Center, an employment, educational, cultural, and social-service facility. CTE closed the Center ten years later and eventually combined services for Hispanics with its other community services. Like the black community, the Hispanic community recognized the importance of increasing political participation and acquiring political power to improve their social and economic status.

Refugees from Haiti comprised the most recent and poorest immigrant group in Stamford. The majority arrived in Stamford during the late 1970s and early 1980s. Their number, estimated at 5,000 to 6,000 in 1981, made Stamford's Haitian community one of the largest in Connecticut. A study prepared for CTE that year indicated that most Haitians lived in poverty, shared crowded lodgings, were unemployed, and did not speak English. Classified as economic rather than political refugees, many were considered illegal aliens and ineligible for government benefits. In an effort to ease their adjustment, churches and agencies like CTE, the Haitian Resource Center, and Family and Children's Services reached out to the Haitian population, providing such services as information and counseling, interpretation and translation, and English language classes.

The city's most recent immigrants, like their predecessors, usually lived in old frame and masonry buildings in the downtown or surrounding areas where rents were low and there was easy access to jobs, shops, and public transportation. Even before black and Hispanic immigration into Stamford began to increase, lodgings and stores in those areas were generally run down after years of neglect and had already become one focus for an urban renewal project to eliminate the "blight and deterioration" in the center of the city.

Stamford initiated the long and deliberate process of extensive urban renewal during the late 1950s, after the Federal Housing Act of 1949 made government funds available for that purpose. To start the project and provide for citizen participation, Mayor Webster C. Givens appointed a 12-member Citizens' Action Council, chaired by community leader and Pitney Bowes President Walter H. Wheeler, Jr. The Council worked closely with the Urban Redevelopment Commission (URC), Board of Representatives, and the Planning and Zoning Boards to develop a proposal for revitalizing a large area in the heart of downtown Stamford.

The redevelopment area included the central business district with the Town Hall and other city offices as well as the Pacific Street area, once the vibrant center of Stamford's immigrant community. The area was bounded by North State Street, Atlantic Street north to the Post Office and west to Washington Boulevard, Broad Street, and Grove and Elm streets. Like the downtowns of many American cities of the late 1950s, the area was characterized by substandard residential and commercial structures, incompatible land uses, narrow streets, inadequate public facilities and parking, crime, fire hazards, periodic flooding, and declining property values and tax base. Incentive for private investment was small. According to the URC, one of the major purposes of urban renewal was "to provide the physical environment which will attract the investment of private capital to the central business district so that the *social* and *economic* potential of the city may be realized."

Working directly with the mayor and Board of Representatives under its own charter, the five-member Urban Redevelopment Commission was responsible for developing and overseeing the entire project. The Planning and Zoning boards reviewed and offered comments on plans but legally could not intervene in the renewal process. In 1959 the URC obtained federal funds for planning and in 1960 selected the developers S. Pierre Bonan of Greenwich and the F.D. Rich Company of Stamford to co-sponsor the project. The sponsors retained the prominent urban planning firm of Victor Gruen Associates to develop a land-use plan for the 130-acre renewal area called the "Southeast Quadrant." S. Pierre Bonan later withdrew, leaving the F.D. Rich Company and its subsidiary, the Stamford New Urban Corporation, as the sole redeveloper. Pat Marshall, who was URC chairman at that time, later recalled the important role of the sponsors: "The URC felt good that we had picked the strongest possible sponsors. They were strong because they had all the requisites: financial ability, entrepreneurship, a good planning consultant, and in relation to the F.D. Rich Company, a real feeling for Stamford. . . . They had more interest in the future of the city than you would have from somebody external."

Both the final cost of the project and the length of time required far exceeded preliminary estimates. The initial cost estimate was $86 million, with nearly $24 million to come from the federal government, $12 million from the city and state, and $50 million from private investors. Before completion almost $400 million had been committed: approximately $100 million from government sources and $300 million from private investors. The redevelopment plan as approved in 1963 called for "seven years to success." Yet the project actually would require 25 to 30 years for completion.

The guiding principle of the plan was to create diversity in downtown Stamford by encouraging varied development: offices, shopping, manufacturing, cultural and entertainment centers, small parks, housing, hotels, and restaurants. Conforming to accepted urban renewal practices of the time, the plan called for demolishing and replacing the majority of structures east of Atlantic Street in a "clearance area" where deterioration was most pronounced. Property west of Atlantic Street became part of a "conservation area," where selected buildings would be demolished and the majority conserved and restored by their owners. Guidelines also called for integrating the old and new downtowns "so that neither functions as an isolated entity." To eliminate street parking and facilitate traffic flow, large parking garages would be accessible from a new inner loop highway encircling the redevelopment area.

The URC used federal funds to plan, acquire land and structures, relocate residents and businesses, demolish structures not marked for preservation, and prepare sites. The city and state shared the cost of improvements: streets and highways, storm drains and sanitary sewers, parking facilities, and installation of utilities and services. The city recovered part of its investment by the sale of cleared land to the redeveloper, who then constructed new buildings. Eventually the city expected to recover its full investment and continue to benefit from increased tax revenues as well as decreased need for services in the area.

The pace of the project was in large part determined by the time required to relocate the 1,100 families living within the redevelopment area. After the proposed plan was made public, some of the families in the area voluntarily relocated and minority families took their places. The relocation issue generated considerable controversy. Some residents opposed the URC proposal that dislocated families be scattered throughout the city. Their low incomes, racial discrimination, and a tightening housing market added to the problem.

Fulfilling the URC goal for finding "safe, decent, and sanitary housing" for all families and individuals required more than 10 years. The last tenant was relocated in 1976. Some found apartments in older houses near the renewal area or in existing public housing; others received assistance to buy their own homes or left town. Many moved into subsidized apartments built during the early 1970s as a result of community action.

Taxpayers' groups who protested that inadequate housing for dislocated families was included within the renewal area sued the city and stopped all activity between 1963 and 1965. To settle a suit filed by "Citizens Against Urban Renewal," the URC and developer agreed to include additional housing. St. John's Towers, three circular 17-story buildings on Washington and Tresser boulevards sponsored by the Roman Catholic Diocese of Bridgeport, contained 352 units of low- to moderate-income housing. New Hope Towers on Tresser Boulevard, sponsored by the Faith Tabernacle Baptist Church, contained 200 units for black families, and 200 or more "market level" rental units were to be constructed by the F.D. Rich Company.

Outside the renewal area nonprofit organizations and the city sponsored other housing projects. "Out of their deep concern for the critical shortage of housing for moderate-and low-income families in Stamford" area churches and synagogues built Friendship House and founded New Neighborhoods, Inc., as a nonprofit housing sponsor. The 89-unit Martin Luther King Apartments, completed in 1971, was the first of New Neighborhood's projects in the West Side and South End. To provide housing for elderly residents, the city built Stamford Manor and several other high-rise facilities. Community efforts

notwithstanding, a critical shortage of affordable housing continued into the 1980s.

Relocation of businesses within the redevelopment area began in 1968 and was completed several years later. Caught in a downward spiral, with little possibility of selling or relocating, some owners welcomed the opportunity to retire or invest their funds elsewhere after the URC had bought their properties. Others chose to relocate in Stamford.

Delays in site preparation resulting from litigation and relocation problems enabled the redeveloper and the city to take advantage of the nationwide trend to move corporate offices away from large cities and high-tax areas and into less costly suburban areas. While lawsuits plagued the downtown project, Robert N. Rich of the F.D. Rich Company developed the campus-style High Ridge Industrial Park south of the Merritt

The work of redeveloping parts of downtown Stamford, begun in the 1950s, has been extensive, time-consuming, and not without its controversies, but the result has been a spectacular change in the city's look. Seen here are two views of the 1970s Landmark Plaza project: partially completed Landmark Tower, and a portion of the Plaza as it looked upon completion.

Parkway, described by *Time* magazine in 1978, as a "showcase of stunning corporate architecture." Tenants included such corporations as American Thread, CBS Laboratories, Citizen's Utilities, Xerox, Conoco, and General Signal. The city also allowed strip zoning for business development along High Ridge and Long Ridge roads. Office complexes for Cadbury-Schweppes, Olin Corporation, and General Electric Credit Corporation arose in parklike settings similar to those occupied by CBS Technology Center. In the 1970s Xerox, Combustion Engineering, and other corporations moved their headquarters to new sites on Long Ridge Road near the Merritt Parkway, while Waldenbooks located on High Ridge Road above Bull's Head.

After building sites in the downtown renewal area were available in the early 1970s, Robert Rich constructed the 21-story Landmark Tower at the corner of Broad and Atlantic streets in an effort to attract corporations to the downtown. His success changed the scope of the urban renewal project and added a new dimension to Stamford's economy. The original redevelopment plan had called for factories; now office buildings and hotels would occupy the area between

Tresser Boulevard and the Connecticut Turnpike. General Telephone & Electronics became the first major corporation in the country to build its headquarters, a striking, inverted pyramid, in an urban renewal area. The Marriott Hotel, Champion International, Singer Corporation, and the legal firm Cummings and Lockwood moved into distinctive buildings in the 22-acre area called "The Stamford Forum." And in 1984, when General Reinsurance Company and a Holiday Inn hotel occupied new structures bordering the renewal area, the area of redevelopment was effectively extended beyond its original eastern boundary. By the late 1970s, southwestern Fairfield County was rivaling Chicago for second place, next to New York, as the home of *Fortune 500* companies.

As redevelopment continued, smaller corporations and business and financial services such as banks, brokerage firms, advertising agencies, legal, computing, accounting, and insurance companies moved into buildings in the Landmark Square complex and on Summer Street. Southwestern Area Commerce and Industry Association (SACIA) president John Mitovich called this "the ripple effect of service firms following their clients here." In 1982 the completely enclosed Stamford Town Center shopping mall opened with Macy's, Penneys, and Saks Fifth Avenue department stores, space for 130 retail shops and restaurants, and a 4,000-car parking garage. As Stamford emerged as a regional retailing center as well as one of the major corporate headquarters centers of the country, the press repeatedly called the city's urban redevelopment project one of the most successful in the nation.

This evolution strained the city's transportation network. The number of persons coming into Stamford daily to work, do business, and shop far exceeded the number leaving. To serve the needs of these travelers, access roads and ramps to the Connecticut Turnpike were improved and the city began in 1983 to construct on the site of the old railroad station a new transportation center with rail, bus, taxi, and limousine services, as well as a large parking garage for commuters.

The later stages of urban renewal were partly shaped by a growing interest in historic preservation, stimulated by activities of the Bicentennial Year of 1976. That year architectural historians and preservationists Renee Kahn and Virginia T. Davis began a survey of Stamford's historic buildings that awakened local interest in Stamford's architectural heritage. "I find that wherever I go," Renee Kahn noted, "people are sympathetic to what I'm trying to do: save some of the buildings." As urban renewal moved into its last stage and work began in the "conservation area" between Atlantic Street and Washington Boulevard, concern for preserving the city's architectural heritage was more evident. In 1983 preservationists sparked the creation of a downtown historic district to conserve and encourage refurbishing and restoration of structures on West Park Place, Summer, Main, Bank, and Atlantic streets.

Stamford's urban renewal generated continuous controversy because it was carried out in a "fishbowl atmosphere." Residents, nonresident commuters, outsiders, and the national media have debated its pros and cons from the beginning. Many residents who were initially opposed to the dramatic changes proposed for their city now express satisfaction with its economic and cultural turnaround. Success has been attributed to an early start, large-scale, comprehensive planning, and the reliance on a single redeveloper who provided

both the flexibility and continuity needed to develop the entire renewal area. Economists have noted that the project created many more jobs than anticipated and was a financial success for the city. Civic-minded corporations have generously donated personnel, space, time, and money to the city's charitable, cultural, educational, and governmental agencies. The employees of corporations and other firms often found traveling into Stamford by car or rail more convenient and faster than going to New York. Stamford's Town Center attracted thousands of shoppers daily, while the Stamford Center for the Arts, renovated Palace Theater, Hartman Theater, Whitney Museum, and other cultural organizations brought more music, theater, dance, and fine arts to Stamford than ever before.

Critics have pointed out that the cost of housing escalated, that the housing shortage became more acute, and that taxpayers failed to realize anticipated tax relief. They contended that Stamford now had two unconnected downtowns, an old and a new, separated by the fortress-like exteriors of new structures and a lack of provisions and amenities for pedestrians. Of concern to many was the absence of people on downtown streets at night and on weekends and the lack of revitalization in areas bordering the new downtown. To the dismay of residents and commuters, traffic congestion steadily increased on most roads as more people commuted to Stamford by car, reaching 28,000 vehicles during the morning rush hours in 1983.

As new businesses came into Stamford, a growing mismatch between the skills of Stamford's resident blue-collar labor force and the requirements of the local job market became increasingly evident. Despite the efforts of both SACIA and SEAC to strengthen the city's industrial base, the number of manufacturing-related jobs increased more slowly than the number of office, service, and retail jobs. Although Stamford's 350 manufacturing firms continued to make a wide variety of products, the majority employed less than 50 workers each. Reasons cited for the slowdown in industrial growth included lack of land zoned for industrial use, the high cost of land and labor, and high taxes.

Stamford, nonetheless, had one of the lowest unemployment rates in the nation during the late 1970s and early 1980s. A study prepared for SEAC in 1981 indicated that locally unemployment was, as in the nation as a whole, highest among minority workers. To increase blue-collar employment opportunities, SEAC President David Anderson proposed that the private sector establish job training and retraining programs and that the city create industrially zoned districts to attract manufacturers.

Changes in the economy and the demanding requirements of urban renewal were only two of the challenges facing Stamford's municipal government after 1960. Providing necessary services and addressing such problems as traffic congestion, crime, and the sale and use of narcotics strained the city's resources. The city nevertheless gave special attention to health, housing, welfare, environmental protection, planning, zoning, and recreational needs. Drug treatment and rehabilitation centers, set up early in the 1960s, continued to operate into the 1980s.

During the process of urban renewal, nine mayors would hold office and each brought in new administrators. Frequent turnover of personnel, the city's rapid development, and its complex needs led to consideration of charter revision. Former mayors and other office holders, 13 charter revision commissions, business leaders, and concerned citizens all offered suggestions for improving governmental operation. Defenders of the existing system cited the high degree of citizen participation and many checks and balances. Critics found the municipal structure inefficient, unwieldy, and unprofessional. Criticism focused on the limited powers of the mayor; the size, power, and inefficiency of the 40-member Board of Representatives; and the large number of independent or semi-independent boards and commissions. Seasoned observers commented that the effectiveness of the government was as dependent on the personalities and politics of the individuals involved as on the system itself.

Some reformers called for a new charter with a city manager and small council to provide continuity and professional management. Others proposed major revisions in the existing charter to enable the city government to deal more effectively with present problems and future challenges. Although proposals for charter revision were placed before the electorate in April, 1984, they were defeated.

Thus Stamford and its people have moved into the postindustrial era aware of their problems as well as their advantages. The town's history, from its origin as a religious settlement in the wilderness to its present status as a major corporation, commercial, and cultural center, is a history of frequent and successful adaptation to change. Strategically located on the border between New York and New England, supported by a strong and adaptable economy, the city has, as its greatest resource, an enterprising and concerned population with vision and determination. Stamford, like the proverbial cat, has had many lives during its long history. The community has changed course on many occasions, and through change, has endured and strengthened.

PARTNERS IN PROGRESS

"Let the great world spin forever down
the ringing grooves of change"
Alfred Lord Tennyson.

More dramatically than any other Connecticut city, Stamford has changed from a tiny plantation of Puritan families, who trekked down from Wethersfield in 1641, to a growing new metropolis that today forms the hub of the third-largest concentration of Fortune 500 industrial company headquarters in the nation.

Like other cities in the state, Stamford started as a farming community clustered around a crude, unheated, one-room church. Its first industries were linked to agriculture-gristmill, sawmill, tannery, shipping. Sailing vessels carried local produce to the New York market, where "Stamford potatoes" became famous.

By 1835 the village had 21 general stores, 12 shoemaker shops, four carpenter shops, three iron-rolling mills, two copper shops, a tinware factory, water-powered gristmill, tannery, newspaper (started in 1829) and print shop, stove shop, carriage maker, silversmith, millinery and hat-making shop, bakery, leather shop, three lumberyards, and a coal yard.

After 1848 the railroad brought the first New Yorkers to Stamford to live and commute, as well as the first foreign immigrants. As time went on, people continued to arrive here by the hundreds from Ireland, Italy, Germany, Poland, Russia, and other countries. New local businesses and industries reflected the importance of immigrants to Stamford's economic and cultural life. In some cases, hard-working immigrants or their descendants started businesses that prospered beyond their wildest dreams.

Nineteenth-century Stamford became an industrial town. Immigrants and farmers found jobs in plants such as the huge Yale & Towne Manufacturing Company, which gave Stamford its erstwhile nickname, "The Lock City." During World Wars I and II local factories converted to wartime production.

But the 1950s and early 1960s saw many plants, including Yale & Towne, moving to lower-labor-cost sections of the country or being acquired or going out of business. The research laboratories and high-technology companies that remained or started up employed fewer blue-collar workers. Stamford became "The Research City."

Today Stamford is, in effect, "The Corporate City." Multinational corporate headquarters began migrating here from New York City in the late 1960s, and the trend accelerated as urban renewal progressed. For a brief time the Stamford area ranked second only to New York in the number of large corporations based here. But acquisitions and moves spirited away several big ones, and Fairfield County, left with only 24 Fortune 500s, slipped back into third place behind Chicago, with 26.

Connecticut banks, under recent deregulation, have entered such nontraditional fields as discount stock brokerage and individual financial-planning. And in their race to do business with the multibillion-dollar corporations, they are compounding their assets through banking mergers and acquisitions.

The influx of large corporations and a multitude of service companies has boosted Stamford employment in the past 10 years alone by more than 30 percent. Today, due mainly to the scarcity of affordable local housing, at least 45 percent of the nearly 70,000 persons employed here commute from other towns. For the third consecutive year, Stamford has had the highest grand list of taxable property of any city in the state.

The organizations whose stories are detailed on the following pages have chosen to support this important literary and civic project. They illustrate the variety of ways in which individuals and their businesses have contributed to the city's growth and development. The civic involvement of Stamford's businesses, institutions of learning, and local government, in cooperation with its citizens, has made the community an excellent place to live and work.

STAMFORD HISTORICAL SOCIETY

Wealthy Colonel Woolsey Rogers Hopkins was a Civil War veteran and the grandson of Moses Rogers, a New York merchant who owned most of Shippan Point. On October 21, 1901, in the library of St. John's Episcopal Church, the 88-year-old colonel called a meeting of about 20 men and women who, like himself, wanted to generate interest in preserving Stamford's history. A week later the group drafted a constitution and elected Colonel Hopkins the first president of the Stamford Historical Society.

The founders came from the local elite: Commodore James D. Smith, yachtsman and former president of the New York Stock Exchange; his daughter Helen, first of the four wives of attorney Homer S. Cummings, then mayor of Stamford; Edward T.W. Gillespie, senior editor of the *Advocate*, and Robert A. Fosdick, president of the horse-drawn Stamford Street Railroad, to name a few.

The present Stamford Historical Society headquarters is the former Martha Hoyt School, completed of fieldstone in January 1914 at 1508 High Ridge Road.

The first afternoon monthly meetings, held in members' mansions, were more social than historical. Members gave historical papers, but they also listened to music and enjoyed elaborate suppers and teas. After March 1902, for reasons unknown, all activities ceased until a reorganization meeting on September 6, 1905, when Colonel Hopkins was reelected president.

On September 13, 1909, the Stamford Historical Society was incorporated. Its first exhibition of about 1,000 Stamford antiques and heirlooms ran for six days, starting on October 30, 1911, at 366 Atlantic Street. The first evening meeting took place in May 1912, and gradually the meetings shifted to evenings.

Stamford is indebted to the Society for pinpointing Settlers' Day as May 16 and for designing the city flag and the city seal. The flag was presented to the city (then town) on May 16, 1914, and the seal on April 12, 1916.

More than a quarter-century passed before the organization achieved its own home—the 1699 Hoyt-Barnum farmhouse, the oldest house still

The first headquarters of the Stamford Historical Society was the 1699 Hoyt-Barnum farmhouse at 713 Bedford Street, the oldest house still standing in Stamford.

standing in Stamford. In 1943 the structure was purchased from the First National Bank for $13,500, and restored in stages through 1973. This tiny red clapboard saltbox at 713 Bedford Street remained the Society's headquarters until the fall of 1984.

Then, to expand its educational activities for children and adults, the group moved to the former Martha Hoyt School, completed of fieldstone in January 1914 at 1508 High Ridge Road. Originally called the Willard School, the name was later changed in honor of its principal, Mrs. Martha Hoyt, who retired in 1933 at age 70.

The 50-year-old former public school, leased from the city for one dollar a year, has ample exhibit and storage space, a meeting room seating 75 to 100, a library and archives, workrooms, offices, and a large parking lot. The Society has refurnished the Hoyt-Barnum House as an early 18th-century farmhouse.

In 1905 the Stamford Historical Society had 58 members and no paid staff. Still growing, it now has 400 members, including 30 devoted volunteers and a paid staff of three.

P. SABINI & COMPANY, INC.

Pellegrino Sabini's ice cream pushcart in 1916 was a Model T Ford truck without an engine. He is shown with three of his children, Joseph, David, and Elbina, perched on the hood.

Pellegrino Sabini arrived in Stamford from Northern Italy around 1900. A small, soft-spoken man, he traveled to this country with a group of Italian immigrants hired to lay the railroad tracks in turn-of-the-century Stamford. He was employed by the railroad for a time, then opened a small watch-repair shop at 207 Main Street, opposite the cannon in Columbus Park.

An entrepreneur from the start, Pellegrino promoted boxing matches with Joe Chimboli, owner of the old Lyceum Theatre in Stamford. He operated a succession of small candy stores on Atlantic Street, then a grocery store on Main near the end of Pacific Street, where he sold ice cream from a Ford Model T truck that had no engine.

In 1920 the enterprising young Sabini switched his business interest to second-hand furniture, opening a store on Canal Street. Dr. A.C. Hexamer owned a building used as a stable for saddle horses around the corner at 275 Pacific Street, and Pellegrino bought it on June 1, 1939, for $15,000. Converting the stable to a store, he

stocked new furniture and appliances, using the Canal Street location as a warehouse for second-hand merchandise. The business was incorporated in 1932 under the name P. Sabini & Company, Inc., with Pellegrino as president and his two eldest children, David and Elbina, as shareholders.

Meanwhile, Pellegrino had purchased property on Shippan Avenue—at the head of the peninsula—which he planned to use as a homesite for his growing family. He also acquired two houses that were slated for demolition, and in 1930 had them barged along the coastline from Old Greenwich to Shippan. The houses had to be slid over a seawall in Old Greenwich and then brought in with the tide at Cummings Park Lagoon and pulled ashore there. The three-story, 14-room house where the Sabini family (including six children) was to live weighed 175 tons. The smaller one

weighed 50 tons.

Four years later, at the age of 54, Pellegrino was killed when his truck collided with a bus on Shippan Avenue as he was on his way to work. Eldest son Dave became president of P. Sabini & Company upon his father's death.

When the Stamford Urban Redevelopment Commission told the Sabini family that the Pacific and Canal streets stores would have to relocate, the Shippan Avenue property was rezoned to accommodate a commercial establishment. A handsome two-story building was constructed next to the 14-room house that had come here by sea. The new store opened for business in 1969.

David served as president of the corporation until his death in 1970. Elbina, the family's only daughter, took over until her death in 1975. Then Angelo, youngest of the Sabini brothers, became president. Joseph, John, and Louis Sabini are also officers of the corporation.

Today P. Sabini & Company, Inc., no longer in the used-furniture business, is one of Fairfield County's most complete home-furnishing stores. In addition to furniture, the firm markets major home appliances and televisions and has a fine appliance-repair department. Its two large furniture trucks and fleet of service vehicles are a common sight on the streets of Stamford. Sabini's now employs 20 individuals, 12 of whom are family members.

Sabini's Furniture and Appliances as it stands today at 614 Shippan Avenue.

SACHS PLUMBING SUPPLIES

Charles R. Sachs opened his first plumbing supplies store in October 1940 at 99 Pacific Street. He pioneered "do-it-yourself" plumbing.

"Charlie Sachs, get yourself a blue-collar job! There's no money in office work." So, urged by his father, a white-collar man who was caught in the 1930s Depression, Charles Sachs went into the plumbing-supply business.

After learning the trade, Charlie opened Sachs Plumbing Supplies at 99 Pacific Street in October 1940. His 20- by 40-foot store was the first he knows of that encouraged people to do their own plumbing by explaining how to "do-it-yourself."

Charlie bought his original stock on credit. He created the illusion of a large inventory by removing merchandise from cartons as it came in and stacking the empty boxes against the wall. His wife and co-proprietor, Goldy, minded the store whenever Charlie went to New York to scrounge the materials that became increasingly scarce during World War II.

Stovepipe and little coal-burning stoves were the most common items for sale. Most-asked-for plumbing supplies included replacement faucets, pipes, and fittings that nonplumbers,

coached by Charlie, could install themselves. Many area households still had claw-foot bathtubs and pull-chain toilets with high wooden tanks. After the war, as equipment and installation methods improved, modern bathroom fixtures became stock items.

By the 1950s, as the economy expanded and the number of do-it-yourself plumbers multiplied, Sachs' business doubled. Growth continued through the 1960s. By 1966, when urban renewal forced the relocation of Sachs Plumbing Supplies, it was none too soon; the increasing inventory overflowed the quarters on Pacific Street. As the old Pacific Street neighborhood was razed, Sachs moved to the new downtown—to three floors at One Summer Place, to be known for many years as Stamford's home-repair district.

Ken C. Sachs started working for his father in 1956, coming in on Saturdays, when he was only nine years old. Ken bought the business from his father in 1974 when Charlie retired. Ken's young children also started coming to the store whenever they could. And Charlie, although officially retired, has continued to advise on a

regular basis.

In 1984 developer F.D. Rich bought the Summer Place property, forcing another move. Ken purchased the former Stolfi Building on Richmond Hill Avenue, a larger facility that could accommodate the ever-growing need for more showroom and warehouse space.

Sachs Plumbing, which started on a shoestring with an inventory of empty boxes, grew, in only 44 years, to stock over 100,000 items. Until the latest move, Charlie, Ken, and general manager Jim Dixon kept track of all those items in their heads. This huge inventory responsibility has since been delegated to a computer.

Today, although a completely modern operation, Sachs Plumbing Supplies continues in the traditon of pioneer and founder Charles Sachs, providing good, old-fashioned "do-it-yourself" advice to the home plumber.

Sachs' personnel pose in front of the firm's many plumbing supplies. They are (left to right) Bill Watrous, Jr.; retired founder Charles R. Sachs; president Ken C. Sachs; bath boutique manager Ellen Sachs Bernblum; Ben Lopez, counter sales; and general manager James W. Dixon.

PARKER TRAVEL SERVICE

Clinton Harvey Parker had such a phenomenal memory that he was able to start a successful travel agency in 1926, with the help of his young wife, Elsie. Few customers who walked into the Parker Travel Service at 73 Elm Street had any idea the handsome owner was utterly blind.

Formerly assistant superintendent of the Lockwood Manufacturing plant in South Norwalk, Clinton Parker in 1924 suffered a severe allergic reaction to fusel oil the plant used to process metal, and he lost his sight overnight. Transportation friends who had marveled at his total recall suggested the travel business. Pulling himself together, Clinton acted on their suggestion. He opened a travel, real estate, and insurance agency in a building owned by his father-in-law, Hugo Noack. Elsie Parker became her husband's eyes.

Because immigration was the focus of Stamford's travel business at the time, the two other travel services here had ethnic orientations. Brennan brought maids over from Ireland. Cappabianca served primarily Italians. Clinton handled his share, too, with Elsie filling out papers for people who wanted to send for relatives abroad. A third-class, round-trip ticket to Europe could be purchased for $130.

The Parkers moved to 433 Main Street in 1935. In 1938 Clinton, not yet 55, died four days after suddenly becoming ill. Some varnish remover had fatally infected a shaving cut on his cheek. Elsie was left to run the business, and her 16-year-old son, Robert N., quit high school to help.

After World War II the switch began from steamships and buses to airplanes. Parker Travel continues to sell bus tour tickets but no longer regular place-to-place bus tickets. It hasn't

Clinton Harvey Parker, before an allergic reaction blinded him in 1924. No longer able to pursue his occupation, he and his wife, Elsie, established a travel, real estate, and insurance agency.

handled real estate or insurance for decades.

Robert Parker's sister, Selma M., came into the business in 1951 and his wife, Edith A., joined in 1953. Elsie Parker retired in 1954. In 1966 Selma's husband, Salvatore J. Ruggiero, joined the partnership. The business had shifted to two other Main Street locations before moving in 1967 to its present address at 205 Atlantic Street in a two-story building owned by the family.

The Parker clan has seen amazing changes over the years. Close to 90 percent of the business today is airline, and of that, 60 to 70 percent comes from Stamford-area corporations. Instead of only three travel services, Stamford now has at least 30. As Robert Parker puts it, "Corporate business keeps us in business."

Elsie Noack Parker, who worked in partnership with her husband, carried on the business after his death in 1938.

EXCELSIOR HARDWARE COMPANY

Elisha Mix, Jr., 1850-1936.

Headstrong Elisha Mix, Jr., a Connecticut Yankee lock maker like his grandfather before him, came to Stamford in 1891 when he was 41 to work with his uncle Frank. Frank Mix had started the cabinet lock division of Yale & Towne, for years the largest factory in town.

Henry Towne had strange theories about heating a factory. The floor was icy cold because all the heat was in the ceiling. Elisha was sick all one winter, and Dr. Samuel Pierson advised him to go away for his health. He returned from Bermuda to find he had been demoted and given a cut in pay because "his department worked so well without him."

Elisha stayed on the job, but in 1897 secretly started his own lock-making business at night in Bridgeport. He stamped his locks "Newark, N.J." so Yale & Towne, which employed four Mixes among its 1,000 workers, wouldn't find out. A year later he told Yale & Towne he was leaving to run his own operation, and the giant company fired his son Moseley, but not his uncle Frank or Frank's son.

Unable to sell his 31 Pleasant Street house in Stamford in a depressed real estate market, Elisha moved his company here instead. With Moseley, he set up shop first in the former Smart Hat factory at 34 Crosby Street, then on East Walnut, and finally in a building he constructed at 39 Woodland Avenue in 1910. That year he incorporated as Excelsior Hardware, named after the Excelsior-type lock for steamer trunks used by steamship passengers.

Elisha, as president of the Stamford Chamber of Commerce, proposed that a trade school be started in cooperation with the state. The town appropriated $3,000, and the Stamford Trade School, predecessor of the present J.M. Wright Technical School, opened in 1919 in a Schuyler Avenue building leased from the Vacuum Panama Hat Company.

Excelsior Hardware was recovering from the Depression when the 1938 hurricane nearly destroyed the firm, flooding the front end of the plant and ruining thousands of dollars in inventory. Business picked up during World War II, with orders for electrical connections for aircraft and locks for military footlockers.

Today, in facilities that extend from Pacific through to Atlantic Street, 100 employees at 39 Woodland Avenue make carrying cases, hardware, millions of metal corners, catches, hinges, and locks.

Elisha Mix, outliving Moseley by one year, was killed in 1936 at age 86 when the car he was driving hit a trolley in Florida. The current president, who in 1978 succeeded Elisha's great-grandson, Coleman Mix, to become the fourth president in the company's history, is former vice-president Reginald E. Connolly. Two members of the third Mix generation and three in the fourth are active in the company today.

Excelsior Hardware has no mandatory retirement age so long as an employee can do the job. Sixteen have worked there 30 years or more. "It's a family-owned firm that's like a family," says corporate secretary John Mix, Elisha's grandson.

Excelsior Hardware Company's products include a steamer trunk lock (left) from the firm's early product line, and its modern 2.5-inch lock for attaché and musical instrument cases and small tool boxes.

THE HISTORY BOOK CLUB, INC.

Ray C. Dovell founded the History Book Club in 1947. After retiring in 1964, he died in 1968 at the age of 80.

Former newspaperman Ray C. Dovell, whose hobby was reading American history, quit his public relations job at Melville Shoe Corporation in Harrison, New York, and founded the History Book Club in 1947 when he was 58 years old.

Gathering an impressive board of historian-editors that included Arthur M. Schlesinger, Jr., Bernard DeVoto, and Frank Dobie, Ray opened an office at 298 Broadway in New York City. Originally he concentrated on American history. The first two books he offered at less than retail price in May of that year were Clifford Dowdy's Civil War history, *Experiment in Rebellion* (main selection), and *Westward Crossings* by Jeannette Mirsky.

From the beginning the book club made selections on the basis of three criteria: The facts must be accurate, the book must contribute something new to the field, and it must be interesting and readable. In 1951 the club enlarged its scope to include all history, not just American.

Ray Dovell lived in the Stamford area and so did two of his executives.

Tired of commuting, they moved their headquarters in 1957 to the top floor of a two-story building at 40 Guernsey Street in Stamford.

With 20,000 members, the History Book Club was just breaking even. Then Ray found some military maps and persuaded Praeger Publishers to compile them into *The West Point Atlas of American Wars*. With this atlas as a premium, membership in 1959 soared to 30,000, and the club began making money for the first time. In 1972 the publishing firm of Harcourt Brace Jovanovich bought the club and has since been pleased with its success.

Today, with 115,000 members in more than 50 countries and with 72 employees in Stamford, the club occupies all of 40 Guernsey Street, as well as the entire third floor of the Visiting Nurse Association building next door. Eighty percent of the members are men, and 20 percent are in the academic world, either as teachers or students.

The club currently offers not two, but eight or nine selections each month. Thus far, 31 selections have won Pulitzer Prizes. Most popular is the Civil War period, followed by the Middle Ages, ancient history, British history, and World War II.

Publishers submit, in manuscript or galley form, at least 1,300 books a year. About 300 that look promising are sent out to readers, all but one of whom are college history professors.

Ten years ago the History Book Club started an Instructor Book Club to help elementary schoolteachers make classroom work more interesting. Three years ago the History Book Club began offering members four 17-day trips a year, with historians as leaders. The trips, which give the club

One of the History Book Club selections, A Distant Mirror by Barbara W. Tuchman of Greenwich, has been a best-seller for some time.

Frank Melville, chairman (left), and John Gibb, president of the club, stand at the entrance to their Stamford headquarters where the organization moved in 1957.

more of a club "feel," provide opportunities for members to meet one another, and they have become so popular that they now have waiting lists.

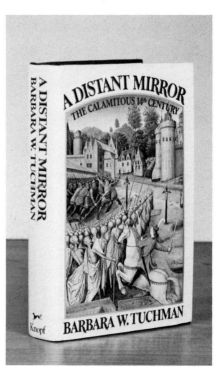

BUSINESS ENVIRONMENTS
Division of Karp Industries Inc.

Polish immigrant Harry S. Karp opened his second store at 411 Main Street. American flags and "America Forever" signs displayed his patriotism in 1916.

Among the merchant princes of Stamford, the name "Karp" endures as one of the most venerable. The Karp enterprise was humbly pioneered by a Polish immigrant named Harry Karp, who, after achieving success as the *Advocate*'s "top newsboy," opened a cigar store near the old fire station on Main Street in 1916. Possessed of little more than a desire to succeed, he gradually expanded his business to include toys, improving his Main Street location twice, first to 411 Main, then to 441. By 1939 he had become the largest toy merchant in town and one of Stamford's most popular citizens. Never without a smile or a cigar, his irrepressible personality contributed significantly to his popularity as a businessman, and as a human being.

Mortimer Karp, with his Dartmouth education, and six valuable years of experience as one of Macy's premier merchandise buyers, joined forces with his father, Harry, in 1945. While Mort's participation immediately raised the fortunes of his dad's toy operation, he was equally quick to recognize the threatening "discount house" phenom-

enon, beginning to sweep the country in the early 1950s. Adroitly, he maneuvered the business away from toys and into office supplies, with an eye toward servicing Stamford's rapidly developing commercial activity. Total immersion into office products came in 1955; a four-story building at 95 Atlantic was leased, and the risky new venture, known as Karp's Office Furniture and Supply, Inc., was launched. By the mid-1970s the enterprise had matured into an unqualified success, having become one of the most respected dealers of office products in Fairfield County.

Harry Karp, who never officially retired, worked productively until he was 82. He died at 86, but not without proudly seeing his grandson, Bob, enter the business in 1975.

Robert Karp, Morty's son, and the third generation of Karps to enter the family concern, graduated from Tufts

---

Mort Karp and son Bob at one of the many office displays located in the four-story showroom center of BUSINESS ENVIRONMENTS at 95 Atlantic Street.

University and spent five years in broadcast journalism. Once at "Karp's," however, he quickly developed an expertise for office planning and design, thus broadening the scope of business operations and adding significantly to the company's overall profit performance.

In 1982 Karp's was sold to a large conglomerate, but almost immediately philosophical differences of conducting business arose. The arrangement was terminated in 1984, enabling the Karps to return to their more accustomed independence.

Mort, now in semiretirement, serves as consultant to the new Karp enterprise called Karp Industries, Inc., a diversified organization presided over by son Bob, who is now president. Bob's first venture under the reorganized Karp banner is BUSINESS ENVIRONMENTS, servicing corporate clients with office furnishings and expertise in office space planning. The company's headquarters and showroom center remain at 95 Atlantic in the same spacious four-story building— which the Karp family now owns.

BONGIORNO SUPERMARKET, INC.

Italian-born John Alphonse Bongiorno earned his American citizenship the hard way, by fighting for it. An enlisted U.S. Army private first class in World War I, he was gassed on the battlefield in France and awarded a Purple Heart.

Returning to Stamford, John rented a bakery on Stillwater Avenue in 1920 and began baking Italian bread, the kind he had learned to make before the war in a bakery on Pacific Street. Soon the hard-working baker was turning out enough dough and taking in enough money to build his own bakery at 195 Stillwater Avenue. In 1923 he added an apartment above the shop for his growing family and in front, a neighborhood grocery.

John's wife, Rose, took care of the grocery, open seven days a week, while he made bread at night and delivered it the next day. John Jr. recalls, "When my father wasn't working, he was sleeping." Nevertheless, on Sundays the family always went to early Mass.

In 1937 John built a bigger bakery on Diaz Street, with a house in front for his family of three boys and two girls, who helped in the business as soon as they were old enough. Three years later, near the new Southfield Village public housing project of 250 garden apartments, he put up a 40-foot by 60-foot grocery at 89 Waverly Place, calling it the Village Food Market.

World War II food rationing convinced the family to phase out the grocery for the duration and concentrate on baking. Eldest son Frank lost his life in combat, but second son John Jr. returned at the end of the war to help his father.

John Sr. died of a lung ailment in 1949, and sons John Jr. and George (a Korean War Navy veteran) bought out the tenant of the food market, reopened in 1951, and sold the bread route to Cassone Bakery. The market—manned by John Jr., George,

PFC John Alphonse Bongiorno, supermarket founder, served in World War I in the U.S. Army's famed "Fighting 69th" Infantry Division and was awarded a Purple Heart.

and their wives, Wilma and Marie, with part-time help on Sundays—stayed open from 7 a.m. to 11 p.m., seven days a week. The new high-rise buildings that doubled the number of Southfield Village apartments more than doubled Bongiorno business.

Forced to move when the Connecticut Turnpike was routed through their property, the Bongiornos built a 4,000-square-foot "superette" at 34 Waverly Place. In 1967 the market had to move again, this time because of growing pains. Today Bongiorno's Supermarket at 288 West Avenue near Southfield Village occupies 40,000 square feet and owns 10 big trucks.

"Our large volume is due mainly to our produce and meat departments," explains John Jr. "Our trucks go wherever necessary to get produce in season—Virginia, Delaware, Pennsylvania, New York State. We don't have any middlemen, and we pass that savings to the consumer. Also, we meet the food requirements of all ethnic groups."

This amazing store, opened originally to serve low-income housing residents, has become the largest-volume single supermarket in the entire Stamford area, attracting customers from miles around. The market's slogan, "Where there's always a good day," is indeed appropriate. To wish someone a good day in Italian, you say, "Bon giorno."

In 1967 brothers John Jr. and George Bongiorno are seen outside the family's supermarket at 288 West Avenue. Today Bongiorno's is the largest-volume supermarket in the entire Stamford area.

ST. AUGUSTINE COUNCIL NO. 41
KNIGHTS OF COLUMBUS

Sister Daniel Marie, St. Joseph Hospital Administrator, accepts a check from Frank J. Robotti (left), and John F. Pryor of St. Augustine Council No. 41, Knights of Columbus. Photo by Scutti.

When 23 Stamford men met in Miller's Hall on May 8, 1887, to accept their charter and install officers of the St. Augustine Council No. 41, Knights of Columbus, they had no idea that the order they were joining would become the largest body of Catholic laymen in the world.

Father Michael J. McGivney had founded the Knights of Columbus only five years before in New Haven as a local fraternal benefit society. But the unique idea that blended Catholic, fraternal, and professional insurance features with a Columbian motif soon spread, eventually attracting an international following.

The St. Augustine Council named John M. Fitzgerald its first grand knight and Father Thomas Keenan its first chaplain. Minutes of the next 20 years indicate that the organization played an outstanding role in the life of the town. Its picnics, Labor Day parades, excursions for members, and the annual ball became fixtures in Stamford's year-round activities.

From the beginning the council met twice a month wherever meeting rooms could be found—Young Men's Temperance Hall on Greyrock Place, Patrick Boyle's Building on Main Street, Pitt's Block at Main and Pacific, Mechanic's Hall at 59 Atlantic, the Ancient Order of Hibernians' Hall at 164 Atlantic, the Quintard Block. Special meetings were held in Miller's Hall and the chapel of St. John's Church of Stamford.

For the first 32 years the Knights had no home of their own. On December 17, 1919, to manage the council's business affairs, they formed the Knights of Columbus Building Association, Inc. For $35,000 in 1920 this association purchased five and one-quarter acres at Elm and Hawthorne streets, including the 100-year-old frame Walsh mansion. The house became a home base for the Knights, but not until it was remodeled could the first council meeting be held there on October 20, 1932.

Since then the Knights have moved twice, first in 1960 to a new two-story brick building at 384 North State Street, and then in 1982 to 453 Shippan Avenue. The Building Association bought the Shippan property after selling the North State Street facility to General Reinsurance Corporation, which built its corporate headquarters there.

"What was done during the Depression when the buck was tight was done with a lot of sacrifice and hard work," says a local Knights of Columbus official. "From the time we started selling parcels of our property we have been able to do more for charity."

Today with 1,100 members, the St. Augustine Council is the largest in the state. This list of its good work in the community could go on for pages. To summarize, just in the past two years it has contributed to many worthy causes, including donations to institutions of learning, hospitals, and charitable organizations. Based on principles of charity, unity, and fraternity, the Knights of Columbus instills in its members a sense of pride in the Catholic contribution to American society.

The Knights of Columbus Center, 453 Shippan Avenue, Stamford.

WILLIAM PITT, INC.

Enterprising William Pitt opened a one-man real estate office in 1949, with a desk and telephone in a room on the second floor of the old brick Pitt Building that stood at the corner of Main and Pacific streets. Only 23, he was believed to be the youngest real estate broker at the time in Stamford.

The structure itself was erected for income purposes in the early 1880s by the realtor's great-grandfather, William Pitt, who owned considerable land here. The present William is the fifth Stamford generation of the Pitt family, originally from England.

Stamford in 1949 was basically a commuter and industrial town, with 20 or 25 firms that, in varying degrees, combined real estate and insurance. William concentrated on real estate. (Today the Stamford Board of Realtors lists 120 member firms.)

The end of World War II saw the beginning of a new era in real estate—the transient market. As business shifted back to normal, big companies began transferring employees to New York City. Many transferees preferred to live in Connecticut

Fifth-generation native son William Pitt was believed to be the youngest realtor in Stamford when he opened his office in 1949 at the age of 23.

The present headquarters of the firm is in the Marriott Hotel complex at Two Stamford Forum. There are also 11 branch offices in Fairfield County.

rather than in New York, and William Pitt enthusiastically encouraged them.

In 1952, as a convenience to house hunters stopping at the Roger Smith Hotel, he moved his office to what was then 49 River Street in a building the hotel owned. By then he had a staff of four or five brokers. Fifteen years later he bought a larger building next door, which became his headquarters for more than eight years.

Meanwhile, unprecedented land development was going on in northern

sections of Stamford. To move closer to that market, William in 1953 opened the first branch office of any local real estate firm. He leased space in a house owned by old-time realtor Arthur Crandal at Long Ridge and Wire Mill roads and later bought it.

Between 1953 and 1984 he opened 10 more branches—Darien, New Canaan, Greenwich, Ridgefield, Stamford (Commercial Division), Westport, Danbury, Norwalk, Wilton, and Fairfield. In 1976 Pitt moved his headquarters to Two Stamford Forum in the Marriott Hotel complex.

The one-man office that began with a desk and telephone has grown into two sizable companies, William Pitt, Inc., Residential Real Estate and William Pitt, Inc., Commercial Real Estate, with a total of 225 employees. The commercial arm brought GTE to Stamford and handled other transactions involving corporations such as Xerox, Combustion Engineering, Cadbury Schweppes, Continental Group, Champion International, General Signal, Coats & Clark, General Re, Price Waterhouse, and a host of supporting attorneys, accountants, and consultants. William Pitt has helped transform Stamford into a home for many of the most important businesses in the nation.

William Pitt's first office occupied one room on the second floor of the Pitt Building, which was constructed by his great-grandfather in the early 1880s at Main and Pacific streets.

PIERSON & SMITH, INC.

The roots of the Pierson & Smith, Inc., real estate and insurance agency go back 100 years in Stamford. On May 22, 1884, Middlesex Mutual Assurance Company of Middletown appointed Harry Bell its Stamford agent "with full power to receive proposals for insurance against loss or damage by fire" in the town, which then had a population of about 13,500.

Harry, son of property owner Andrew Jackson Bell (who named Bell Street), had started working at the First National Bank of Stamford in 1886 and eventually would become the bank's president. He was an eighth-generation direct descendant of Francis Bell, one of the leaders of 29 Wethersfield men who founded Stamford in 1641.

Later the Harry Bell Agency was taken over by Arthur McCoy and became the McCoy Agency, which ultimately was purchased by the founders of Pierson & Smith in 1967.

The father of one of the founders, Samuel N. Pierson, had entered the real estate business in the early 1920s. Following Pierson's death shortly after World War II, his son, Samuel F., wanted to concentrate solely on real estate. Therefore, Richard H. Smith became his partner in 1948 to handle the insurance end of the business, which until then had consisted mainly of personal insurance. Subsequently the agency expanded into commercial insurance as well. In 1981 Richard H. Smith retired, selling his share of the business to his son, Richard H. Smith, Jr., and Jon Rudiger. They were joined in 1979 by a third partner, Michael G. Watts.

Today Pierson & Smith provides a wide range of commercial and personal insurance, risk management, and financial services through more than eight different insurance companies, including the original Middlesex Mutual. For many years it has served the local United Way and boards of many social service agencies, as well as the Ferguson Library. More than 70 percent of the United Way agencies are insured through Pierson & Smith, which ranks in the top two percent of independent insurance agencies in the United States.

On the real estate side, Samuel F. Pierson implemented the corporate office park concept in Stamford, integrating corporations into the community in campus-like settings. He negotiated major real estate transactions that have brought to Fairfield County the corporate headquarters of some of the nation's largest companies—General Electric to Fairfield; Stauffer Chemical, Westport; Richardson-Vicks, Wilton; and Union Carbide, Danbury.

In Stamford, Pierson & Smith aided in the development of CBS Technologies' facility, Olin Corporation's headquarters, and the new Pitney Bowes corporate center in the South End, as well as negotiating lease transactions

---

Pierson & Smith, Inc., handled the real estate transaction that brought Olin Corporation to Long Ridge Road in Stamford in 1968-1969.

Pierson & Smith's roots go back 100 years to the Harry Bell Agency. Harry Bell signed this contract with Middlesex Mutual Assurance Company in 1884.

for the High Ridge Office Park.

But the agency itself hasn't moved. Its offices remain at 65 Broad Street on the second floor of a brick building that occupies the former site of the frame house in which the late Samuel N. Pierson was born.

ST. JOSEPH HOSPITAL

An American Hospital Association report in the 1930s revealed that Stamford had 17.5 percent fewer hospital beds than a town with a population of nearly 60,000 ought to have. Convinced that a second hospital—primarily a Catholic hospital—was needed here, the Reverend Nicholas Coleman, pastor of St. John's Church, presented a plan for the construction of a Catholic hospital to the Most Reverend Maurice F. McAuliffe, Bishop of Hartford.

Agreeing, Bishop McAuliffe signed a contract to purchase for $14,000 the seven-acre Strawberry Hill estate of Mrs. Hugh L. Cooper, widow of the American engineer who designed Russia's famed Dnieper River Dam. A campaign in 1939 raised $350,000, with $100,000 of it pledged by the Diocese of Hartford, then encompassing Stamford.

The hospital was named St. Joseph in honor of the Sisters of St. Joseph of Chambery (an order founded in France in 1650), who came from their provincial house in West Hartford to staff and operate it. First Administrator was Mother Sacred Heart from St. Mary's Hospital in Waterbury.

On November 2, 1942, the four-

Sister Mary Teresita, C.S.J., R.N., the first operating room supervisor, is seen here outside St. Joseph Hospital in 1942, the year the hospital opened.

story, T-shaped facility officially opened at 128 Strawberry Hill Avenue, not with the 50 beds originally planned, but with 85. Mrs. Francis Williams, so honored to deliver the first baby at St. Joseph, named her 7-pound, 10-ounce daughter Josephine.

Since then the hospital has had four major fund-raising campaigns supported by businesses, corporations, organizations, and individuals: in 1947 the Coleman Wing to double the number of beds, one million dollars; in 1976 a new emergency and ambulatory care center, $3 million; in 1982 a

new operating and recovery room suite, $1.9 million; in 1983 a C-T scanner, $750,000.

In addition, the Hospital Auxiliary, composed today of more than 1,000 members, has thus far contributed $1.25 million for equipment. Parishes in the Diocese of Bridgeport (Stamford became part of the Bridgeport Diocese when it was formed late in 1953) provided funds to construct the eight-story, 200-bed Marian Pavilion, which was dedicated on March 24, 1968. Attached to the hospital, the Marian Pavilion also houses the Queen of Clergy Home for retired priests.

Today St. Joseph Hospital treats 7,500 patients a year and has 260 beds and 600 employees.

Although Stamford has a Catholic population of some 57,000, approximately 50 percent of the Hospital's patients are Catholic. St. Joseph Hospital welcomes persons of all races and creeds.

In the words of Sister Daniel Marie, current Hospital Administrator, "In the delivery of health care, St. Joseph Hospital has a dual role: providing quality care in a spiritual environment. The Sisters and staff of the Hospital fulfill an invaluable role not only in the professional aspects of service but also in the apostolic role; in reaching out to people we are carrying out the healing mission of Christ."

The original 85-bed hospital has grown to 260 beds today. The eight-story Marian Pavilion can be seen in the right background.

STAMFORD GLASS & MIRROR WORKS

Early in the 1920s 16-year-old Anthony Arbini traveled from Milan, Italy, to San Francisco. He was uncertain whether he would be able to stay in the United States, but he wanted to try. He worked very hard, from 14 to 16 hours a day, at the job his uncle had helped him obtain at a glass shop. There he learned to cut, polish, bevel, and silver glass.

After being granted citizenship, Anthony journeyed to St. Louis, Chicago, and New York, learning as much as he could about the glass business. In 1936 he was employed at the Marchand Co. in New York and was asked to join the firm in its relocation to Stamford. An adventurous young man, Anthony didn't mind the move, but he never considered that it might be an eventful one. Here he met his future bride, Aida Fasoli, and they raised a family of three children.

In 1940 Anthony opened the Stamford Glass & Mirror Works at Bulls Head on the northeast corner of Long Ridge and Cold Spring roads. He silvered and beveled mirrors and built mirrored furniture, pouring on the silvering by hand.

During World War II Anthony closed the shop during the day while he worked at a local war plant, moonlighting after hours at Stamford Glass. But in 1954 he had to close the firm when he became ill. He is now retired, residing in Florida and Stamford.

Anthony Arbini founded the family glass business in 1940 at Bull's Head, later moving to West Main Street. With their father are (left to right) Adelaide, Mary, and Joe.

Joseph Arbini, Anthony's son, attended Wright Technical School and graduated as a mechanic, but he had learned so much from his father about the glass business that he decided to work for a glass company in town. He was determined not to let the business he grew up in stay closed forever. Joe reopened Stamford Glass & Mirror Works in 1970 on Hamilton Avenue, concentrating on mirrors, storefronts, and insulated windows. Today mirrors are silvered automatically by spray guns and Joe buys mirror sheets that he cuts to size. In 1974 he moved his operations to a larger building he purchased at 874 East Main Street, where he displays 100 or so framed mirrors, mirrored walls, and mirrored bars.

Stamford Glass, the largest firm of its kind in the city, has a station wagon and five trucks that can be dispatched in just minutes. It employs 12 people and is very much a family business. Joe's mother, Ida, and wife, Carole, have both managed the office in the past. Currently, Joe Jr. is the vice-president at Stamford Glass. Daughter Chris, who attends college in Massachusetts, assumes managerial responsibilities during the summer months. Anthony, who started it all, frequently can still be found in the shop, sharing his knowledge of the glass trade.

Connecticut Glass Dealer of the Year in 1982 and president of the Connecticut Glass Dealers' Association for three years beginning in 1980, Joe Arbini believes in giving something back to the industry and city that "have given so much" to him. "When somebody tells me they need a sponsor for a kids' baseball team or hotdogs for a kids' picnic, I'm glad to help. I love the glass business and I love Stamford."

Today owner Joe Arbini has five trucks equipped with radios for commercial emergencies. The firm is the largest glass and mirror company in Stamford.

BARNES ENGINEERING COMPANY

Foreseeing that infrared technology would make important contributions to industrial and government electro-optical research programs, physicist Dr. R. Bowling Barnes founded the firm that was to become Barnes Engineering Company on January 16, 1952, in four small rooms with one telephone on the second floor of the Singer Building at 77 Bedford Street. He borrowed two chairs, a wastebasket, and an ashtray from a friend. Stamford's skilled labor base and favorable climate for new high-technology ventures aided the company's growth, and by 1955 Barnes Engineering had become a public company and moved to its present location on Commerce Road.

Scientists at Barnes pioneered many diverse applications for infrared instruments, which detect and measure thermal radiation. At any given time, Barnes technicians could be engaged in activities as different as gauging the thickness of red-hot billets in a Detroit steel mill or tracking the fiery reentry path of experimental missiles from a ship in the South Atlantic. Thermography, the creation of infrared images, was developed at Barnes and became an important medical diagnostic aid. Barnes' infrared instruments have revealed the presence of

Dr. R. Bowling Barnes, who founded Barnes Engineering in 1952, concentrated on infrared physics and electro-optical technology.

intruders in bank vaults, inspected the quality of welds in helicopter blades, and determined the extent of crop disease.

With the explosive growth of the nation's space program in the '60s, Barnes' technological skills found exciting new outlets. One of the company's best-known products, which today accounts for almost half of its $20-

million in annual revenues, is the infrared horizon sensor. This device detects the warm edge of the earth in contrast with the cold of space and orients orbiting spacecraft so that antennas and on-board instruments point precisely toward the earth. Over 650 horizon sensors have been designed and fabricated to such demanding standards of quality and reliability that Barnes states with justifiable pride that its products have never caused a mission failure.

Barnes' instruments also serve as scientific payloads on spacecraft to determine characteristics of the surface of the planet below. The dense clouds of Venus were probed in 1964. A comprehensive thermal map of the surface of the moon was compiled from the *Apollo 17* command module. Daily temperature measurements of the earth's atmosphere at all altitudes are made from Air Force and NASA meteorological satellites. Recently delivered instrumentation will investigate the balance between incoming solar radiation and heat radiated away from the earth to predict long-term climatological trends.

Barnes today offers new, expanded technological capabilities. Nuclear power plants, corporate offices, and military establishments rely on the firm's computer-based, high-level electronic security systems. A new micro-imaging system for the integrated-circuit industry will analyze thermal patterns of miniscule silicon chips to eliminate faults in design and fabrication. Innovative optical components from Barnes' materials research laboratory are leading the way in laser countermeasures.

Barnes Engineering Company is proud of its contribution to science and Stamford's reputation as the "Research City."

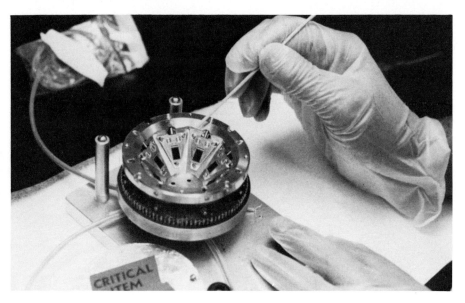

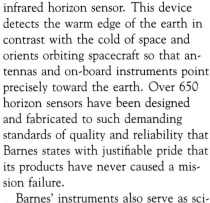

Infrared detectors of extraordinary sophistication are the heart of Barnes' commercial instruments and spacecraft systems.

HARRY BENNETT & ASSOCIATES, INC.

During the 1980 hostage crisis in Iran, Harry Bennett gave away 3,000 yellow ribbons, a symbol that was displayed until the hostages were returned to America. Here Harry Bennett ties a ribbon on a pillar in front of the firm's headquarters at 828 High Ridge Road.

Never before had Greenwich High School seen a student with the business creativity of grocer's son Harry Bennett. He founded the weekly tabloid *GHS News* and fattened it to as many as 60 pages. Long before today's coupon blitz, he ran coupons good for reduced rates at local theaters, thereby selling more papers than the school had students. His class of 1936 voted him the student who "has done the most for the school" and also the one "most likely to succeed."

After Harry worked his way through New York University and took graduate courses, the high school called him back at $25 a week to teach commercial subjects and be the newspaper's faculty advisor. Next he worked for G. Fox and Co. in Hartford, then volunteered for the service as a private. He came out of World War II an Air Force captain.

In the postwar housing shortage

Harry saw a good opportunity. He built a model house on the corner of High Ridge and Crystal Lake roads, offering to duplicate the house on customers' lots anywhere from Greenwich to Wilton, and went on to develop or build Lakewood Park, Hemlock Hills, and Bentwood, as well as being consultant on at least 10 other projects.

Because his scurry for lots boosted land prices, Harry in 1950 became a real estate broker as well as a builder, setting up an office in the model house. Although he built about 100 houses, it was as a broker, developer, and investor that he hit the jackpot.

Harry soon went after commercial opportunities he spotted in New York State and throughout New England, eventually handling transactions for more than 30 shopping centers. He put together the real estate package for Caldor's store at Broad and Summer streets as well as for most of the first 40 stores Caldor built elsewhere.

Harry takes particular pride in his idea for converting the vacant Trinity Episcopal Church on High Ridge Road into the Ferguson Library's Turn of River Branch. City-owned Dorothy

Heroy Park was a rugged, swampy North Stamford tract until Harry leveled it and sold it originally to the Italian Center for a day camp. Among others, he has sold 21 properties, some of them two or three times, on Summer Street and on Washington Boulevard—reputedly more on those streets than all the other brokers in Stamford combined.

He has held many civic and religious offices, including justice of the peace, director of the Chamber of Commerce, president of the Stamford Board of Realtors, and consultant to officers of Temple Beth El. Listed in *Who's Who in the East,* Harry has also invested in properties and buildings in Stamford.

Although the farsighted Realtor handles 50 times more residential than commercial transactions, he says the profits are in commercial investments. He also says that for most of his life he has worked 100 hours a week and now intends to cut back to 60.

Harry Bennett opened his first real estate office in 1950 in this split-level model home he built at High Ridge and Crystal Lake roads.

UNION TRUST COMPANY

Stamford Trust Company, the first local bank to provide both banking and trust services, was chartered on June 11, 1889, and opened on July 1, 1891, the year that Stamford's 16,000 residents celebrated the town's 250th anniversary. The bank occupied the ground floor of a building constructed in 1868 at the northwest corner of Main and Atlantic streets. On this same property nearly 250 years before had lived Stamford's second Congregational minister, the Reverend John Bishop, who had walked here all the way from Boston.

In 1889 there were only eight other banks in Connecticut empowered to act as trustee, executor, administrator,

In 1985 the Union Trust building is to be remodeled with an addition (center and left) and ground floor retail stores as shown in this architect's sketch.

Stamford Trust Company opened in 1891 on the ground floor of this building, which was constructed in 1868 on the northwest corner of Main and Atlantic streets. Courtesy of the Stamford Historical Society.

guardian, and conservator for individuals and companies.

Walter D. Daskam, formerly with the Stamford National Bank, founded Stamford Trust and became its first treasurer. First president was John A. Brown, former town and borough official and member of the Connecticut legislature. They opened the bank with a capital stock of $50,000, and in three months assets had grown to $271,000.

In 1912 the bank built a two-story marble edifice in simple Greek style at 300 Main Street and moved a few doors west of its original corner. In 1928 it expanded the building on both

sides and added six stories of offices on top.

Stamford Trust in 1957 merged with three smaller banks in Old Greenwich, Norwalk, and Greenwich and, as of January 1, 1958, changed its name to Fairfield County Trust Company. Eleven years later it changed its name again, this time to Union Trust Company, after a merger in 1969 with Union and New Haven Trust Company, which has New Haven roots going back to 1868. Today Union Trust, with 1,400 employees and 60 offices (36 the result of mergers) is the third-largest bank in the state.

In the late 1960s the Federal Reserve System permitted the formation of holding companies that could own stock of a bank or banks and, unlike banks, could form subsidiaries. In 1971 the officers of Union Trust formed Northeast Bancorp, Inc., a holding company, with Union Trust as one of its bank subsidiaries and Security Bank & Trust of Bloomfield, purchased in 1982, the other. Northeast also has a finance subsidiary in Hong Kong and a mortgage company in New Haven.

So far, none of the Connecticut banks is big enough to be the banker to Stamford area Fortune 500 corporations, because Connecticut banks are permitted to lend no more than 10 percent of their capital to any one borrower.

For that reason, Northeast Bancorp in 1983 signed a merger agreement with the Bank of New York, $12 billion in assets to Union Trust's $1.5 billion. As soon as laws permit, the Bank of New York will buy Northeast Bancorp. At present, the state legislature prohibits such mergers outside New England.

In 1985 Union Trust will finish remodeling its Main Street headquarters and a new eight-story addition on the west side of the building. This expansion reflects chairman Thomas F. Richardson's optimism for the future of the central business district in downtown Stamford.

GATEWAY BANK
(Formerly Citizens Savings Bank)

In 1874 Citizens Savings and First National Bank of Stamford, who shared quarters, moved to this building at 166 Atlantic Street. Courtesy of the Stamford Historical Society.

Citizens Savings Bank opened in 1869 in the Seely Block of Main Street, which was constructed in 1861. Before being razed in 1935, the building housed The Rome Company. Courtesy of the Stamford Historical Society.

Most savings banks that opened in the first half and middle of the 19th century were charitable ventures organized by community leaders, the same men who also founded hospitals and supported churches. They wanted to help poor people who were moving in great numbers from farms to cities. These people were accustomed to the barter system, not money. Instead of saving, they tended to spend all they earned, too often on gambling and drinking.

Many savings banks shared quarters with commercial banks, which did not then duplicate services. It was no surprise, therefore, when the Citizens Savings Bank opened on July 2, 1869, in the ground-floor offices of the First National Bank of Stamford, located in the "block" built in 1861 by Albert Seely on the south side of Main Street east of Atlantic.

Generally a civic leader would become the bank's part-time president, and the secretary/treasurer would actually run things. Citizens Savings' first president was Wells R. Ritch (also an incorporator of the First National

Bank), with secretary/treasurer William C. Hoyt handling day-to-day operations.

Citizens Savings initially accepted deposits of no less than one dollar and, in any one year, no more than $400. The theory was that if any trouble arose, the customers wouldn't lose too much, and if a few depositors withdrew all their money, the bank wouldn't lose much, either. On opening day the savings bank took in $517.50 in deposits, which a year later had risen to $129,206.06. The annual dividend paid was 3 percent.

In 1874 both Citizens Savings and First National moved to the first floor of an ornate new facility at 166 Atlan-

On December 2, 1913, Citizens Savings moved to its present neoclassical-revival facility of limestone on the southwest corner of Bank and Atlantic streets. Courtesy of the Stamford Historical Society.

tic Street across from the Town Hall. Then, on December 2, 1913, Citizens Savings moved to its own building, the attractive neoclassical-revival structure of limestone on the southwest corner of Bank and Atlantic streets. This triangular property was purchased from Benjamin Harris, who had bought it from the Congregational Church that had stood on the site before being razed in 1911.

Citizens Savings opened three branches—at Ridgeway Center, Glenbrook and Shippan. When the law allowed, it began accepting checking accounts as of January 1, 1976.

In 1984 the bank merged with another mutual bank, South Norwalk Savings, to become Gateway Bank. Citizens Savings in 1983 had $176 million in assets and South Norwalk Savings had $383 million. Today, with 19 offices throughout Fairfield County, Gateway is the eighth-largest savings bank in Connecticut and offers a full range of consumer and business services. It no longer has a limit on the amount of money that can be deposited.

ASHFORTH PROPERTIES, INC.

When Lord Louis Mountbatten decided to rent out for two months each summer his deceased wife's 19th-century stone castle, Classiebaum, on the Irish coast, his sole American real estate agent was Albert B. Ashforth, Inc. Following Mountbatten's assassination aboard his fishing boat offshore in 1979, his daughters took charge of the castle.

Although new to Stamford in 1980, the Ashforth organization goes back to 1896 when its founder, Albert B. Ashforth, opened a real estate office in Manhattan. Innovative from the start, Albert organized the city's first cooperative apartment house in 1904. When the public accepted it he built several more.

After Albert died in 1929, son Henry Adams Ashforth took over and developed a large national brokerage department. Convinced that New York property owners were interested in real estate in other big cities, he was a broker for properties from coast to coast. The company is also a part owner of a group of buildings in Seattle.

But perhaps the most innovative Ashforth of all is the founder's grandson, Henry Jr., current president and native of Greenwich. In 1965 he bought the Greenwich Railroad Station and its air rights from the New Haven Railroad for $326,130, and in 1970 completed the Greenwich Plaza complex in its place. This was one of the first office buildings in the area to offer space to other than local corporations.

In 1973 Henry Jr. restructured his organization into a holding and development company, Ashforth Properties, Inc. It has three wholly owned subsidiaries, Albert B. Ashforth, Inc. (the original real estate firm), A.P. Construction, Inc., and A.P. Services, Inc. "A.P." stands for Ashforth Properties. The headquarters of the organization is based at 3001 Summer Street in Stamford Square, which the com-

pany built and owns. One hundred additional staff members work in Manhattan.

Albert B. Ashforth, Inc., manages about 80 properties, mainly in New York City, and is a leading commercial leasing broker in Fairfield County. A.P. Construction erects buildings such as Stamford Square and One Milbank, the luxury condominiums in Greenwich. A.P. Services, with 250 employees, operates cleaning and security services in office buildings.

Why a cleaning service? When Henry Jr. began looking into maintenance and security for Greenwich

Founder Albert B. Ashforth built the first cooperative apartments in New York City.

Henry Adams Ashforth, son of the founder, brokered properties in major cities from coast to coast.

Plaza and Stamford Square, he decided he could do the job better by forming his own venture. A.P. Services is a cleaning contractor that handles not only the two company-owned buildings but also Stamford Catholic High School, several banks, and a General Electric Company building in

Henry Adams Ashforth, Jr., the third generation of the family heading the firm, bought the Greenwich Railroad Station and built Greenwich Plaza, Stamford Square, and One Milbank.

Bridgeport.

In buying, leasing, building, managing, and/or servicing many kinds of properties, the Ashforth organization today runs an operation that is unique in Fairfield County.

PARSONS, BROMFIELD & REDNISS

All of the permit processing for Stamford's first planned development district, Newbury Commons, was handled by Parsons, Bromfield & Redniss. The complex is on West Washington Street and has 261 designed residential units.

Late in the 19th century a Stamford city engineer laid the foundation for today's surveying, engineering, planning, and environmental consulting firm known as Parsons, Bromfield & Redniss.

Harold A. Parsons, a tall, thin, taciturn Yankee, founded Parsons Engineering in 1893. From 1900 to 1913

The present partners, Richard W. Redniss and Raymond L. Redniss, in front of Parsons, Bromfield & Redniss' offices at 22 First Street.

he was city engineer, and part of that time also held the same job in Darien and Milford. During the Depression, when surveying declined, he sold women's stockings.

Later Harold surveyed, among other properties, the Old Barn Road and Case Acres developments. Until he was 83, he still went out in the fields in a jacket, vest, and tie, discarding the jacket only in the hottest weather. He was elected first selectman of Stamford in 1951, holding the post until he died of a stroke in 1957 at age 86.

Llewelyn Bromfield, a portly, sweet-tempered Yankee who loved to play the organ, started his engineering firm in 1910 and was town engineer before the town and city consolidated in 1949. In the construction boom of the '50s he handled many subdivisions, as well as the Ridgeway Shopping Center.

Robert L. Redniss, a World War II U.S. Air Force aerial photographer, was building houses in 1957, using Parsons Engineering for surveying. After Harold's death, he bought the firm from widow Martha Parsons. When Llewelyn Bromfield retired in 1964, he bought his practice, and the firm became Parsons, Bromfield & Redniss. Raymond L. Redniss also worked for the firm at this time. Richard W. Redniss joined the venture in 1978, diversifying the scope of services to include planning, zoning, and environmental

consulting. Richard and Raymond have managed the business since then, with Robert retiring in 1982.

Parsons, Bromfield & Redniss has worked directly for the City of Stamford, providing all the original mapping and survey work for the entire Urban Redevelopment Commission southeast quadrant and the design of Washington Boulevard, Harbor Drive, the City Marina bulkhead, Smith House, and the hurricane barrier.

It is impossible to view Stamford's downtown without appreciating the firm's involvement: the Town Center, Landmark Square, Stamford Forums, Champion International's headquarters, St. John Towers, the GTE building, New Hope Towers, the Marriott, and many others.

Parsons, Bromfield & Redniss has also been active in other parts of Stamford, as well as throughout Fairfield and Westchester counties. In addition to countless residential complexes, the concern handled the complete permit processing for Stamford's first planned development district, Newbury Commons, on Washington Boulevard. These 261 rental apartments will be the largest single private residential development here.

Parsons, Bromfield & Redniss engineered Stamford's first designed residential district of large single-family homes, Doral Farms on Roxbury Road, and coordinated the approvals for the first designed residential district of attached units, Middlebrook Farms on Intervale Road. Designed districts allow for the creative grouping of dwellings where they fit best on the site, maximizing the open space and other amenities.

"One of the reasons designed districts are more desirable today," says Richard Redniss, "is that family patterns have changed. There are more single-parent homes, more people without children, and they want a place they can call their own."

COLONIAL INSURANCE AGENCY, INC.

Lawrence F. Smith, founder of the Colonial Insurance Agency, and his wife, Eleanore, in front of the firm's present headquarters at 43 Hoyt Street.

It was in this house, at 395 Glenbrook Road, that Lawrence Smith was born, raised, and eventually began his insurance agency in 1956.

Lawrence F. Smith, former director of research and development of the National Association of Insurance Agents, started his business in 1956 at 395 Glenbrook Road in the house where he was born. Confident that he could lower many automobile insurance premiums by giving young people all the credits they were entitled to, he began writing high-risk policies that most insurance agents did not want. On the *Advocate's* sports page Larry ran two-inch ads headlined "Attention, Young Drivers!" Sunday mornings after church he'd find teenagers waiting in his driveway to submit their applications.

Both his father, James J. Smith, and his grandfather, Frank A. Graf, had been life insurance agents. For 12 years, until the mid-1940s, his grandfather had also served on the Stamford Board of Education. To no one's surprise, Larry majored in insurance at Boston University.

In 1957 he married Stamford native Eleanore "Ele" Faryniarz, a business

administration graduate of the University of Connecticut. She took care of his Stamford agency, located by 1960 on Summer Street, while Larry opened and managed the New York office of Bayly, Martin and Fay, the world's largest motion picture insurance brokerage firm. He left that position in 1965 to become insurance manager of 20th Century Fox Film Corporation in New York.

While working in Manhattan, Larry wrote an unusual $3-million policy for the Los Angeles Dodgers, the first major league baseball team to own an airplane. He insured the team for $250,000 per game for every game lost as a result of a plane crash or any other incident involving the cancellation of a game at home. The policy had a one-game deductible and a maximum 12-game indemnity for any series of games lost.

In 1969, after 18 years of commuting, bolting his dinners, and going out nights and weekends on calls in Stamford, Larry focused solely on his Colonial agency here. Today he and his staff of 14 are headquartered in the two-story brick building he owns at 43 Hoyt Street. In 1971 he purchased

Reynolds, McOwen & Smith, Inc., a Miami, Florida, insurance agency with nine employees.

Although Colonial Insurance handles all kinds of policies, Larry still specializes in difficult-to-place insurance such as product liability for pharmaceutical companies and workers' compensation for hazardous industries. Eighty percent of the business is commercial and 20 percent personal lines. Its combined gross premiums of more than five million dollars annually, plus an additional one million dollars in life/health insurance, make Colonial one of the five largest insurance agencies in Stamford.

Larry recalls one particular teenage driver unable to afford the premium another firm charged. Giving him the credits he was entitled to, Larry lowered his premium. The young man went on to MIT and now owns a successful research/engineering business in Connecticut; Colonial insures the whole company—including the owner's automobile.

MALLOZZI CONSTRUCTION COMPANY

No one knows Stamford underground better than Ottavio "Otto" Mallozzi, founder of one of the more successful excavating contracting firms in the city. Wherever there is major construction in the area, Mallozzi equipment can be seen at work: Landmark Square, GTE, Marriott Hotel, Forest Mews, Stamford Police Department, YMCA, Holly Pond Plaza, and Saks Fifth Avenue are just a few of the many building jobs the firm has helped complete. Veteran's Memorial Park, in central Stamford, and the newest and largest cemetery in Fairfield County, Queen of Peace in North Stamford, reflects the Mallozzi trademark.

Otto started in the business world as a landscaper in his father's company. Soon afterward he became interested in the field of excavation. At the age of 16 Otto tackled his first job—replacing a waterline across Adams Avenue near North Street. "I started taking all the work no one else wanted," Otto explains, "digging deep holes where there's no room to work or where there were large amounts of water and rock." By 1960, at the age of 20, he had incorporated. He had one employee.

Not limited to excavation, Otto is very well known for blasting of difficult areas. One such area was the renovation of the Armory Building. Built at the turn of the century, the owners wanted to remove the left wing and dig to the original ground level, and this required blasting a ledge. The owner knew there was only one person who could handle this blasting; Otto was promptly called, and did indeed handle the difficult project.

The largest undertaking Mallozzi Construction had performed thus far was the deepest—the Landmark Square complex 25 feet down. A large majority of the excavation for Stamford's urban renewal had been done by Mallozzi.

Mallozzi Construction has 14 permanent employees, and in this age of big corporations, it has been able to maintain the old tradition of a family business. Otto's wife, Toni, is very active as administrator for the company, and their grown children—Lisa, 21, Joseph, 20, and Tavio-Gregory, 16—have an active part in the business when not attending college and local schools.

In addition to excavating and blasting, the firm performs many specialized jobs such as erosion control, storm and sanitary sewers, waste treatment, and demolition. Mallozzi Construction prides itself in staying in step with modern technology and has a fleet of excellent heavy equipment to perform almost any job.

While Stamford was being rebuilt, Mallozzi Construction was being built, as Otto say, "through good, old-fashioned hard work," which justifies its claim to being "A Company That Performs."

BLOOMINGDALE'S STAMFORD

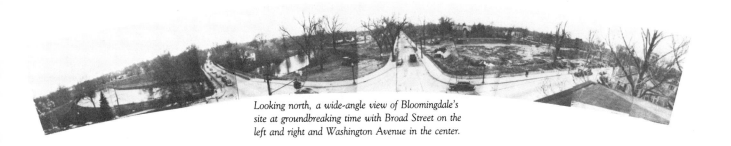

Looking north, a wide-angle view of Bloomingdale's site at groundbreaking time with Broad Street on the left and right and Washington Avenue in the center.

The first large out-of-state department store came to Stamford 30 years ago, preceding the influx of Fortune 500 corporations by nearly 15 years. On February 17, 1954, Bloomingdale's opened its third and, at the time, largest branch on the corner of Broad Street and the former Washington Avenue, now Washington Boulevard. The Manhattan-based store already had a branch in New Rochelle, New York, and another in Fresh Meadows, Long Island. (Today it has 14 branches in nine states.)

Local merchants were concerned at first about the effect Bloomingdale's would have on their sales. They needn't have worried. Says Thomas C. Mayers, first general manager of the Stamford store, "Our coming resulted in improved business for the other merchants because so many more people came in to Stamford to shop."

Bloomingdale's has a policy of encouraging its employees to take an active part in the community. Tom Mayers became so active and so well known that, resigning from the store, he was twice elected mayor of Stamford, an office he held from 1963 to 1967.

Back in 1872, the store's founding brothers, Lyman and Joseph Bloomingdale, had started a bargain-basement business at 938 Third Avenue in New York City. As business boomed, they moved farther and farther uptown, eventually buying the whole block between 59th and 60th streets, where Bloomingdale's flagship store stands today. They concentrated mainly on home furnishings, rather than ready-to-wear.

In 1929, instead of remaining a partnership, Bloomingdale's became part of the new Federated Department Stores, Inc., along with Abraham & Straus, Filene's, and Lazarus & Co. of Ohio. During the Depression Bloomingdale's was the only major New York department store that showed a profit. Afterward, as the Upper East Side attracted more affluence, the store upgraded its image to meet the tastes of its clientele.

Around the time the Stamford store opened, Bloomingdale's was putting more emphasis on ready-to-wear merchandise. Perceiving what their customers wanted, buyers set a precedent by asking manufacturers to create specific items in specific ways, just for them. Buyers also began searching in foreign countries for unique, exciting items for the store's special promotions.

The Stamford store's sales in the past 10 years have more than doubled, with the volume of ready-to-wear and home furnishings about equal. Bloom-

ingdale's regional vice-president, James McCullagh, credits this to "our unending desire to give our customers a level of service, excitement, and assortments that few, if any, retailers can match. But the real backbone of our success has come from our employees, many of whom have been with us for years."

Bloomingdale's opened here 30 years ago with about 350 employees, and 17 of them are still with the company. Today it has approximately 600 employees, 30 of whom have accrued more than 25 years of service. No wonder that, as a retailing institution in southwestern Connecticut, Bloomingdale's is more dominant today than ever before.

Bloomingdale's opened in 1954 at Broad Street and what is now Washington Boulevard. It has since been remodeled twice and a third floor has been added.

FAG BEARINGS CORPORATION

Norma-Hoffman Bearings Corporation, FAG's predecessor, moved from Long Island to this plant on Hamilton Avenue in Stamford in 1926.

This German-owned company has a complex heritage with roots in both the United States and Germany. FAG Bearings Corporation (FAG stands for Fischer Aktien Gesellschaft, which translates to Fischer Joint Stock Company) traces its American root back to 1911, when W.M. Nones opened a small office in New York City to import precision bearings from the Norma Company of Germany. He called his enterprise the Norma Company of America.

Nones began manufacturing his own bearings in 1914 in a plant on Long Island. The venture grew and, in 1922, Hoffmann Manufacturing Company of England acquired the controlling interest, changing the name to Norma-Hoffmann Bearings Corporation. In 1926 Norma-Hoffmann moved to a large new plant on Hamilton Avenue in Stamford.

Still another change came in 1953 when a holding company, Universal-American Corporation, purchased the English interests but retained Norma-Hoffmann's identity as a subsidiary. Then, in the 1960s, Gulf & Western Industries took over Universal-

American, and Norma-Hoffmann became, briefly, a Gulf & Western subsidiary. FAG bought Norma-Hoffmann in May 1969 and changed the name temporarily to Norma FAG to retain the association for customers. When FAG became accepted in a couple of years, the "Norma" was dropped.

The firm's much deeper but, in some respects, less complicated German root goes back to 1883 to Schweinfurt, West Germany. There Frederich Fischer, manager of a small bicycle-repair shop and son of Phillipp Moritz Fischer who constructed the first pedal bicycle, invented a mill that ground bearing balls between two horizontal disks turning in opposite directions. A much more accurate process than grinding balls on a lathe, its basic disk principles are used to mass-produce bearing balls throughout the world today.

In 1909, 10 years after Frederich Fischer's death, Georg Schaefer, owner of another Schweinfurt ball bearing factory, acquired Fischer's factory and merged it with his own. The combined organization, whose complete name is FAG Kugelfischer Georg Schaefer KGaA (kugel means "ball") has been under the exclusive personal direction of the Schaefer family ever since.

Both the German and the Ameri-

can roots have made vital contributions to the development of the bearings on which the mechanized world turns. Besides inventing the ball mill, the German company in 1912 achieved a breakthrough with the first barrel-type roller bearings held between integral inner-ring shoulders and spherically ground inner and outer raceways.

The American company in 1921 introduced the ball bearing cup mounting, forerunner of all small "self-protected" ball bearings. It made the first heavy-duty cylindrical roller bearings for diesel-electric railroad traction motors in 1928. Ten years later it introduced the first cartridge-type ball bearings ideally suited for electric motors. Other contributions include the earliest aircraft control pulley bearings and precision aircraft supercharger roller bearings.

The present FAG Bearings Corpora-

The original centerless ball bearing mill invented in 1883 by Frederich Fischer, manager of a bicycle-repair shop in Germany.

FAG Bearings Corporation headquarters, completed in 1980 at 118 Hamilton Avenue. FAG also has a 100,000-square-foot distribution center.

tion in Stamford has a history not only of ownership changes but also, more recently, of a dramatic change in function. For 53 years it was a manufacturing facility that employed during peak times as many as 1,600. In 1979, with 325 employees remaining, FAG closed the factory because it was no longer economically efficient to manufacture the product line of bearings here. Now FAG employs 150 in its corporate headquarters, completed in 1980, and its nearby 100,000-square-foot distribution center, both located at 118 Hamilton Avenue.

All of FAG's U.S. manufacturing is done in its Joplin, Missouri, plant, built in 1970. Although FAG's bearings can range anywhere from less than .04 inches across the bore, which are assembled under high-power microscopes, to the world's heaviest at 234,000 pounds, which was designed to support an 11-story reel of steel pipe, the Joplin bearings generally measure from about 4 to 14 inches. They are used for automobile water pumps, traction motors for locomo-

tives and subway cars, machine tools, and rolling mills. None of the parent organization's 20 plants (17 in Europe and one each in Canada, Brazil, and the United States) duplicates another. It's more efficient to make long production runs of one type, using an automated process.

No company in the world makes more kinds of bearings than does the FAG parent, and all 70,000 configurations can be ordered from the distribution center here. With this tremendous inventory on tap, sales volume of FAG Bearings Corporation since 1969 has grown 400 percent.

After closing its Stamford plant,

FAG, at company expense, refurbished the three buildings into an industrial park and leased the space to a half-dozen small manufacturers. In so doing, the firm provided the manufacturers with industrial space they otherwise might not have been able to afford in the Stamford area. The industrial park, with a working population of 500, has more than replaced the jobs lost when the plant closed, even though the 500 are not on the FAG payroll.

FAG bearings come in as many as 70,000 different configurations. Shown are examples of ball and roller bearings.

THE AMERICAN THREAD COMPANY

Probably the first spinning mill ever humidified, Willimantic's No. 2 was built of riverbed stone in 1862. Photo of painting by A.N. Wyeth.

Back in 1854 in Willimantic, Connecticut, manufacturer Austin Dunham and three partners organized the Willimantic Linen Company to make crash toweling, napkins, and shoe thread from imported Russian flax. Soon the Crimean War cut off the flax supply, and in 1856 the fledgling enterprise switched to producing three-cord cotton sewing thread, instead.

Around the time of the Civil War, the increased demand for thread brought the Willimantic Linen Company its first financial success. In 1862, out of stone dug from the Willi-

mantic River bed, the company began constructing Mill No. 2 and in 1865 completed a new stone office building in front of the mill.

No thread finer than a three-cord thread had ever been made in the United States because the dry atmosphere in fall and winter generated static electricity that broke the thread. The sewing machine, just coming into general use, required a smoother, rounder thread like the six-cord made in Scotland. The enterprising Willimantic Linen Company, by installing steam pipes and atomizers to raise the humidity in Mill No. 2, produced six-cord thread as good as any in Scotland.

The firm also pioneered better working conditions and other types of employee benefits hitherto unknown. Running time was reduced from 66 to 60 hours a week. Women were given cups of bouillon at their work. Employees enjoyed attractive cottage housing. The Dunham Library was started in a company building where evening classes were held so employees could learn to read and write English. Any worker home sick received a bouquet of flowers.

Meanwhile, a dozen smaller thread companies had sprung up in New England. In the 1890s competition among the firms was intense. Eventually all the concerns (including Willi-

The American Thread Company moved from New York City in 1970 to this building in High Ridge Park.

mantic, which by then had five mills) decided they would have to consolidate or face financial hardship. They approached the prestigious English Sewing Cotton Company Ltd. across the Atlantic.

English Sewing agreed to buy the assets of the 13 American companies and pay their debts. In 1898 the 13 firms were incorporated as The American Thread Company, and an American, Lyman R. Hopkins of Holyoke, Massachusetts, was elected the first president. The British parent received 1,193,800 shares of American Thread common stock.

American Thread remained headquartered in Manhattan until moving to High Ridge Park on October 5, 1970. It is a member of the Tootal Group, which also includes English Sewing Ltd. Tootal, a leading international textile company based in Manchester, England, controls more than 50 manufacturing facilities worldwide.

Today American Thread has 2,500 employees in the United States and operates six modern manufacturing facilities located in the Carolinas. Its Sylvan, North Carolina, plant, built in 1964, was the first all-electric spinning plant in the world.

American Thread is among the country's leading manufacturers of industrial sewing thread and also produces sewing thread, sewing notions, hand-knitting and rug yarns, and crafts for consumer use. It has two wholly owned subsidiaries—ATCOT Corporation and Calico Printers Associates, U.S.A. Ltd.

SMS ARCHITECTS

The founding partners of SMS Architects, looking over a company project, are Lester W. Smith, FAIA, Thorne Sherwood, FAIA, and Willis N. Mills, FAIA. Photo circa 1960. © Robert Stahman.

Three World War II veterans from the U.S. Navy, Marine Corps, and Army Air Force formed an architectural partnership in Stamford in 1946. Hiring a part-time secretary, they opened an office at 187 Main Street, above what was then Racanello's Florist Shop, and called their firm Sherwood, Mills & Smith, Architects.

The Navy man was Thorne "Tony" Sherwood, an architectural graduate of Columbia University. The Marine was Willis N. "Plumber" Mills, who had met Tony while teaching architecture at Columbia. The nickname "Plumber" originated at Kent School, where Willis had gained an adolescent reputation for "lousing things up." Air Force veteran Lester W. Smith, a Princeton Phi Beta Kappa in architec-

ture, had met Plumber before the war, in Trinidad, where a military base was being built.

In 1948 the trio moved to West Park Place over the former Partee typewriter shop and hired a couple of employees. Next they moved to 65 Broad Street (where Pierson & Smith Real Estate-Insurance is now) and worked their way up to a staff of 40. By 1960 their sizable architectural firm had moved to larger space at 777 Summer Street and hired 10 more people.

How it happened that Sherwood, Mills & Smith—the undisputed leader in architectural design in Fairfield County—changed its name to SMS Architects, converted a former New Canaan woodworking mill into offices, and moved to 59 Grove Street in New

In 1984 the officers of the architectural firm include (left to right) Andrew J. Santella, Robert C. Steinmetz, AIA, Willis N. Mills, Jr., FAIA, and Lee A. Wright, AIA.

Canaan on May 1, 1972, illuminates a page of Stamford's recent history.

The three veterans began by designing houses. Their third commission was a bathhouse for the Stamford Yacht Club, for which each received a free membership as part of the fee (but only for a year or two). It was their 74th job, designing New Canaan's South School in 1948, that put them on the map. After that came 140 schools, 30 in Fairfield County. (In Stamford the partners designed Roxbury, Turn of River, and Newfield public schools, and King, Low Heywood-Thomas, and Long Ridge private schools.)

As the 1970s approached, fewer babies being born meant fewer schools being built. Suddenly the architects had to change direction, designing not just schools but libraries, office buildings, condominium projects, nursing homes, and recreational facilities. A few examples: the Greenwich Public Library addition; Waldenbooks headquarters, and the 1600 Summer Street office building in Stamford; Lyon Farm Condominiums and the Round Hill Community Church in Greenwich; Waveny Care Center in New Canaan; the Stamford Jewish Center; and recycling Greenwich High School into the Greenwich Town Hall.

The principals, who lived in the suburbs, became disenchanted with the way Stamford was developing, especially with increased rush-hour traffic. Although continuing to handle Stamford projects, they felt no requirement to be located here. The firm's name was abbreviated to SMS Architects because, as the receptionist says, "I was answering the phone that way anyway."

All three founders have retired, leaving the firm in the hands of principals Willis N. Mills, Jr., FAIA, the managing partner; Robert C. Steinmetz, AIA; Lee A. Wright, AIA; and Andrew J. Santella, construction contract administrator.

AL KOPROSKI REALTY

Al Koproski's grandparents came here from Poland in 1895 and, along with other Polish immigrants, settled in the South End-Waterside section. In 1904 they opened Koproski's Market on Harbor Street, where groceries, meats, and vegetables were sold until the market closed in 1970. Nevertheless, it was real estate, not groceries, that attracted Al Koproski because, he says, his father owned several pieces of

Al Koproski bought the vacant McCall's factory building in 1960 and started his own real estate business in the president's suite. He sold the facility in 1983.

property here.

Al went to work for old-time realtor Sam Silberman, owner of what was then the largest commercial and industrial agency in Stamford. Sam told his trainee, "You can make a good living in real estate sometimes, but the secret of success is buying, not selling. The people who make money in real estate are the ones who invest in it."

Taking Sam's advice, Al started his own business in 1960 by buying the McCall's factory building on Pulaski Street and moving into the former president's suite. He kept the huge McCall's sign on the roof but along the side of the structure, where the woman's magazine used to be printed, he painted, "Al Koproski Real Estate—Industrial & Commercial Specialists" and "2,000-160,000 square

Al and Pat Koproski outside their 36 Pulaski Street real estate building, which also serves as the Polish Slavic Information Center.

feet available immediately." The Cannondale Corporation, manufacturers of hiking gear, eventually rented the entire building.

In 1975 Al bought a house across the river at 36 Pulaski Street and moved his office there. He sold the McCall's building in 1983 to Bernard Manger, owner of Manger Electric Company.

From the start Al set a goal of buying one piece of property a year. Today he owns 17 properties, including five Stamford apartment houses and the Oceanview Beach and Tennis Club in Shippan. He may have sold the club by the time this book appears because, he says, taxes have risen so high that a three-month operation can scarcely make a profit. His business is 95 percent industrial and commercial and 5 percent residential.

In Polish-American circles the realtor is better known for volunteer work than for real estate transactions. In 1976 he was responsible for having the name of Dyke Park, on the tip of the South End, changed to Kosciuszko Park in honor of the Polish general who fought for freedom in the American Revolution. He and his business partner/wife, Patricia, known as Pat, run the Polish-Slavic Information Center and edit the monthly *Polish-Slavic Newsletter* in their realty office. Without charge they help people coming here from Poland find housing and jobs.

Active in the Americares for Poland Foundation, based in New Canaan, Al has helped raise money for children's medical supplies and recently for two million disposable diapers sent to Poland. Because of the acute shortage of both regular diapers and antiseptic soap, disposable diapers appreciably lower the incidence of infectious diseases among Polish babies. Al and Pat have made several trips to Poland to make sure the gifts are getting into the proper hands, and are satisfied that they are.

JOHN A. DRENCKHAHN, INC.

John A. Drenckhahn, at age 83, is the oldest electrical contractor in Stamford.

The electric lights that replaced kerosene lamps in his family's Riverside home in 1914 so intrigued 13-year-old John Drenckhahn that three years later he went to work as a $5-a-week apprentice at New England Engineering Company on Atlantic Street. It was managed by G.E. Risley, who later started his own electrical firm. A journeyman electrician's wages then were $18 for a 44-hour week.

John came from a hard-working family. His father, a former sausage maker in Germany, had bought 100 acres in the Quaker Ridge section of Greenwich. There the Drenckhahns produced sausages, bacon, hams, butter, and eggs for market. In 1910 they sold the farm and moved to Riverside.

Early during the Depression John dug ditches and did odd jobs to earn a living. Then, in 1931, he borrowed $1,500 and, with another unemployed electrician, Edward MacDonald, bought out Risley. They went into partnership as electrical contractors on the ground floor of Redman's Hall on Federal Street, hiring two electricians and, to keep the books, Mrs. Risley.

In 1939 John sold his interest to MacDonald and went into business for himself in his home at 882 Hope Street. His first vehicle was an old Chevrolet car. In 1945 he put an office addition on the house, and when his sons, Fred and John Jr., left the Army after World War II, they joined the business. It was incorporated in 1957, with John Sr. as president.

During the explosion of school and church construction in the '50s and '60s, the company employed as many as 35 electricians. Besides its commercial work, it wired 12 Stamford area schools and six churches. In 1954 John Sr. had moved his headquarters to a two-story brick facility he constructed at 886 Hope Street, next to the house, and in the late '60s he put an addition on the building. He has done work for the Southern New England Telephone Company since 1931 and the Stamford Hospital since 1957.

The Olin Corporation became a Drenckhahn customer during a crisis. Early Saturday morning, July 25, 1981, fire raced through the south wing of Olin's corporate headquarters, knocking out the entire communications system (not installed by Drenck-

hahn). In newspaper ads Olin thanked the local fire departments and, among others, John A. Drenckhahn, electrical contractors, for the emergency service that enabled Olin to conduct business as usual by 8 a.m. the following Monday.

At age 83, John Sr. is the oldest electrical contractor in Stamford. He has been treasurer of the Kiwanis Club of suburban Stamford from the time he joined, and each year cooks the roast beef for the club's Christmas party.

In his lifetime the founder of John A. Drenckhahn, Inc., has seen amazing changes besides electric lights replacing kerosene lamps. Gone are most of the factories that used to line Hope Street. Gone, too, is his Chevrolet car. In its place stand 10 green trucks and a cherry-picker. The rate paid electricians today is $500-plus for a 35-hour week.

At day's end the green Drenckhahn trucks are a familiar sight next to the firm's building at 886 Hope Street.

CRYSTAL ROCK WATER COMPANY, INC.

The plant and offices of the Crystal Rock Water Company stand behind a 1910 house on Long Ridge Road that Henry E. Baker purchased in 1939.

Back in 1914, 19-year-old Henry E. Baker hitched his horse to a small open wagon in Danbury and courageously ventured for the first time all the way to Stamford. At a log cabin on Vine Road he asked directions to town, then stopped at a house on the north end of Summer Street to board his horse and rent a room for himself.

The tall, thin young man was in the spring water business with H. Ray Bailey of Danbury. Later he and Bailey jointly leased the Crystal Rock Spring on the C.A. Lockwood farm near the present Stamford Museum, where Henry filled half-gallon bottles, loaded them in the wagon, and delivered them around town, at 25 cents for six.

Although a reservoir and water mains had begun to replace wells in Stamford as early as 1871, many people still liked to fill their bottles at local springs. Henry saved them the bother, bringing spring water to their doors. The idea caught on, and by the 1920s there were at least 11 small companies in the bottled water business here.

On November 13, 1922, Henry had an accident that was described in the *Advocate*. The neck of a bottle broke as he was washing it and gashed the fleshy part of his right thumb. Dr. Ralph W. Crane put in seven stitches and told Henry not to use his hand for a while. Nevertheless, he continued to serve his customers, with one arm in a sling.

In 1939 Henry paid $9,000 to Elizabeth Keane, the last of five spinster sisters, for six acres and a 14-room house built in 1910 at 313 Long Ridge Road. Drilling a well there, he unexpectedly tapped an excellent water supply. So he built a small plant to bottle artesian well water.

Henry's wife, Gladys, did his bookkeeping, and when he died in 1947, she took over the business. Henry Jr., their only son, was 15 at the time. Working nights and weekends at the plant until he finished school, he has been on the job ever since and today is company president.

As more office buildings went up here and more people began to appreciate good drinking water, Crystal Rock's business boomed. Incorporated in 1965, Fairfield County's only bottled water company now serves about 9,000 customers throughout Fairfield, Westchester, Putnam, New Haven, and part of Litchfield counties. It has 40 employees and 12 big blue-and-white trucks to deliver bottled water and nonperishable, snack-type refreshments every 10 working days. Four service vans take care of refrigerators, small microwave ovens, and other coffee-break equipment provided to customers.

Henry Jr. built a new plant in 1968. Before putting on an addition in 1982, he let volunteer firemen set the original plant building on fire so they could practice putting out the blaze. He and his three sons, who work in the business, are volunteer firemen. A fire radio continuously plays at low volume in his office, and his sons wear pagers. As Henry Jr. says, "When your neighbor needs help, he needs it right away."

Henry E. Baker, Sr., founder of Crystal Rock Water Company, started his business by delivering bottled spring water in this horse-drawn wagon.

THE STAMFORD SAVINGS BANK

As the Industrial Revolution began luring workers away from farms and the barter system to factories and cash payrolls, a Presbyterian minister in frugal Scotland organized the first mutual savings bank in 1810. The idea soon spread to this country, and the first savings bank in Stamford opened on September 20, 1851, a little less than three years after the railroad came to town. Called The Stamford Savings Bank, it shared a converted grocery store on Main Street west of Atlantic with the Stamford Bank, the first commercial financial institution founded here in 1834.

Twenty-six prominent Stamford men had petitioned the state legislature to charter the bank, and one of them, Theodore Davenport, was elected the first president. The only paid officer was secretary/treasurer Charles G. Rockwood, who drew a salary of $200 per year. He also served as cashier of the commercial bank, which, unlike the mutual savings bank, paid no dividends and had been organized for the profit of its stockholders, not its depositors.

Hezekiah Satterlee made the first deposit, five dollars, and as deposits grew, the bank was able to lend money. One borrower took out a $1,200 loan, offering as security "a house and lot opposite Silas Brown." In a town of 5,000, everyone knew where Silas Brown lived.

By April 10, 1852, the Stamford Savings Bank had a total of $8,708.48 from 75 depositors, who received a 5-percent dividend (later reduced as a result of financial crises and the Civil War). Loans totaling $7,659 had been paid out to seven individuals.

In 1886, when the city's population had reached 15,000, the bank moved into its new three-story red brick Victorian building with a massive round tower on the triangle at Main and Bank streets. The commercial bank, renamed the Stamford National Bank, moved along with it to what became known as "The Old Red Bank," paying a rental of $1,200 a year. The Stamford Safe Deposit Company, formed in 1887, set up its vault in this structure.

Then in 1940 the bank erected its present red brick facility of modified Georgian design at 160 Atlantic Street

The present home of The Stamford Savings Bank, at 160 Atlantic Street, was erected in 1940.

The Stamford Savings Bank, at Main and Bank streets, also housed Stamford National Bank until 1905, when Stamford National built the six-story skyscraper next door. Courtesy of the Stamford Historical Society.

on the site of the former First National Bank of Stamford. The Old Red Bank was razed in March 1969.

Today The Stamford Savings Bank has, in addition to its main office, five branches: Summer Street, High Ridge, Springdale, Darien, and Greenwich. Its assets have more than doubled to $338 million in the past 10 years. These days it offers checking accounts and other services legally permitted to savings banks, and in 1980 was the first bank in the Stamford area to write variable-rate mortgages. Since 1973 its mortgage loans have increased 150 percent.

Although some Stamford banks have recently sought mergers, Richard E. Taber, Stamford Savings president, emphasizes, "We will retain our independence and our focus to the local community. We want to remain the local bank that can handle the family's banking needs. We are not interested in merging with any out-of-town banks. Economically, we don't need to, and we plan to keep it that way."

CLAIROL

In 1931 a 33-year-old New York manufacturing chemist named Lawrence M. Gelb discovered in Paris an amazing formula that was to revolutionize hair coloring. Instead of just coating the outside of the hair, the new formula, called Clairol, actually penetrated the hair shaft for a far more natural color effect. Larry quickly obtained the rights to sell the preparation in the Western Hemisphere and bought $200 worth to test in New York beauty salons.

Defying the Depression, the enthusiastic entrepreneur opened a one-man New York office and began mixing, bottling, labeling, demonstrating, and taking orders. As he put it, "Women will always seek ways to look more beautiful, no matter how hard the times."

By a stroke of genius he called his

product "Clairol Oil Shampoo Tint," avoiding the dreaded word "dye." No "nice" woman of the time, except perhaps an actress, would admit to bleaching or dyeing her hair, but "tinting" seemed acceptable.

By 1938, when annual sales to hairdressers had reached $300,000, Larry saw trouble brewing in Europe and bought the formula for $25,000. He hired a Ph.D. biochemist to head his laboratory and a hairdresser to help with presentations and train the fledgling sales force.

Clairol's research, manufacturing, and distribution operations in 1940 rented space on Fairfield Avenue in Stamford and hired 25 local employees, most of them women. The corporate and marketing headquarters remained in New York. Sales were still well under one million dollars.

In 1950 Clairol launched a retail breakthrough—"Miss Clairol Hair Color Bath"—the first formula to lighten, condition, and color the hair in one simple application that took only 20 minutes. It looked more natu-

Lawrence M. Gelb, founder of Clairol discovered a formula in Paris in 1931 that revolutionized hair coloring.

ral than ever, and for the first time women could do the job at home.

That year Clairol moved its 100 Stamford employees to a new building on Commerce Road, and Larry's sons, Richard L. and Bruce S., began working there. From Commerce Road the operations expanded to Stamford's first urban redevelopment project (so-called East Meadow) on Jefferson Street and Harbor View Avenue.

The famous question, "Does She . . . Or Doesn't She?" (Hair Color So Natural, Only Her Hairdresser Knows for Sure) brought hair coloring into the mass market in 1956. *Good Housekeeping*, which had previously refused to touch the subject of hair coloring at all, in 1959 awarded Miss Clairol its coveted seal of approval.

Clairol's steady growth and proven success made it an attractive candidate for acquisition. Bristol-Myers Company offered the best long-term possi-

Standing, left to right, are Bruce S. Gelb, Bristol-Myers' executive vice-president; Richard L. Gelb, chairman and chief executive officer; and John Melton, then president of Clairol as they honor Stamford's 43-year retiring employees in early 1984.

bilities and on April 13, 1959, acquired Clairol for $22.5 million in cash. Larry became chairman of the board of Clairol, with Richard, president, and Bruce, executive vice-president.

But by 1963 the company was bursting its Stamford seams and seriously considered moving out. Newly elected Mayor Thomas C. Mayers sat down with management to explore ways to keep the city's second-largest private employer (after Pitney-Bowes) here. They found the last big parcel of land, which had been zoned for another purpose.

Rezoning accomplished, Clairol in 1965 purchased the former Daycroft School property (at one time the 46-acre Schuyler Merritt estate) on Blachley Road. Later the firm gave part of the property to the city, along with a cash donation to straighten the dangerous Cove Road "S" curve. On May 1, 1968, 1,400 employees moved into the world's largest hair-coloring, toiletries, and cosmetics manufacturing and distribution center, which has a production floor larger than two football fields. In 1970 the Clairol researchers came over from Commerce

Clairol's Blachley Road production and distribution facilities received one of Modern Manufacturing Magazine's *"Ten Top (new) Plants of the Year" awards in 1969.*

The 1950s brought a retail breakthrough for Clairol. The "Miss Clairol Hair Color Bath" promised to lighten, condition, and color the hair in one 20-minute application women could do at home.

Road to a new laboratory across the way.

Today, with annual sales upwards of $400 million, Clairol has about 60 percent of the hair-coloring market. Its top sellers are "Nice 'n Easy," a shampoo-in hair color, and "Loving Care," which colors only the gray, leaving the rest natural. More than 30 percent of women nationwide now color their hair.

The firm has expanded into shampoos, conditioners, and hair sprays;

skin-care products; and personal-care appliances such as "Clairol Kindness" (a curler with heated rollers), the "Nail Works," and, for tired, aching feet, the "Foot Fixer."

Clairol started as a family enterprise, and a family spirit persists. Larry died in 1980, but now Richard is chairman and chief executive officer of Bristol-Myers, and Bruce is executive vice-president.

In Stamford the company has between 1,400 and 1,500 employees, of whom 36 percent are female and 20 percent minority. Many are related to one another. Thirty-five active employees have 25 or more years of service, and 21 retirees have had at least 25. Robert M. Phillips, a Stamford resident, succeeded John Melton as president of Clairol on September 1, 1984.

As one of Stamford's largest taxpayers, Clairol has made significant long-term contributions to the city, including rescuing of the New Hope subsidized housing project, for which it received a citation from the Urban League and the NAACP. Many local employees volunteer on community boards and committees. A Clairol spokesman assures, "The company that sells products to make women more attractive from head to toe expects to play a strong role in Stamford's future."

GENERAL ELECTRIC CREDIT CORPORATION

In the depths of the Great Depression, General Electric Company was mass-producing refrigerators, ranges, and washing machines even though the average citizen lacked the cash to buy them. Credit was hard to obtain. Banks tried to avoid this kind of risk, and independent finance companies required manufacturers to assume most of it.

Tackling the problem, assistant treasurer George F. Mosher proposed that GE provide customer credit by setting up a captive finance company. And so, on January 1, 1933, General Electric Contracts Corporation, with Mosher as president, opened at 120 Broadway in Manhattan, moving seven months later to larger space in the GE Building at 570 Lexington Avenue. This Depression "child" filled such a big need that by the end of the year its total financing had reached $6,580,000.

During World War II, when GE switched from consumer to defense production, the Contracts Corporation was supplanted by the present General Electric Credit Corporation, an investment company empowered to lend money and deal in commercial paper.

The postwar economic boom brought a change in social attitudes. The stigma of "being in debt" had evaporated, and nearly 50 percent of American families were using some kind of installment financing.

The 1960s saw dramatic changes as GECC, while still a wholly owned GE subsidiary, shed its "captive" role and began to diversify with financial services to consumer, commercial, and industrial markets that had nothing to do with GE products. Under Charles "Ticker" Klock, named president in 1961, GECC enjoyed remarkable growth.

GECC moved into this 192,000-square-foot facility at 260 Long Ridge Road in 1970 and completed a 40,000-square-foot building next door in 1984.

In 1970 Klock moved the firm's administrative offices and several hundred employees to a new building at 260 Long Ridge Road here. Fourteen years later, there were over 1,100 GECC employees working in Stamford. In 1984 the company completed another building next door to the north.

John W. Stanger, who became president in 1975, began a new era of accelerated diversification and growth. GECC's total net income since then has increased annually by an unprecedented 25 percent. Compared to GECC's net earnings assets of $2.4

Shown here (left to right) are Charles "Ticker" Klock, second GECC president; John W. Stanger, current president; and George F. Mosher, founder and first president.

billion in 1970, its 1983 net earnings assets have more than quintupled to $13 billion. (GECC was responsible for 13.5 percent of parent GE's 1983 net earnings.)

The commercial and industrial financing division accounts for the lion's share—52 percent—of GECC's net earnings assets. Distribution sales financing accounts for 27 percent, real estate financial services, 13 percent, and subsidiaries, 8 percent.

While not as actively dealing direct with consumers, GECC, in creating money for business, affects nearly all segments of society. Most people are unaware, for example, that many airplanes they fly in are actually owned by GECC and leased to the airlines. GECC owns many oil tankers and locomotives that it leases, as well.

THE CONNECTICUT BANK AND TRUST COMPANY

No bank existed in Stamford until 1834, when the Connecticut Legislature chartered the Stamford Bank, local ancestor of Hartford-based The Connecticut Bank and Trust Company (CBT). For many years the legislature, as a condition to granting a charter, required a contribution to a worthy cause. The bank agreed to pay Wesleyan University $5,000 in two installments.

There was no national currency prior to the Civil War. Instead, banks in all 34 states printed their own state bank notes—1,600 different kinds of money that could fluctuate in value from week to week.

The Stamford Bank opened on September 10, 1834, in an old house at the head of the canal while bank president John W. Leeds' former grocery near Atlantic Square was being remodeled into a banking house. For the next half-century the bank did business behind three impressive gothic arches across the front.

In 1863 Congress passed the National Bank Act to help finance the ongoing Civil War and promote a stable national currency. Like many other banks, Stamford opposed going national. Nevertheless, two directors and the cashier left to help organize the First National Bank of Stamford, fourth in the entire country to join the national system. When a tax was imposed on state bank notes in 1865, the Stamford Bank quickly capitulated and became the Stamford National Bank.

On July 12, 1919, the two commercial banks merged into the First-Stamford National Bank, electing as president Schuyler Merritt, for whom the Merritt Parkway is named. In 1929 it became the First-Stamford National Bank and Trust. The bank moved on June 23, 1930, from its 1905 six-story building at 303 Main to the eight-story "skyscraper" at One Atlantic Street, for years Stamford's tallest building. Today it is CBT's Fairfield

The Stamford Bank opened in 1834 in a converted grocery store at 303 Main Street. In 1865 it reluctantly became The Stamford National Bank.

County headquarters.

The bank in 1933 absorbed Depression-hit People's National Bank of Stamford to protect the bank's depositors. In 1947 First-Stamford opened its first branch, in Glenbrook, initiating an expansion by means of new branches and acquisitions throughout

The Connecticut Bank and Trust Company's Stamford executive offices occupy this eight-story building constructed in 1930 at One Atlantic Street.

Fairfield County and beyond. In 1958 it merged with Greenwich Trust Company, and in 1962 became the State National Bank. Around-the-clock automatic teller service was introduced in 1971.

By 1977 State National was actually the oldest national bank in continuous service in the United States. Charter Nos. 2 and 3 had been surrendered, and Charter No. 1 had gone through a long period of inactive status before resuming operation.

On December 31, 1983, the holding company of State National was acquired by the holding company of the larger Connecticut Bank and Trust Company, dating back to 1792. Today, with total assets of more than five billion dollars and 150 offices throughout the state, the new CBT is the largest bank in Connecticut.

And it may well become the second-largest in New England. A planned merger of CBT Corporation and Boston-based Bank of New England Corporation, of almost equal size, is currently in litigation. This merger would create a banking institution with assets of more than $10 billion.

F.D. RICH COMPANY

Not since the great days of Yale & Towne, 100 years ago, has any single business venture so affected the economic vitality of the city of Stamford as has F.D. Rich Company.

Today a nationwide real estate development firm with continuing and past project involvement from coast to coast, Alaska, and the Caribbean, F.D. Rich Company has the reputation of being the sole redeveloper of the urban renewal of downtown Stamford.

Fittingly enough, the company that has so distinctively shaped the new city has its origins in Stamford. F.D. Rich, Sr., chairman emeritus, founded the enterprise in 1920. An immigrant from Italy at an early age, he, his brothers, and relatives combined their strong arms and ambitions into a business that became in a short period of time a nationwide operation. The firm's first Stamford landmark is Sacred Heart Church, built in 1923. It still stands today as a symbol of the founder's devotion to contributing to the good life of his community. Now operated by succeeding generations of the Rich family, F.D. Rich Company still cherishes those original principles of its founder.

While the firm has, during its six decades of existence, developed and constructed in both near and far locations, it is best known for its reputation as the builder of the Stamford of today and tomorrow. The company's involvement in the renewal of Stamford began in 1961, with the award of the urban-renewal contract. Based upon F.D. Rich Company's abilities, resources, and community involvement, the city, in effect, entrusted the firm with the responsibility of shaping Stamford for future generations.

Starting in 1961 with a grand scheme that envisioned Stamford as the regional center for Fairfield and Westchester counties, F.D. Rich Company had, by 1984, transformed the city into such a reality. To create this center and to design the distinctive buildings that have since characterized downtown Stamford as a city of the 21st century, the company engaged world-class architects such as Gruen, Safdie, Guirgola, Bisharat, Erikson, and Pelli. This effort has brought into being, in the once-deteriorating core of the city, nine high-rise office buildings, a million-square-foot Town Center Mall, a hotel, and over 1,000 units of housing.

According to Robert N. Rich, now president of F.D. Rich Company, the key ingredient to Stamford's urban-renewal success was the establishment of a public-private partnership. "Public and private interests working together

Ten Stamford Forum

for the common good is a long-standing Connecticut tradition.

Through the terms of seven mayors and continuously changing city boards, the company and the community's representatives have maintained a constant devotion to seeking and creating the best for the City of Stamford."

The execution of the firm's contract for urban renewal will continue well into the 1990s. Scheduled for construction and development during the next decade are an additional two million square feet of office space, approximately 1,000 units of housing, and more than 100,000 square feet of retail space to serve the growing downtown population. In addition to another hotel for the area, the existing Marriott Hotel is being expanded to over 500 rooms and will feature a revolving rooftop restaurant, providing panoramic views of Long Island Sound and the New York City skyline.

During the first decades of the renaissance of Stamford, the prime effort has been to revitalize the downtown commercial and business environment. With the business vitality of the region now surging to greater heights, the public-private partnership is beginning to direct its attentions to creating activities that will serve to reinforce the quality of life for the community. Recently, under the leadership of the Coliseum Authority, Champion International, Pitney-Bowes, and F.D. Rich Company, the community has mobilized its resources to create the Stamford Center for the Arts, a vital cultural center that will serve all segments of the community. F.D. Rich, Jr., chairman of F.D. Rich Company and president of the Stamford Center for the Arts, commented, "Just as urban renewal was a community effort, so will be the creation of the new Center for the Arts. With two major performing theaters and supporting areas, the Center for the Arts will be the cultural focal point for the region. This will in fact make Stamford truly a complete city."

Succeeding generations of the Rich family are now working together with the community to complete the grand scheme envisioned by the mayors, public boards, and the corporation during the late 1950s and early 1960s.

During the last decade of the 20th century, F.D. Rich Company will have completed its work and the inhabitants of Stamford in the 21st century and beyond will be able to judge whether the firm and the Rich family have met the urban-renewal challenge as responsible and sensitive citizens of their community.

One Landmark Square

STAMFORD HOSPITAL

In 1892 bachelor farmer Judge John Clason, a former Stamford judge of probate and a member of the Connecticut legislature, donated $45,000 "to give the community something it needed and something that would be of the greatest possible benefit to all," a community hospital. By the fall of 1895 community contributions had raised the total to $100,000, making it possible for the Stamford Hospital to open a 30-bed facility on May 7, 1896, in the former Huntington-Brooks mansion on Noroton Hill. Four horse-and-buggy doctors comprised the original "visiting" staff and one, Samuel Pierson, M.D., served until his death in 1937, long after the automobile had replaced the horse.

Support for the hospital was strong from the beginning. Since most public hospitals then depended on affiliated women's groups for necessities they couldn't afford to buy, the Stamford Hospital Aid Society was organized. The Training School for Nurses opened at the hospital in 1901, continuing as its primary source of nurses until 1976, when the school closed because of the increasing popularity of college-degree nursing programs.

New industries moved into Stamford between 1900 and 1910, bringing 10,000 new residents. The Stamford Hospital expanded to meet their needs, moving in 1913 to a new five-building complex on the present 18-acre tract on West Broad Street.

Over the years more major building programs were needed, including the 1983 $23-million project. Now a 323-bed general community hospital serving lower Fairfield County's approximately 160,000 residents, the Stamford Hospital and its over 250 attending physicians provide a wide range of acute care, emergency, and outpatient services for medical/surgical, obstetric, pediatric, and psychiatric patients. The most modern facilities include the Altschul Clinical Laboratories, a liner accelerator, ad-vanced diagnostic cardiology equipment, a C-T scanner, six operating suites, obstetrical facilities with a neonatal intensive care nursery, and a 24-hour emergency center.

The Stamford Hospital is the only major teaching community hospital in lower Fairfield County, and its commitment to education is long-standing and far-reaching. There are active affiliations with Yale University School of Medicine, and Columbia University College of Physicians and Surgeons, as well as a major institutional affiliation with New York Medical College.

In order to ensure its continuing ability to meet the changing needs of the community and to bring greater financial flexibility, the hospital underwent a corporate restructuring in 1983. A parent corporation, the Health Corporation of Greater Stamford, was formed to support and encourage the development of comprehensive, integrated health care-related services by providing financial management and other assistance to its affiliates.

According to Philip D. Cusano, president and chief executive officer, "The modern hospital has become the focus for a level of health care expertise that cannot be found in any other environment. Nowhere else is there

Stamford's first public hospital opened in 1896 in the former Huntington-Brooks mansion on East Main Street. A horse-powered buggy awaits a doctor, right foreground.

the quality of professional expertise, the availability of high technology, or the variety of medical discipline brought together in such a coordinated fashion—all directed toward the prevention of illness and the diagnosis and treatment of disease. With the community's help we will continue to take significant steps toward providing the kind of facilities and services that will be essential in dealing with future directions of health care."

Aerial view of the Stamford Hospital in 1976. By 1985 the brick buildings on the left will have been replaced.

PEOPLE'S BANK

New England's largest mutual savings bank, with six branches in Stamford, began in 1842 as Bridgeport Savings Bank in the store of iron merchants George and Sherwood Sterling on Bridgeport's Water Street. The first account was opened on December 24, 1842, by the Fayerweather lighthouse keeper for his daughter, Miss Helen Moore. Four months passed before a single depositor withdrew any money—one dollar.

The bank's charter set a $400 limit on the amount any one person could deposit at a time, and no deposits could be made to an account after it had reached $1,000. This policy, in effect for 50 years, discouraged deposits from wealthy people. Today, of course, the bank doesn't limit savings or checking accounts.

In 1843, for an annual rent of $12, the little savings bank moved to a second-floor room near the corner of Water and Wall streets. Two weeks before Christmas in 1845, a fire spread from an oyster saloon and burned half the downtown section to the ground. Virtually overnight the business center moved from Water Street to Main Street, where it remains today.

The bank purchased its present location at Main and State streets in 1850 for $2,100. Today on this site stands the classic three-story columned bank building, erected in 1918, and, next to it, the modern 11-story glass and steel structure, completed in 1965.

After the Civil War, famous showman P.T. Barnum bought six big farms in East Bridgeport and became the first large-scale developer the savings bank helped to finance. Barnum would supply a Bridgeporter with at least 80 percent of the cost of home construction, so long as that individual gave up smoking and drinking.

In 1843 the bank paid $12 a year rent for this second-floor room (stars in windows) near Water and Wall streets in Bridgeport.

In 1927 Bridgeport Savings and another Bridgeport bank, People's Savings, merged to become Bridgeport-People's Savings. During the Depression the bank advanced more than one million dollars to pay delinquent taxes of borrowers so they wouldn't lose their homes. It also made the first FHA loan in the state.

After merging with Southport Savings in 1955, the bank continued to expand aggressively through acquisitions. It came to Stamford in 1981 by acquiring First Stamford Bank and Trust. Its Stamford offices are at 120 Bedford Street, the Town Center, 945 High Ridge, 324 Hope, 328 Shippan, and 2586 Summer streets.

In 1965 People's became the first bank in the nation to provide Pay-by-Phone service to its customers, and in 1981 People's established its first commercial banking department offering commercial checking and loans. Today people's has five regional commercial banking offices throughout Connecticut. Also in 1981, People's acquired a mortgage banking company, PB Mortgage Corp., Inc., which now has 16 offices in five states.

In 1983 the name was shortened to People's Bank. Its new discount brokerage subsidiary, People's Securities, Inc., was admitted to the New York Stock Exchange in 1984.

Today, with assets of $3.9 million, 64 offices in five Connecticut counties, and 2,000 employees, People's is New England's largest residential mortgage lender. Its original basic philosophy of personalized individual service has been strengthened and expanded to include new dimensions of consumer and commercial banking services.

People's Bank, New England's largest mutual savings bank, today has a Stamford office on the third floor of the Town Center and five other local branches.

COLLINS DEVELOPMENT CORPORATION

After obtaining a degree in architecture from Princeton University, Arthur Collins worked for a Manhattan real estate firm founded by his late father. He set his sights on becoming a developer because, he says, "A developer has the pride of ownership, along with tax advantages. An architect provides a service but has to pay too much taxes."

Arthur spent 15 years commuting to New York. Then in 1970, drawing on his expertise in site work, architecture, and finance, he formed Collins Development Corporation in Greenwich in partnership with Arthur D. Emil, senior partner in the law firm of Surrey and Morse of New York City. During the next decade, as his original staff of three grew tenfold or more, he created three residential projects in Greenwich: Lyon Farm, The Common, and Palmer Point, including Jardine's restaurant. He is the restaurant's landlord.

In 1980 the developer moved his company to Harbor Plaza in Stamford. He bought the Shippan property, where he built and owns one of the most distinctive office environments in Fairfield County—a location bordered by hundreds of boat slips. His Harbor Plaza tenants include Continental Group's corporate headquarters in three buildings, the Westinghouse headquarters in a fourth, and American Maize and others in a fifth.

Collins Development has its own headquarters at 43 Lindstrom Road in the former Heede International warehouse, remodeled into bright, airy offices, also next to boat slips. (Heede International used to assemble construction equipment shipped over from Sweden.)

About six years ago Arthur and his partner bought 40 acres and a large Jacobean mansion in Princeton, New Jersey. There he built and sold 60 condominium units for around $300,000 each. They also bought Palmer Square and the Nassau Inn in the middle of town and "has been happy

Arthur Collins founded Collins Development Corporation in 1970. Photo by Ing-John.

doing a whole bunch of things—adding 200 rooms to the inn, building a 600-car garage, etc." In Connecticut he is about to complete the South Norwalk Historic Restoration Project of 17 buildings with shops.

Since going into business for himself, Arthur has constructed some 10 different projects in the Stamford-Greenwich area. They encompass one million square feet of office space and about 800 residential units. Besides Harbor Plaza, they own an office building at 9 West Broad Street. Arthur also has an interest in the building started on Long Ridge Road at Bull's Head and another at Main and Washington Boulevard where the Firestone Tires store used to be.

Arthur Collins III, with a degree in landscape architecture from the University of Pennsylvania, has joined his father's firm. He does site work and has helped manage sales of the 80-unit Palmer Landing residential condominium project on Shippan. During Palmer Landing's opening weekend in May 1984, 10 of the $250,000 units were sold.

"As a developer you have to pretty much know the entire field yourself," explains Arthur Sr. "This comes only with experience. It's a risky business but it's fun, and it's profitable if you know what you're doing."

An aerial view of Harbor Plaza—the most impressive local Collins project. The Continental Group corporate headquarters buildings are in foreground.

HOLY NAME OF JESUS CHURCH

Stamford's Polish community dates back to 1874, when Stanislaw Podrazick and his wife Franciszka arrived here and settled on Liberty Street in the west end. Polish immigrants in increasing numbers worked in local factories, when they could get jobs. In 1898 they founded the Mutual Aid Society of King John III Sobieski, named for the 17th-century Polish monarch whose forces had stopped the Turks from conquering Europe. In 1903 a Catholic parish was authorized for Stamford's Polish population of 50 families.

The first Holy Name of Jesus Church, built of clapboard early in 1905, stood near the corner of South and Atlantic streets (today a Pitney-Bowes parking lot). It included a convent and parochial school classrooms. The present Italian villa-style rectory was built in 1852 for Charles Quintard, who sold it to famed cabinetmaker Duncan Phyfe. The church bought the residence in 1909.

Confusion characterized the first two decades of the church. Its first three pastors had little understanding of American business. The fourth understood business, but his severity alienated young people, as well as the five Resurrection Sisters of the school, who left.

Then quietly, on June 22, 1922, the Reverend Francis M. Wladasz arrived to calm a stormy parish. The fifth Holy Name pastor had a judicious blend of wisdom, tact, and authority. He staffed the school with five Bernardine Sisters and obtained the first curate, Father Stanislaus Nalewajk. Also, he encouraged the formation of the Polish American Business and Professional Club, today known as the Polish American Cultural Society, which sponsors events to promote Polish culture in the community; the Holy Name Athletic Club, Stamford's oldest athletic club; Boy Scout troops, the Central Committee of Combined Polish Societies, and many other groups.

Under Father Wladasz' leadership the parishioners gave visible proof of their generosity, buying a new convent (1926) and building the Holy Name Parochial School (1930) and the beautiful Byzantine Romanesque Holy Name Church (1925), all located on what is today Washington Boulevard. The former 18-acre Untermeyer estate on Sky Meadow Drive was acquired in 1947, becoming Villa Maria, Provincial House, and Retreat Center of the Bernardine Sisters.

After these remarkable achievements, the parish went into shock on July 26, 1959. Father Wladasz was being invested as Right Reverend Monsignor at the Holy Name altar when he suffered a fatal heart attack.

Soon thereafter, Father Felix Werpechowski began his third tour in the parish, this time as pastor. Retiring in 1971, he was succeeded by Monsignor Alphonse J.V. Fiedorczyk, Chaplain (Brigadier General) U.S. Army Retired, also a former Holy Name curate.

Monsignor Fiedorczyk, who edited the magnificent 176-page book commemorating the 75th anniversary of the church, estimates that today there are 11,000 to 12,000 Polish Americans in Stamford and 900 families in the Holy Name Church. The Holy Name Parish remains officially an ethnic Polish parish and, although not all those attending the church or the parochial school are Polish Americans, there is no disposition to change that designation.

— Sponsored by the Holy Name Church, Holy Name Athletic Club, and Polish American Cultural Society.

The Reverend Francis M. Wladasz, pastor of the Holy Name of Jesus Church from 1922 to 1959, pulled the predominantly Polish parish together.

The beautiful Byzantine Romanesque Holy Name of Jesus Church was completed in 1925 on what is today Washington Boulevard.

CONNECTICUT NATIONAL BANK

The Stamford Morris Plan Company, original local ancestor of Connecticut National Bank, opened in 1917 at 207 Atlantic Street to handle loans and investments.

The city's second mayor (1895-1897), attorney Edwin L. Scofield, became the bank's first president. Scofield died in 1918 and was succeeded by Dr. John J. Cloonan, a practicing physician for 40 years and former member of the Stamford Board of Education. In his honor, Woodland School was renamed Cloonan School. When a new middle school was built on North Street, it became Cloonan.

On January 2, 1963, the Morris Plan Bank began operating under its new national charter as the Lincoln National Bank of Stamford. Lincoln had its main office at 1122 East Main Street in Fairlawn and a branch at 36 Atlantic Street. A trust department was added, along with three more branches.

Lincoln National became Hartford National Bank on December 12, 1969, when it was acquired by the newly

formed parent, Hartford National Corporation, after a market study showed Stamford to be a major growth area. Hartford National Bank was Hartford's first and only financial institution for 22 years from the time it opened in 1792.

In 1982 the corporation acquired Connecticut National Bank of Bridgeport, founded in 1806, and merged it with Hartford National Bank, which was three times the Bridgeport Bank's size. The merged bank was named Connecticut National Bank because of its statewide connotation. Hartford-based Connecticut National Bank has Fairfield County headquarters at One Landmark Square and eight other branch offices in Stamford. From these regional headquarters offices, the bank serves consumers, institutions, and small middle-market and large business customers.

Connecticut National Bank set up

its Discount Brokerage Service in 1983 and also the Private Banking Center, which provides individual banking attention to customers who need more than traditional banking services. Most Private Banking customers here are corporate executives.

Early in 1984 the aggressive Hartford National Corporation acquired FirstBancorp of New Haven. That action merged First Bank of New Haven, New Britain Bank and Trust Company, and Terryville Trust Company into Connecticut National Bank and added $800 million in deposits. Pending is an interstate merger with Arltru Bancorporation of Lawrence, Massachusetts. Regulatory agencies have approved, but a court suit is delaying the merger.

Through internal growth and acquisition, Connecticut National Bank has had a tenfold increase since Lincoln National was acquired in 1969. With assets of $5.4 billion, it currently has the largest bank network in Connecticut and is the only bank operating in all six of the state's major metropolitan areas.

Serving both consumers and businesses, Connecticut National Bank's lower Fairfield County regional offices are located on the main floor of Stamford's Landmark Tower.

John Caldwell was the first president of the first bank founded in Hartford in 1792. Today Connecticut National Bank is the state's largest banking facility.

THE ADVOCATE

Stamford's oldest business started here Wednesday, April 8, 1829, when the first four-page weekly *Stamford Intelligencer* came off a Washington flatbed handpress in a little office on the south side of Main Street near Summer. A year's subscription cost two dollars, payable quarterly.

The publisher-editor-editorial staff consisted of Albert Hanford, a printer formerly connected with the failed *Norwalk Gazette*. Within 10 months the *Intelligencer* had gone through a second publisher and was ready for a third, 29-year-old William Henry Holly, whose Stamford ancestors went back to 1647.

During the next 18 years in which Holly, for the most part, edited and published the paper, he changed its name each time he changed his politics—starting with *Stamford Sentinel*, then *Democratic Sentinel*, *Farmer's Advocate*, and under another editor, *Farmer's and Mechanic's Advocate*. The name that stuck was "Advocate."

The 1860s brought in the Gillespie dynasty for 117 years. First of the Scottish-Irish brothers to come down from Canada was 21-year-old William Wright Gillespie, who began in 1860

Between 1871 and 1895 the newspaper occupied this building on Advocate Place, near the site of today's Landmark Tower. Courtesy of the Stamford Historical Society.

---

as mechanical foreman and by 1867 owned the paper. Brothers Edward T.W. and Richard H. turned the *Advocate* into a daily (except Sunday) in 1892, the same year E.T.W. published the historic book, *Picturesque Stamford*. In 1941, after sons Richard Jr. and Schuyler had died, the fate of the paper depended on their youngest brother, Kingsley.

A chemical engineer with no newspaper experience, Kingsley A. Gillespie, 46, switched overnight from directing research at the Stamford Rubber Supply Co. to publishing, playing a large role in community organizations. In his 37 years at the *Advocate*, circulation doubled. The paper

won a Pulitzer Prize in 1977 for investigative articles by reporter Anthony R. Dolan.

In 1977, Gillespie sold the family ownership of the *Advocate* and *Greenwich Time* (purchased in 1958) to the Times Mirror Corporation of Los Angeles.

The Times Mirror has changed the *Advocate* as dramatically as Stamford has changed: a large new building and computer processing for better, faster reproduction, with frequent use of color, and a fast-growing Sunday edition as of September 1981. Weekly pages increased 50 percent, advertising lineage tripled, and staff doubled.

As well as emphasizing local news, the paper gives good coverage to local arts, business, government, and sports. In its circulation category of under 50,000, it has for the third consecutive year won an AP national award for best Sunday sports section and UPI awards in New England for editorial, spot news photography, and coverage of the Mianus River bridge collapse. Among its many community activities, the *Advocate* sponsors many championship games for the Fairfield County Interscholastic Athletic Conference.

"Stamford is the hub of the *Advocate*'s identity," says publisher Steven L. Isenberg, who was master of ceremonies at the Ferguson Library's 1984 Book and Author Luncheon. "We are a local community daily."

In 1981 the Advocate moved to its 11th location, the new 75 Tresser Boulevard building. The 100-foot copper beech tree dates back to the 1890s. Photo by Tom Ryan.

CHAMPION INTERNATIONAL CORPORATION

The family tree of this Fortune 500 manufacturer of fine paper, wood products, and paper packaging—Stamford-based since 1975—has roots that reach back to 1893 and to the tiny dots of halftones. That year an Ohio printer-publisher named Peter G. Thomson decided to apply a smooth coated surface to paper so the half-tones, a graphic arts photographic breakthrough of the 1880s, would reproduce better.

To accomplish this, the publisher sold his publishing house in Cincinnati and, with the $100,000 proceeds, founded the Champion Coated Paper Company in Hamilton, 20 miles away. Spurred by success, he decided to manufacture the paper he coated, and so he purchased the Eagle Paper Company in nearby Franklin. This step lured Peter Thomson into pulp manufacture and ultimately into ownership of timberland itself.

A move back to the source also characterized a second root of Champion International's family tree. In 1919 enthusiastic salesman Lawrence Ottinger borrowed $500 and founded the United States Plywood Company in New York City. A wholesale jobber, he marketed casein glue and World War I surplus plywood, a relatively new building product at the time. Until then, customers had to obtain plywood cut to order directly from the mills. U.S. Plywood, by 1925, had chalked up its first million-dollar year.

Although originally against "owning brickbats," as he put it, Lawrence eventually succumbed to the lure of manufacturing. In 1937 he bought Aircraft Plywood Company of Seattle and its Douglas fir plywood mill. In 1940, when USP sales had reached five million dollars, he bought the Algoma Plywood and Veneer Company in Wisconsin, including some timberland. Now Lawrence Ottinger, too, was tied to the tree.

The roots of Champion's paper packaging division go back to 1906,

Peter G. Thomson (right), founder of Champion Paper Co., visited President Calvin Coolidge (center) and Chief Justice William Howard Taft in Washington in 1925.

when Michael W. Waldorf, borrowing money from friends and relatives, opened Waldorf Boxboard Company in St. Paul, Minnesota. He pioneered the commercial recycling of used paper, from which he made folding cartons and paper labels. In 1966 Waldorf merged with Hoerner Boxes, Inc., a manufacturer of corrugated containers that had been founded in Keokuk, Iowa, and had grown rapidly throughout the Midwest. The merged packaging company was known as Hoerner Waldorf, Inc.

Down through the years there have been mergers, acquisitions, and new-plant construction to strengthen and thicken the three main roots. Then in 1967 came the big merger—Champion Papers and U.S. Plywood—followed in 1977 by the important merger with Hoerner Waldorf.

Champion's headquarters at One Champion Plaza was designed by Ulrich Franzen.

The Champion greenhouse, a jewel-like glass pyramid on the third-floor terrace, is an attractive, free educational resource for the entire community. Photo by Eric Kamp.

Champion's businesses are based on the tree. The firm owns or controls 3.3 million acres of timber in the Northwest, Rockies, Upper Great Lakes area, and the Southeast. These forests supply nearly half its timber needs.

There was a period when Champion branched out into other businesses, not all of them profitable or related to wood products. Then shrewdly, over the past 10 years, the concern shed 16 such businesses, redeploying the assets into the area it knows best—forest products. Its 1983 sales came to more than four billion dollars.

Champion's decision to build at the corner of Atlantic Street and Tresser Boulevard stemmed from the desire to keep its roots in the East, and in a convenient location. Champion chairman Andrew C. Sigler chose the four-acre downtown site as part of his commitment to the revitalization of down-

The Fairfield County branch of the Whitney Museum of American Art is open to the public, free of charge, on the ground floor of Champion's headquarters. Photo by Stan Reis.

town Stamford.

One Champion Plaza, a handsome 15-story building clad in pewter-colored aluminum, has brought together for the first time under one roof the key management team of the entire operation. Of the firm's 40,000 employees—32,000 domestically and another 8,000 at Canadian and Brazilian subsidiaries—750 work here.

Champion encourages its employees to volunteer in the community and has set up the Champion Fund for Community Service. The volunteers can request money from the fund for specific projects to help community organizations they work with. For example, employees volunteering for the Red Cross asked for funds to buy addi-

tional mannequins used in teaching CPR lifesaving techniques. Fifty employees donate their time preparing and serving Salvation Army breakfasts to people who would otherwise go hungry.

In 1981 Champion International's family tree grew a branch of a museum. New York's Whitney Museum of American Art established its first permanent branch in a 3,600-square-foot gallery space especially designed for that purpose off the main floor lobby in the company's headquarters. Whitney-supervised art exhibitions change every two months. The museum is open to the public from 11 a.m. to 5 p.m. Tuesdays through Saturdays, and the public may park at no charge in Champion's eight-story garage, except on Saturdays when the garage is closed.

Late in 1983 Champion grew a jewel-like botanical garden in a permanent 1,600-square-foot glass pyramid on the third-level terrace. Its lovely floral displays and special exhibits change regularly. And, like the Whitney branch, the greenhouse is open at no charge during the same hours, with free parking except on Saturdays.

A successful enterprise has a kind of underlying culture, an emphasis that permeates its operation. At Champion International Corporation, the emphasis is on excellence.

SHAMROCK MAINTENANCE CORPORATION

In 1964 Stamford was changing from its sleepy industrial background to a prime corporate office relocation area. In the ensuing years many businesses announced their plans to relocate in Stamford.

Years earlier, in 1958, Carl Shanahan had arrived here from his native Ireland. He obtained employment as an engineering draftsman, first at Machlett Laboratories and then at Pitney Bowes. In the evenings he moonlighted at St. Mary's Parochial School as a janitor. As he cleaned St. Mary's at night, Carl realized there was no local janitorial company to service the many new buildings that the corporations were expected to occupy.

From that humble beginning Carl got the idea for his new maintenance venture, calling it Shamrock Maintenance. This was the start of what is today a multimillion-dollar corporation.

With his limited janitorial background Carl decided that being a local enterprise would be the key point of his marketing program. After he was awarded his first contract for the 1515 Summer Street building, owned by Steve Day, Carl was able to establish a reputation for the businesses arriving in Stamford. In quick succession Shamrock was awarded contracts for Xerox, The American Thread Company, Continental Oil, and General Electric.

The firm's reputation for first-class work spread throughout the area. Today Shamrock employs over 700 workers who service 80 buildings for 70 corporations with over $7.5 million in annual sales. A security division was formed in 1976 as an added convenience for Shamrock's clients. Today the division has over 100 employees servicing many customers.

Carl does everything he can to make his employees feel secure. "We try to assign them to the building most convenient to where they live," he says. "We adjust their hours if they have to catch a bus or a train after work; we pick them up if they get stuck in a snowstorm." Although he had no previous managerial experience, he found he had a flair for it. From the very start Shamrock's policies were employee-oriented.

All workers, including part-timers, participate in a profit-sharing program; employee-incentive awards that send two employees and their guests to Florida each year, all expenses paid by Shamrock; and an employee-of-the-month program with gifts given to the winners. Of course the winners are achievers, as performance of duties determines who is eligible. Shamrock and Carl Shanahan believe that people should be recognized and rewarded for their accomplishments.

Carl believes he's been very fortunate to have personally grown in conjunction with Shamrock's growth. He attributes that to his natural ability for working with and receiving the best from his people. His motto today is the same as when he started Shamrock Maintenance: to provide quality and service at the best possible price.

Born and raised in another country, Carl Shanahan attributes his success to the opportunities that are available to everyone who wants to work in this country, and he feels that the free-enterprise system is our greatest blessing.

Copy supplied by Shamrock Maintenance Company.

Shamrock president Carl Shanahan (center) with maintenance supervisors Juan Amarillo and Hattie Green. While working for Shamrock Maintenance, Ms. Green has put her six children through college.

Among the 100 Shamrock Security Group employees are Vernon Williams and Janice Sotire. The security force guards several buildings around the clock.

PATRONS

The following individuals, companies, and organizations have made a valuable commitment to the quality of this publication. Windsor Publications and the Stamford Historical Society gratefully acknowledge their participation in *Stamford: An Illustrated History*.

The Advocate•
The American Thread Company•
Ashforth Properties, Inc.•
Barnes Engineering Company•
Harry Bennett & Associates, Inc.•
Bloomingdale's Stamford•
Bongiorno Supermarket, Inc.•
Business Environments,
    Division of Karp Industries Inc.•
Michael & Maureen Cacace
Champion International Corporation•
Citizens Utilities Company
Clairol•
Collins Development Corporation•
Colonial Insurance Agency, Inc.•
The Connecticut Bank and Trust
    Company•
Connecticut National Bank•
Crystal Rock Water Company, Inc.•
Day, Berry & Howard
John A. Drenckhahn, Inc.•
Excelsior Hardware Company•
FAG Bearings Corporation•
The Ferguson Library
Gateway Bank
    (Formerly Citizens Savings Bank)•
General Electric Credit Corporation•
Hallmark Properties Inc.
The History Book Club, Inc.•
Holy Name of Jesus Church•
Paul G. Hughes
Al Koproski Realty•
Mallozzi Construction Company•
Parker Travel Service•
Parsons, Bromfield & Redniss•
People's Bank•
Pierson & Smith, Inc.•
William Pitt, Inc.•
F.D. Rich Company•
P. Sabini & Company, Inc.•
Sachs Plumbing Supplies•
St. Augustine Council No. 41
Knights of Columbus•
St. Joseph Hospital•
Shamrock Maintenance Corporation•
SMS Architects•
Stamford Glass & Mirror Works•
Stamford Hospital•
The Stamford Savings Bank•
Union Trust Company•

•The histories of these companies and organizations appear in Chapter X, Partners in Progress, beginning on page 146.

A NOTE ON THE ILLUSTRATIONS

Although the responsibility for selecting and captioning the illustrations for this book has been largely mine, it hardly needs saying that the finished product represents the work of many people. I would have been at a complete loss without the cheerful, unstinting work and guidance of members of the Stamford Historical Society, including, but not limited to, Ann Hermann and Greg Mecca. I am particularly indebted to curator Lois Dater, whose conservation of the society's collection over the years and valuable advice enabled me to find the best and most appropriate illustrations.

The active involvement of the authors—often calling for extra research beyond the work they had already done for the text—was also crucial, especially as far as the captions are concerned. Preservationist Renée Kahn and the staff of the Ferguson Library, especially Debbie O'Hara, deserve a word of thanks, as does our superb photographer, Simon Wolfe, who made so many trips from New York to Stamford, caring much more about quality than expediency. Many people came forward with pictures and caption information of their own, and the book is richer for their contribution. One person who must be singled out is George Samaha, the owner

of the oil painting showing St. John's Episcopal Church in the mid-19th century. His willingness not only to let us reproduce the painting here—and we believe this is the first time it has ever been published—is particularly welcome because no one in Stamford, besides Lois Dater and perhaps a few others, even knew of its existence until Mr. Samaha sent a color transparency of it. As far as I could determine, this is the loveliest depiction of Stamford in its first 200 years, and possibly 350.

It is always a regret, even in the thickest volume, that more material could not have been included. I was sorry to have to leave out some wonderful turn-of-the-century pictures for which there was no room; I also wish there existed illustrations for more of the significant or interesting incidents in Stamford history. I have tried to choose pictures which collectively show as many aspects as possible of Stamford life over the centuries. Inevitably there are gaps. But even the gaps can be useful: they may stimulate even more thought and curiosity about Stamford's past and present, which is all to the good.

—Lissa Sanders

SELECTED BIBLIOGRAPHY

Allen, Irving L., et al. *Metropolitan Connecticut: A Demographic Profile*. Urban Research Report No. 8. Storrs: University of Connecticut, 1965.

Bell, C.W. *Stamford's First Century of Banking, 1834-1934*. Stamford: Gillespie Bros., 1934.

Bender, Andrew W. "An Analysis of the Structure of Local Government in Stamford, Connecticut." Master's thesis. New York University School of Public Administration, 1972.

Cahn, William. *The Story of Pitney Bowes*. New York: Harper Bros., 1961.

Cresap, McCormack & Paget. *Stamford's Public School: A Survey of Organization and Administration*. New York, 1957.

Feinstein, Estelle F. *Stamford in the Gilded Age, 1868-1893*. Stamford: Stamford Historical Society, 1973.

Franklin, Robert. "The Consolidation of the Town and City of Stamford, Connecticut." Master's thesis. University of Connecticut, 1952.

Gillespie, Edward T.W. *Picturesque Stamford*. Stamford: Gillespie Bros., 1892.

"Hometown of Hardware —Stamford, Connecticut." *Hardware Consultant and Contractor Magazine* 14 (1950):8-20.

Hunter, Lorraine. "History of the Catholic Church in Stamford, Connecticut, 1849-1974." Unpublished manuscript, 1974.

Institute of Educational Research. Division of Field Studies. "Report of the Survey of the Public School System of the Town of Stamford, 1922-23." New York: Teacher's College, Columbia University, 1923.

Leonard, Lee. P., ed. "Stamford Post Offices and Postmasters, 1790-1977." Stamford: Stamford Historical Society, 1977.

Lobozza, Carl. *Stamford, Connecticut: Pictures From the Past*. Stamford: Stamford Historical Society, 1970.

————. *Stamford, Connecticut: Journey Through Time*. Stamford: Stamford Historical Society, 1971.

————. *The Changing Face of Stamford*. Stamford: Stamford Historical Society, 1979.

Majdalany, Jean. *The History of the Cove in Stamford, Connecticut*. Stamford: Stamford Historical Society, 1979.

"The Making of Modern Stamford." Biographies, notes, ethnic studies, bibliographies. 33 boxes. Hartford: Connecticut State Library.

McCann, Guy. "Stamford: Corporate Headquarters Phenomenon." *Fairfield County Magazine*, January 1974.

Mazza, David L. "Homer S. Cummings, the Dawn of a Reformer." Master's thesis. University of Connecticut, 1972.

Moving In: This is Stamford. Stamford Weekly Mail. Special edition of November 13, 1981. Vol. 48, No. 19.

"Origin and History of Yale & Towne Manufacturing Company, 1868-1918." Stamford: Yale & Towne Manufacturing Co., 1918.

Pendery, Joyce S. "Women's Secular Voluntary Associations and Their Leaders in Stamford, Connecticut, 1860-1910." Master's thesis. Sarah Lawrence College, 1978.

Sherwood, Herbert. *The Story of Stamford*. New York: States History Company, 1930.

Sinrich, Phyliss. "Stamford, Tuning up for Tomorrow." *Fairfield County Magazine*, February 7, 1977: 24-34.

Spencer, Thomas T. "Homer S. Cummings and the 1932 Presidential Campaign." *Connecticut Historical Society Bulletin* 48 (1983):1-9.

Stamford American Association of University Women. "Guide to Stamford's Schools." Editions of 1964, 1967, 1970. Stamford: AAUW.

Stamford Area Commerce and Industry Association. *Membership Directory and Business Reference Guide*. Yearly: 1963-1983. Stamford: SACIA.

Stamford, Connecticut, Bicentennial Committee. *Stamford Past and Present, 1641-1976*. Stamford: Stamford Bicentennial Committee, 1976.

Stamford Chamber of Commerce. "Stamford Keeps Pace With Tomorrow. Stamford: Chamber of Commerce, 1965.

"Stamford Collects the Facts: A Study of the Social Work Program in Stamford." Stamford: Gillespie Bros., 1938.

Stamford, Connecticut, Community Chests and Councils of America. "Families in Trouble, 1950." Stamford: The Council, 1950.

Stamford High School Civics Class. "Stamford: A City and a Town." Stamford: Stamford High School, 1929.

Stamford Historian. Vol. 1, No. 1 and No. 2 (1954). Stamford: Stamford Historical Society, 1954.

Stamford Junior Chamber of Commerce. "Stamford, Connecticut, A Plus City: Gateway to New England." Stamford: Junior Chamber of Commerce, n.d.

Stamford League of Women Voters. *Stamford, Our City*. Stamford: United Publishing and Printing Corp., 1959-1983.

Stamford League of Women Voters. "Know Your High School." Stamford: League of Women Voters, 1977.

"Stamford's Welcome to the Soldiers and Sailors of the Great War, October 10, 11, 12, and 13, 1919." Stamford: Gillespie Bros., 1919.

Stamford Issue. County Magazine. August 15, 1968.

Stamford Issue. Fairfield County Magazine. May 1974.

Stokes, Charles J. "Fairfield City, 1990." *Fairfield County Magazine*. January 1972: 15-19.

Suplee, Henry. "Henry R. Towne." *Proceedings of the American Society of Mechanical Engineers (1924)*: 933-940.

Twenty-Five Years of Progress, 1910-1935. Stamford: Instituto Italiano, 1935.

Updegraff, Marie. *History of the Roxbury Community Church, 1870-1970*. Stamford: Roxbury Community Church, 1970.

————. *The Story of the Stamford Hospital, 1896-1971*. Stamford: Stamford Hospital, 1971.

————. *The Story of the Stamford Hospital School of Nursing, 1901-1976*. Stamford: Stamford Hospital, 1976.

Walton, Alfred. *Stamford Historical Sketches*. Stamford: by the author, 1922.

Zeranski, Joe. "Historical Calendar of Stamford." Unpublished manuscript prepared for the Stamford Historical Society, 1980.

Index